CAREER DIRECTIONS

Second Edition

Donna J. Yena
Johnson & Wales University

IRWIN
CAREER
EDUCATION
DIVISION

Burr Ridge, Illinois

Executive editor:	Carol A. Long
Senior developmental editor:	Jean Roberts
Developmental editor:	Anna Drake
Marketing manager:	Lynn M. Kalanik
Project editor:	Karen J. Nelson
Production manager:	Bob Lange
Cover designer:	Maureen McCutcheon
Designer:	Larry J. Cope
Art coordinator:	Mark Malloy
Compositor:	Carlisle Communications, Ltd.
Typeface:	10/12 Palatino
Printer:	R.R. Donnelley & Sons Company

Library of Congress Cataloging-in-Publication Data

Yena, Donna J.
    Career directions / Donna J. Yena. — 2nd ed.
        p.   cm.
    Includes bibliographical references and index.
    ISBN 0-256-13145-7
    1. Vocational guidance. I. Title.
    HF5381.Y46   1993
    650.14 — dc20   92–41863

Printed in the United States of America
    4 5 6 7 8 9 0 DOC 0 9 8 7 6 5

Preface

The goal of your career education is to prepare you for a career in your chosen field of study. *Career Directions*, Second Edition, is your guide to managing your own career throughout your lifetime. Although you may receive assistance from your school in securing a job, you need to master job search skills so that you can make successful career moves on your own. Technical skills are only one part of a successful career. You also need to develop your self-confidence, career focus, communication skills, and job search skills. Mastery of these areas will enable you to stand out in today's competitive and changing work environment. *Career Directions* puts you in control of your future!

WHO CAN USE THIS BOOK?
Students in career schools can use this book in professional development courses or workshops. Students in colleges or universities can use this book to direct their own career planning and job search efforts.

Career Directions provides instruction and resource materials that will help you find your first job, enter a new profession, or move to a new job within an existing career. Regardless of what stage you are in, *Career Directions* can help you assess yourself and take the right next step in your career.

HOW TO USE THIS BOOK
The material in this book can be studied in a variety of ways. You may complete all of the material at once in your professional development course or study certain topics through a series of professional development workshops offered at your school. It is also possible to study *Career Directions* independently. It is best first to complete all the material thoroughly so that you master the process of managing your career. At various stages of your career, you may find it helpful to go back to certain chapters that can help you with a particular decision.

There is a deliberate sequence to the material presented in *Career Directions*. Unit One focuses you first on preparing for your career through self-assessment, personal development, and an overview of career paths open to you. Unit Two provides job search techniques including résumés and job applications, letters to write during your job search, interviewing techniques, and advice on accepting a job. Unit Three assists you with managing your career from your first months on the job and gives advice on growing with your job. Unit Four introduces you to contemporary issues in the workplace that may affect you in your work environment.

Unit Five is your personal career handbook, which contains tools you can use to successfully direct your career. Chapter Thirteen, "Career Paths," provides an opportunity to review the many career options available to you. It also shows you the jobs you may hold as you move through your career in a particular field. These career paths should be explored along with the information in Chapter Three, "Career Paths Overview," and can be referred to again when considering future career moves.

The "Glossary of Terms Used in Job Descriptions" (Chapter Fourteen) is designed to help you understand the job descriptions in the "Index of Job Descriptions" (Chapter Fifteen).

This glossary can be used in conjunction with Chapter Four to help you express your qualifications more effectively in your résumé. The "Index of Job Descriptions" provides a brief description of what each job listed in "Career Paths" entails. This gives you an idea of what the actual day-to-day responsibilities are in the jobs that might interest you.

Finally, Chapter Sixteen, "Career Resources," contains a list of resource materials that you can use to supplement much of the information presented in *Career Directions*. Should you want to explore one or more topics in depth, you can start by using some of these additional resources.

SKILLS YOU WILL DEVELOP

The most important benefit you will gain from studying *Career Directions* is mastery of the essential skills necessary to managing a successful career. You will learn how to:

- Identify your personal and professional strengths and weaknesses. Relate your values, interests, personality, and skills to your career choice.
- Compare your professional qualifications with employer expectations.
- Set goals for self-improvement.
- Improve your communication skills.

- Convince an employer you are the right candidate for the job.
- Present your best professional image.
- Evaluate the many career paths available to you.
- Conduct an independent job search.
- Write effective résumés.
- Complete job applications.
- Write job search letters.
- Secure a job interview.
- Conduct a successful interview.
- Complete proper follow-up after an interview.
- Accept the best job.
- Be successful on the job.
- Deal with workplace issues.

SPECIAL FEATURES OF CAREER DIRECTIONS

In addition to "Contemporary Issues in the Workplace" and the "Career Handbook," there are other special features that will be useful to you. The Interview Hall of Fame . . . and Shame in Chapter Six depicts some real-life stories of great things you can do to conduct a successful interview. It also illustrates some real-life mistakes people have made in their effort to impress an interviewer.

A summary of growing career fields gives you an idea of some of the industry trends influencing job growth over the next five years. Tips on how to recession-proof your career teach you how to stay marketable during tough economic times.

These special features provide you with specific information so that you can make better career choices, market yourself more competitively to prospective employers, and successfully manage your career in a changing environment.

ACKNOWLEDGMENTS

The content of this text incorporates my own work experience with the valuable input I have received from students, employers, and placement professionals throughout the country.

During my 13 years of involvement with students, they have willingly shared their most common concerns about their careers during individual career counseling sessions and in personal and professional development courses I have taught. The hundreds of employers I have worked with over the years have applauded our students' clear focus, realistic attitudes, and professional experience, and have offered candid assessments of students' strengths and weaknesses as they prepare to enter the workplace.

My thanks to the many placement professionals I have met throughout the country at placement workshops I have conducted, who have openly discussed their challenges and successes with assisting students in job placement.

Specifically, I would like to thank the reviewers whose input has allowed me to refine this edition:

Edythe Evans, John Hancock Financial Services

David D. Hatch, PepsiCo

Kathy Hughston, Bradford School

Elizabeth M. Hummel, American Business and Fashion Institute

Chad J. Layton, Footlocker

Shirley C. Lowery, Barnes Business College

Sheila M. Powell, Commonwealth College

Jann Underwood, Eldorado College

Finally, I would like to thank the Irwin Career Education Division for the professional guidance and support they have given me throughout this project. I am particularly grateful to the marketing professionals and sales representatives for their input from the market. I owe personal thanks to the Executive Editor, Carol Long, and Developmental Editor, Anna Drake, for the partnership we developed as we worked to produce this manuscript. My thanks also to Louise Phaneuf for her expertise and hard work in producing the final manuscript.

The success of *Career Directions* is shared by everyone who contributed to making it a practical and complete guide to helping students launch their careers. Thank you!

Donna J. Yena

Contents

The World of Work in the 21st Century

TOMORROW'S CAREERS

QUALIFICATIONS FOR TOMORROW'S CAREERS

Technical skills   +   High energy level
Positive attitude
Flexibility
Brightness
Hard-working attitude
Willingness to learn

Although technical skills are important, they must be balanced with interpersonal skills.

Patricia Aburdene, co-author with John Naisbitt of
Re-Inventing the Corporation

Business leaders report that students with solid basic skills and positive attitudes are more likely to find and keep jobs than students with vocational skills alone.

New technology has allowed us to access information in greater volume than ever before. The Information Age is here. New technology has allowed us more leisure time, increasing the amount of time we spend dining out, traveling, and generally using various sources of entertainment. Our lifestyles are changing, and the way we communicate with each other is changing. These changes, and many more, in the way we live are shaping the world in which we work and the skills we need to compete.

THE CHANGING WORKPLACE

As you prepare to enter the workplace, you should be aware of how that environment is changing. A major part of your professional development will occur as a result of your ability to respond and adapt to some of these changes.

Increased *competition* for jobs is a result of more qualified **candidates** entering the work force for the first time and experienced workers changing jobs for better opportunities.

Teamwork is the process that brings together workers with different ideas and skills to accomplish a particular job through the *new management team*. Many companies are using the team approach because it is effective in accomplishing company goals.

Customer service involves providing what customers need in the best way possible so that they keep coming back to that company for the products and services they need. Good customer service also helps attract new customers.

Quality goes hand in hand with customer satisfaction. Keeping the company as the number one choice among customers requires the constant improvement of products and service to ensure they are of high quality.

Cultural diversity in the workplace is growing, creating a work environment that is composed of people from a wide range of different cultures. It is also becoming easier for people from all over the world to travel and relocate to different countries. This is resulting in a more *global work force* made up of more people from outside the United States.

There is a need for you to commit to *lifelong learning* to heighten your awareness of how the environment is changing and to develop ways to deal with these changes in order to have a successful life and career.

Competition

Competition for jobs will remain high. Tomorrow's jobs will be many in number, but increased competition for those jobs from career changers and more entry-level candidates may make it more difficult to be chosen for high-quality career opportunities.

For you, this means that you must have strong qualifications and know how to market them in order to stand out as the right candidate for the job. You must develop competitive skills, a clear goal, and a careful plan for achievement in your chosen field.

The New Management Team

The new management team involves closer working relationships between management and support staff. There are no longer sharp differences in the importance of different jobs, but rather, recognition that each person performs a critical function for the organization. Such support positions as data entry operators and secretaries have grown in responsibility and taken on a new significance in the management of information and services within companies. Managers work more directly with support staff than ever before in setting and achieving company goals. Managers and support staff work together to create the new management team.

THE NEW MANAGEMENT TEAM

Management   +   Support staff
(Accountants, computer specialists, reservationists, sales representatives, distributors, cooks, night auditors, front desk clerks, secretaries)

With an increasing number of professionals seeking top-management jobs, there is a decline in the number of qualified support personnel in organizations throughout the country. That's where many jobs will be. Businesses are recognizing the importance of support personnel that are committed to quality, customer service, and teamwork. To be successful, it is no longer necessary to "climb to the top," but rather to become the best at whatever you do to keep the day-to-day operations of the business thriving. Your ability to work with a team will be important throughout your entire career.

Customer Service and Quality

W. Edwards Deming, a leading expert on quality in business, says that "Quality is defined by the customer. Improvements in products and processes must be aimed at anticipating customers' future needs."

Today's businesses compete primarily on the basis of customer service and quality because customers consider these to be important when deciding which products or services they want to use. We hear a lot about the service economy that exists today. This simply means that the business of most companies is focused on delivering some type of product, such as computer equipment, or providing a service, such as delivering your clothes by mail, to customers. In the past, companies focused more on actually making the goods than showing how they could be used. The focus on service means that the jobs available to you will probably require good product knowledge and an ability to communicate well to customers about how the product can benefit them.

By treating the customer right the first time and providing a high-quality service or product to that customer the first time, a company can attract and retain good customers. *You* will be the link between the customer and the company that will either cause the customer to come back again or to go elsewhere to fill his or her needs. Your ability to relate to others is critical to success in your career.

Cultural Diversity and Globalization

"By the year 2000, minorities and immigrants will hold 26 percent of all jobs, 60 percent of all women will be working, and the average age of the work force will be 39 years old."[1] The composition of the workplace is changing dramatically as the number of minorities and immigrants working in the United States grows. This blending of culturally diverse people into the workplace brings new skills and different perspectives to a business.

Culturally diverse work settings mean that you need to learn to appreciate and recognize others' different educational experiences and cultural values. For example, as women continue to become a greater part of the work force, you may find yourself noticing more changes in the work environment, such as more flexible work schedules and programs that address family care issues, including child care and elder care programs. Another example of differences in the workplace is the need for you to adjust to working with older and more experienced workers in jobs similar to yours. This is because more older workers are employed than in the past due to an overall increase in our nation's older population. In this case, your ability to bring new techniques and fresh perspectives to your co-workers and employer can give you a competitive edge.

Learning to Learn

The ability to think, learn, and create new ideas is the new basic skill for the 21st century. Believe it or not, the one thing that may not remain constant is the need for the skills you are learning now. With further advances in technology and in the way we live, new equipment and procedures will require new skills periodically. You may need to retrain several times during your career.

As technical skills for new jobs change, your abilities to work well with people, to market your skills, to see others' points of view, and to work with a team will always remain important as you progress through your career. Your success will always depend on the right combination of technical skills and people skills. Both will remain important parts of your "package" of qualifications. Learning how to put together the best package you can is the art of managing your own career. *Get ready—the world of work is changing.*

---

[1]"Riding the Tide of Change," *The Wyatt Communicator*, Winter 1991, pp. 4–11.

PREPARING FOR YOUR CAREER

Chapter One

Self-Assessment

Self-assessment is the process of identifying your values, interests, personality traits, and skills; relating them to your definition of success; and comparing how well you meet employer expectations. Once you do this, you can set your own goals for self-improvement to bring you closer to reaching your individual personal and professional goals.

UNDERSTANDING YOURSELF

Having a clear understanding of yourself helps you choose a career that meets your individual needs. Your unique talents and needs all influence your choice of career and your overall lifestyle.

Values

Your values are the standards you choose to live by. Your values affect most of the choices you make every day. The sum total of your own personal values or standards makes up your value system. Values by themselves are not right or wrong. What is an acceptable choice for one person may be unacceptable for you because of your value system. For example, one person may feel little or no obligation to spend time helping others through some sort of community work. For you, this may be very important because one of the standards you have set for yourself is helping others. Some examples of values include:

- Time with family
- Financial reward
- Community service
- Professional position
- Personal relationships
- Social status
- Where you live

One way to clarify what values are most important to you is to ask yourself: What are the top priorities in my life? These priorities may tell you a lot about the values you have. The examples listed above may reflect some of your values. There are probably some you would add to or subtract from this list. Knowing what's important to you makes you aware of your own value system.

Values and Your Career Choice Your values affect your career choice in many ways. For example, if you value nights and weekends with your family, you'll probably require a career with a workweek that does not include much overtime or weekend work. Frequent travel is also something you may prefer to avoid. If your career choice is to be a secretary, you will generally find that spending time with your family will be possible because most secretarial jobs have standard workweeks, with work hours of 8:30–4:30 or 9:00–5:00 Monday through Friday.

When your career choice seems to conflict with your values, take a second look. For example, if you are considering a career in sales, you may need to travel and work some nights and weekends. Perhaps if you rethink what is important to you, you may realize that time with your family, rather than a standard schedule, is what really counts and that good planning gives you the free time you want while you pursue a sales career.

Interests

Interests are the activities you choose to do because you enjoy them. Your interests may lean toward individual or group activities. Most people enjoy some combination of both. A variety of interests helps you develop and grow and is a good source of fun and relaxation.

POSSIBLE INTERESTS

Hiking	Baseball	Skiing
Basketball	Jogging	Dancing
Reading	Sewing	Writing
Fixing cars	Drawing	Computer games

Interests and Your Career Choice How you spend your free time says a lot about you—your likes, dislikes, and motivation. This information can provide you with leads to the career that's best for you. For example, if you spend some of your free time as an officer in a club or organization, you may have an interest in a job that puts your leadership skills to work. If you enjoy fixing cars or repairing computers or household items during your free time, you may be suited for a career as a technician. An interest in writing may mean you are suited for a career as a claims analyst or administrative assistant. Pay attention to what you enjoy doing, and you may discover interests that apply to a variety of careers.

Personality

Personality can be your biggest asset as you prepare for a career in the service industries. Your personality is the sum total of the way you act and react to everyday events. A personality trait is a distinguishing quality or characteristic that belongs to you. A look at some traits that are generally positive on the job is a start to assessing your own personality.

EXAMPLES OF POSITIVE PERSONALITY TRAITS

Confident	Persuasive
Committed	Influential
Competitive	Mature
Detail-oriented	Persistent
Extroverted	Motivated
Energetic	Positive
Interested	Reliable
Introverted	Responsible
Imaginative	Responsive

Personality and Your Career Choice Certain types of personalities may be better suited for certain careers. For example, if you are pursuing a career in retailing, you will need a high energy level and an outgoing personality. In contrast, if you are pursuing a career in court reporting, you may be quieter by nature and able to work at a set pace for a long period of time. Both careers offer excellent opportunities but are better suited to different personalities.

The more you develop your positive personality traits, the more you'll be viewed as someone that other people like to be with. A pleasing personality is a plus when looking for any job because many employers see this as one indicator of your own confidence in yourself and your ability to get along with others. Of course, while there is much more to career success than a pleasing personality, it is a big advantage to bring to any professional setting.

Skills

As you assess your skills, you will find they generally fall into one of the following three categories: personal, interpersonal, or technical. A skill is an ability you have developed or an area in which you have expertise. Personal skills are your own way of dealing directly with situations. For example, organizing your time or work well, being able to solve problems on your own, and seeing a project through from start to finish are personal skills that can help you succeed in your job. Interpersonal skills are your methods of dealing with others. For example, being a good listener or a great public speaker helps you communicate well with others. Technical skills are the abilities you can demonstrate through work with your hands. With a little effort, most of us can learn new skills that may help us in our personal and professional lives.

TYPES OF SKILLS

Personal	Interpersonal	Technical
Memorizing	Listening	Word processing
Organizing	Teamwork	Shorthand
Problem solving	Understanding	Filing
Initiating	Sales	Reception work
Completing	Public speaking	Computer operation
Planning	Negotiation	
Prioritizing	Teaching	Letter writing
Budgeting	Training	Drafting
	Coaching	Cooking

Skills and Your Career Choice   You may find that you are interested in a career that uses the skills you already have, or you may wish to develop new skills that will set you in a different career direction. For example, if you are understanding and a good listener, you may have what it takes to be a customer service representative for an airline. You may need to learn computer skills as well. By combining the skills you already have and the ones you want to develop, you can begin to make yourself a stronger candidate for the job you want. If you are unsure about whether you will fit into the career field that interests you, remember there is a wide range of jobs that may suit you within each field.

If you tend to have many mechanical "hands-on" skills, such as machine repair or computer operation, you may enjoy a job as a technician. If you have good interpersonal skills, such as working well as a team member or teaching, and prefer using them on a daily basis, you may enjoy a job that focuses more on dealing with people. Within every career field, jobs range from high people orientation to high task orientation. The travel/tourism field is a good example. If you are in a travel/tourism program in school and you find that many of your good skills are interpersonal ones, you will probably enjoy a job such as a tour escort, where you would deal with people a lot. If you find your personal and technical skills to be stronger than your interpersonal skills, you may enjoy a job as a data analyst in the travel industry. The tour escort spends most of his or her time working with the public individually and in groups, while the data analyst may independently review population trends in a city and write a recommendation on whether or not to build a new hotel or restaurant there.

Both jobs are in the travel/tourism industry, but each is very different and may require a different type of person.

Defining Success

Everyone has his or her own definition of success. You won't get to where you want to go with someone else's dream—you must create your own. For many people, success is defined as carving out your own niche—finding something you want to do and doing it well. Your idea of success may be to reach a feeling of personal fulfillment, or it may be to reach a certain financial status. As you attempt to define your own success, think about what's important to you, not to those around you. Don't limit yourself to traditional ideas of success, such as a top position in a large corporation, but broaden your idea to something you can really feel in your gut! When you feel the drive for something that strongly, you must want it badly enough to really go after it.

Changing Perspectives Over the years, there have been changing perspectives on success. Talk to some successful people and ask what their definition of success was when they first started their careers. They might say something like:

"I'd like to be earning $100,000 a year by the time I am 30 years old."
"I'd prefer to be my own boss."
"I want to own a vacation home on one of the islands."
"I want to own a new sports car."
"I'd like to get my book published."

Then ask if that definition of success has changed over the years. In almost all cases, the answer will be yes. People who are well established in their careers will probably give some very different answers, like:

"I'd like to balance my time between job, family, and friends."
"I'd like to be challenged in my work."
"I'd enjoy helping someone else reach one of his or her goals."
"I want to be the best secretary in my department."
"I'd like to be debt-free."

Your changing values affect your attitudes about success. Both your age and the society in which you live affect your values. At an early age, your symbols of success may be focused on approval from others and independence demonstrated by owning material things. As you grow older and gain more experience, your symbols of success may change as your value system changes. You may experience a shift away from needing outside sources of approval toward wanting inner satisfaction. For example, some of the new symbols of success are having more control over one's time, viewing work as fun, receiving affection and understanding from others, involvement with community work, and teaching or helping others.

As you progress through your career, changes in your personal life and in the world around you will have an impact on your goals. An emphasis on human resources will cause employers to develop new approaches to rewarding performance in the workplace. The traditional meaning of the words *reward, recognition,* and *compensation* will change to meet the new values of the worker in the 21st century. The values of tomorrow's workers—including you—are changing the work force as we've known it in the past. For these reasons, successful lifelong career planning involves periodic review of your definition of success and your strategies for achieving it.

As you plan your career today, decide what your definition of success is right now and base your immediate decisions on that. If success to you right now is being hired by one of the leading employers in your field, focus on achieving that. Just understand that by looking ahead and at least thinking about the lifestyle you may want in the future, your present decisions may take a different focus.

Qualities of Success   Some qualities of success include setting goals, a positive attitude, risk taking, enthusiasm, and motivation. Successful people share many common characteristics. By having *goals*, they take each one of their small successes and use them to build bigger successes in the future. Successful people make the most of their intelligence. They have and use common sense. They are willing to explore new avenues of information. Some of the most interesting individuals are those who read extensively, listen well, and absorb all the facts they can from the world around them. Successful people are usually *positive*, a trait which attracts people to them. They have ways of preventing disappointments and setbacks from becoming obstacles to their goal. Along with a positive attitude comes the ability to trust and believe in oneself and others. Successful people are good *risk takers* and are willing to accept failure as part of the course. They think you fail only when you are not able to cash in on the experience you have.

Successful attitudes are built on *enthusiasm*. Enthusiasm is the demonstration of a strong interest in something. It comes from within and has a strong effect on other people. Enthusiasm lends credibility to what you do and results in your own satisfaction. It builds spirit around an idea and is a great basis for creativity. A fantastic idea that is presented with little enthusiasm can be rejected in favor of another idea that is delivered more enthusiastically.

Successful people are usually highly motivated. *Motivation* is an inner drive that makes you do something. Motivation makes you productive and allows you to work well independently. If you are motivated, you have a healthy interest in yourself. Motivation goes hand in hand with a love for what you do. All these qualities of success must come from within. They are not something anyone else can give you. Above all else, *success is really an attitude*. It is a choice you make to respond to problems as opportunities, to see alternate routes to your goals when others see only a path with a dead end.

Success and Your Career Choice   As you decide on the career you will pursue, think about how well it will allow you to meet your individual definition of success. For example, will it provide you the level of financial stability you are looking for? Will promotion eventually require a higher level of education than you are currently pursuing? Will it enable you to satisfactorily maintain your family relationships? Ultimately, you must ask yourself if your career choice will allow you to have the overall lifestyle you want. A successful career helps you lead a successful life.

EMPLOYER EXPECTATIONS

Generally speaking, employers prefer candidates who possess some combination of the positive personality traits, skills, and qualities of success just discussed. Some employers may have additional expectations when considering you as a job candidate. The following sections will give you some information about these expectations and how important they are to employers.

Goals

When you have goals, an employer may recognize your commitment to your career, believe you will stay in a job for a reasonable length of time, and realize where your self-motivation will come from.

Positive Personality

A person with a positive personality has certain characteristics, including a good attitude, poise, self-confidence, decisiveness, and a tendency to be extroverted. Having one or more of these attributes may convince an employer that you can do the job well.

Appropriate Technical Skills

Employers must first be concerned with filling their job openings with candidates who possess the basic aptitude to do the job. Whether or not it is important that your skills be fully developed depends on the job, but in most cases you must demonstrate at least the basic skills to start in the job. An employer will evaluate how much more training you need and decide whether it is possible to provide you with this additional training. You must be sure to convince an employer that you can perform the tasks the job requires. Remember that the attitude you present with those skills may convince an employer to hire you even when more technical training is needed on the job.

Application Skills

Human resource professionals often agree on what various industries are looking for from students with a postsecondary education. Many repeat all the qualities discussed so far but unanimously agree that these three attributes are most important: The ability to *analyze* information, *apply* how it can be used, and then take appropriate *action* were the most necessary skills for success in their corporations. These "think and do" skills are the most basic to any business situation because they are a source of ideas that develop new products, and they ensure that workers learn how to act independently on the job, providing growth for themselves and for the company.

Work Ethic

Proving you have a strong work ethic may include giving examples that show you are willing to work hard and perform to the best of your ability on a regular basis. Even if you haven't had a lot of work experience, the hard work you put into your studies or into a project or hobby are good examples of your strong work ethic.

Realistic Expectations

Realistic expectations of job candidates about starting salaries and job responsibilities are important to employers because they may improve job satisfaction. When a job candidate fully understands what is expected of him or her on a day-to-day basis, there is less chance of disagreement or disappointment about the job.

Maturity

Employers evaluate maturity in a variety of ways. Your ability to remain poised in different situations, tolerate differences of opinion, and assume responsibility with little supervision are some examples of how an employer may evaluate your maturity level. Immaturity in the workplace can lead to personality conflicts, poor performance, or inappropriate social behavior. Employers try to avoid hiring immature workers because they may be disruptive or unproductive in the workplace, show less likelihood of success, or require more supervision and training than an employer is willing to provide.

Enthusiasm

Enthusiasm is one indicator of how excited you really are about your career and about life. Employers prefer candidates who seem genuinely excited about their job, because usually people perform best when they are doing what they like to do. Lack of enthusiasm may be interpreted as a lack of interest or confidence on your part.

Focus

Your ability to be focused on your career goals tells the employer you have already thought through many options and have decided to make a commitment to a specific career. This means there is a greater chance that you are choosing a job you really want, and that you will concentrate on doing what is necessary to be successful.

Scholastic Record

Your scholastic record is one way an employer may judge whether you have developed skills appropriate to the job. Reviewing your record will indicate if the courses you studied provided the skills you will need, and good grades in these courses will indicate an understanding of the subject. Good grades may also be concrete evidence that you have the motivation, enthusiasm, and focus needed to succeed.

Company Knowledge

Your ability to convince an employer that you understand and like the business field you are about to enter is important. When you have thoroughly investigated both the industry and the company you may be dealing with, you demonstrate sincerity about wanting to work for that company and give the impression that you're not just shopping around for any job that comes along.

Follow-Through

An ability to independently follow directions on projects is important. Employers want to know you can complete your work on your own without constant supervision. When you need to be supervised constantly, you take away from the time the supervisor has to do his or her own job and you cost the company money.

Handling Conflict

Think of some times you successfully handled conflict. Such incidents may have occurred within your family, with friends, or between co-workers. Conflicts between people happen frequently in the workplace, and an employer needs to know that you are able to handle them on your own. This is both a sign of maturity on your part and a time-saver for the employer, who would prefer not to waste valuable time settling differences between people instead of getting the job done.

Self-Discipline

Self-discipline is helpful on the job because it helps keep you focused on your job until it is completed. The ability to avoid distraction and be self-driven helps you perform your job well.

Outside Interests

Employers look at how involved you are in activities outside the classroom in order to understand your likes and dislikes, your level of initiative, your leadership potential, and your ability to manage your time well. Employers understand if you simply have not been able to explore many outside interests because you've been working or have family responsibilities, but they often prefer some evidence of involvement beyond the classroom. It is important to realize that very often an employer will accept a candidate with weaker skills over another because the candidate seems to be the *right type* for the job. Usually, the right type is someone who demonstrates positive personality traits and qualities of success, and meets the employer's overall expectations.

Loyalty

You should be able to give a prospective employer examples of situations that demonstrate your ability to be loyal to your employer. An example might be a time when you defended the reputation of your company, which had just gotten negative publicity in the newspaper. Another example might be a time when you knew a co-worker was recording more hours on his or her time card than he or she had actually worked, and you told your supervisor about it.

Good Speaking Skills

MARKETING
ASSISTANT
Responsible for handling clerical functions for Director of Marketing, Membership Manager and Database Manager, including:

• correspondence
• travel arrangement
• preparation of reports
• coordination and transmission of communication during Director of Marketing or Department Manager's absence
• assist in other duties as assigned to ensure the smooth running of the Marketing Division

Good communication and organizational skills necessary. Computer experience important. Strong keyboarding ability necessary. Accuracy and promptness a must.

The Society is an equal opportunity employer and provides excellent benefits. The building is wheel-chair accessible. Interested applicants should send resume and salary requirements to:

Personnel Manager
American Mathematical Society
PO Box 6248
Providence, RI 02940

Equal opportunity Employer

Being able to express yourself verbally to an employer can give the impression that you will interact well with others on the job and that you can promote your skills and your ideas confidently. A good appearance may leave the employer thinking you really care about the impression you make on others and that you would present a positive image of the company.

Reviewing this list of qualities is one way to understand what employers look for in job candidates. Another way to understand employer expectations is to read the classified ads. Employers may indicate certain personality traits they are looking for or give other clues as to their expectations by the way they have described the job and the person they are seeking to fill it. Read the qualifications sought for a wide variety of careers in and out of your chosen field. List all of the common attributes that appear in the ads. Do you see many similarities or much repetition? This is a good indication to you that, regardless of differing technical skill requirements, employers expect candidates to demonstrate certain qualities. These qualities are important to the employer because they are, to a large measure, predictors of success.

SETTING GOALS FOR SELF-IMPROVEMENT

Throughout this self-assessment process, you have identified your own values, interests, personality traits, skills, and ideas of success. You have also reviewed those that many employers prefer in the professionals they hire. Preparing for your career involves evaluating how well you compare to what employers expect and then setting goals for self-improvement so that you will better meet employers' expectations.

Characteristics of a Goal

A goal is the difference between where you are and where you want to be. Careers move in a positive direction when you set goals. Before setting your goals for self-improvement, you should be aware of the basic characteristics of successful goals. A goal should be:

Conceivable: Can you picture the goal in your mind?

Believable: Do you really believe it can happen?

Desirable: Do you really want it?

Achievable: Is your goal realistic?

Measurable: When will your goal be accomplished?

Goals provide you with the *motivation* or drive to produce top performance on a daily basis. This drive can come from having a clear idea of the direction in which you want to go. It is much easier to get excited about what you are doing if you can see the end results. In the case of personal goals, the end result can be both gaining personal satisfaction and becoming more qualified for the job you want.

Setting Goals into Action

In developing your personal goals, you will develop an *action plan* and identify *action steps* for each area you want to improve. For example, if one of the personality traits you want to develop is confidence, your action plan may be to offer your opinions more often, even when they are different from others'. Your first action step may be to do this more in class, while your second action step may be to speak up more in social conversations as well. With each action plan, you should decide how you want to monitor your progress and determine how you will really know you've achieved your goal. The act of speaking up more in class may be a way to develop your confidence, but the final measure of whether or not you've developed confidence may be the level of comfort and ease you feel with your new actions. The measure of success as well as the strategies for achieving that success will vary with everyone. What is important is that you think through how you are going to work on your goals and how you will know when you've achieved them.

The process of setting goals for self-improvement really involves turning a weakness into a strength. In the process, remember that acknowledging your weaknesses in a positive way can be important to you and to a prospective employer. Being comfortable with your weaknesses is the result of having a plan for improving them. With this plan, you gain control of the areas you need to improve, rather than letting those areas control you. Your ability to express your weaknesses in a positive way to an employer can mean the difference between the job you really want and the job you may settle for. If an employer asks what your major strengths and weaknesses are and your thoughts are "I am an excellent typist, but my shorthand is only 60 wpm," your response should be "I am an excellent typist. I am working at bringing my shorthand speed up by practicing on my own (or by taking an extra class, or by asking my boss to let me use it more on the job I have now). I like shorthand and realize it is an important skill. I am confident that my speed will improve with practice."

Through this process of setting goals for self-improvement, you can honestly turn something that may sound negative into a positive response. This is easier to do if you already have your action plans and success measures in place!

PROOF BY EXAMPLE

Now that you have assessed what skills you have and compared them to what employers look for, you need to focus on how to *convince* an employer that you have excellent qualifications for the job. An employer must be able to *visualize* your value to his or her organization. It is essential that you *create* a *word picture* of your skills, abilities, and past accomplishments and that you link these to the employer's needs.

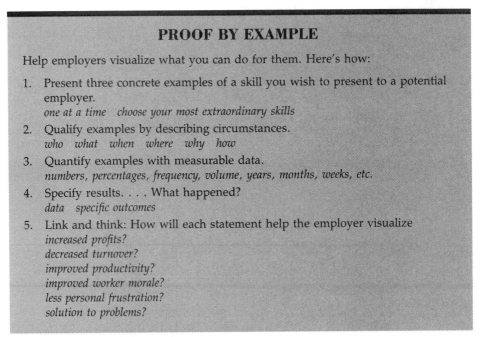

PROOF BY EXAMPLE

Help employers visualize what you can do for them. Here's how:

1. Present three concrete examples of a skill you wish to present to a potential employer.
   one at a time   choose your most extraordinary skills
2. Qualify examples by describing circumstances.
   who   what   when   where   why   how
3. Quantify examples with measurable data.
   numbers, percentages, frequency, volume, years, months, weeks, etc.
4. Specify results. . . . What happened?
   data   specific outcomes
5. Link and think: How will each statement help the employer visualize
   increased profits?
   decreased turnover?
   improved productivity?
   improved worker morale?
   less personal frustration?
   solution to problems?

Excerpted from Career Development Seminars, Robert Morris College.

Chapter Two

Personal Development

Personal development is the process of improving your image. It is an important part of your professional development, because projecting a positive image of yourself is key to working well with others. A positive image also helps you when you are being considered for a promotion. Professional development is the process of establishing yourself in your career. Personal development involves developing effective communication skills, proper grooming and dress, time management, stress management, business manners, role models, and awareness of the world around you.

COMMUNICATION SKILLS

You may spend more than 85 percent of your day communicating with others.[1] Communication takes many forms: speaking, writing, listening, and body language. Each interaction we have with others results in either a positive or a negative impression. First impressions consist of things people notice about you when they first meet you. *It takes only two to four minutes to make a first impression.* First impressions are important because they can lead others to pay further attention to you or disregard you before they get to know you. Communication skills are necessary to enhance your technical skills. Excellent communication skills may even make up for weaknesses in technical skills with some employers. For example, if a secretary must spend a lot of time dealing with clients, strong communications skills may compensate for a slow typing speed. This is because it may be easier for a good communicator to improve typing skills through practice than for a poor communicator to become an effective communicator.

Speaking

Speaking is a form of communication. The spoken word can be powerful, depending on the content of the message and the style in which it is delivered. Being aware of what you sound like can help you know how you may be coming across during a job interview, an oral presentation, or a one-on-one discussion. Factors that influence how your voice is received include: how fast you speak

---

[1]Janet G. Elsea, "The First Four Minutes," *First Impression, Best Impression* (New York: Simon & Schuster, 1984).

(rate), how high or low your voice is (pitch), how positive you sound (tone), and how clear your speech is (articulation).

What you say is not always as important as *how* you say it. The quality of your message should ultimately make the difference in whether or not your message is credible to others. However, the relationship between how you say something (your voice) and what you say (your message) is critical. Learning how to match your voice with the content of your message is key to being an effective communicator. Let's look at some examples of the relationship between the two.

Say the following sentence two times, putting verbal emphasis on the italicized word(s). "Did you know he *succeeded* on the third try?" "Did you know he succeeded on the *third* try?" Most people would interpret this same statement in two distinct ways, given the different verbal emphasis in each case. The first statement emphasizes the word *succeeded*. The thought that he was successful is foremost in the listener's mind, regardless of how many times he tried. The second statement emphasizes the word *third*. The thought that it took three attempts before this person was successful is emphasized. The tone of each sentence implies different meaning.

As you move forward in your career, you will have many opportunities to create a positive impression by how you speak. When you use the telephone to respond to a want ad or ask people for career advice, your voice is your only tool for making a good impression. Let someone hear a smile in your voice by being enthusiastic. Speak slowly and clearly pronounce all your words. Project your voice so you can be heard. If you have an accent, you should be conscious of how well you are understood by others. If the clarity of what you say is not diminished by your accent, there is no need to work on eliminating it. If your accent sometimes interferes with your ability to deliver a clear message, you should work on changing it.

Listening

Listening is the communication skill that is most often overlooked. Listening is paying attention to what someone is saying. A good listener hears the message being conveyed and evaluates the meaning of the message. Good listening is a form of learning because it reveals knowledge of others. Hearing what is being said but not concentrating on what it means is called *passive listening*. *Active listening* means hearing what is being said and interpreting its meaning as well. Active listening makes you a more effective communicator because you react to what you have heard.

As you are planning your career, you will find listening to be helpful in many ways. Listening to business and personal acquaintances may lead you to a new contact. Listening to how someone talks about their company can tell you a lot about how the company is run and the morale of the employees that work there.

Good listening skills include being able to distinguish fact from fiction, detect inconsistencies in information, and understand the main points of a message. When parts of a message are unclear, the best thing to do is to take notes, jot down your questions, and wait until the entire presentation or discussion is finished. It may also be appropriate to provide comments about what was presented or to provide feedback on what was said and how it was said. Remember that many times we have difficulty listening to what is being said because we are distracted by things that are bothering us or by the environment around us. Another distraction can be our own emotions about what is being presented or about the speaker. The key to overcoming these distractions is concentration. By developing basic communication skills, you will become more confident in yourself and more effective in your interaction with others.

TEST YOURSELF—ARE YOU A GOOD LISTENER?

- Are you attentive?
- Do you maintain eye contact?
- Do you ever start speaking before another person has finished?
- Are you tuned in to the other person's facial expression, gestures, body language, and tone of voice?

Writing

Writing effectively can also help you gain a competitive edge in your job search when writing letters or résumés or completing a job application. Throughout your career, almost any job will require you to produce written documents. You may also want to show a prospective employer a report you did for one of your classes. People form an impression about you through your writing. Well-organized thoughts and good grammar, spelling, and punctuation show the reader that you care about the quality of your work. The neatness of any document you produce is important. This means having no white-outs, erasures, or bent or soiled papers.

You can take several steps to become a good writer. These include deciding on the content, sequence, and style of your writing. *Content* is the first thing you need to think about. Focus on what you want your message to be. Ask yourself what you are really trying to tell someone. To get started, jot down some of the key words or phrases that begin to define your message.

Sequencing the information you want to convey means listing your key points in the order you want to present them. Look to see if there is a flow in the thought process you are using, and be sure there are no gaps.

Style of writing can be chosen to reflect the personality of the writer or to fit the degree of formality required in different situations. When writing is required as part of your job search, you should be sure to let your individuality come through. Very often, how you express yourself in the written word can differentiate you from others saying the same thing in writing:

Factual: "I have all the necessary qualifications to work at your company."

Professional: "My education, coupled with my work experience, makes me a well-qualified candidate for the job you offer."

Distinctive: "The secretarial award I won for my typing accuracy and speed and the A I received in my Communications class make me an excellent choice for your administrative assistant position."

Notice that in the last statement, the human resource manager may learn about the unique qualifications you personally bring to the job. Being specific about the skills you offer when presenting yourself to an employer may help you stand out among other applicants.

In general, the writing style for almost all job-search situations should be professional. To develop an effective professional writing style, you should know your reader, know your message, and be concise. Having this type of focus helps you get to the point so that what you say is clearly understood. Sound confident. Your confidence helps the reader feel that you can support what you say. Use proper form (grammar, spelling, punctuation), so that the quality of your work will not be questioned. Keep the language simple. When you do this, the reader can understand what you say better, and there is less chance of confusing the reader. Proofread your own work so that there are no mistakes. Have someone else proofread your work. You will want the opportunity to correct errors and make improvements on your work before it is in final form. It is not proper form to use slang or abbreviations in your professional writing. Avoid copying form letters. Form letters should serve as a guide for you to get started with your work, but what you say and how you say it should be original. Sound enthusiastic! You will sound more convinced and you will be more convincing when you are enthusiastic.

Body Language

Body language is a form of nonverbal communication conveyed by certain body movements. Body language includes your facial expression, poise, posture, and mannerisms. When someone looks at you, certain clues can be detected through your body language as to how you feel or what you may be thinking. Facial expressions can reveal your inner thoughts and feelings or present a controlled reaction by choice. Facial expression can show a variety of emotions. These are just a few simple illustrations of how you communicate with your face, before any words are spoken:

Facial Expression	*Message to Others*
Smile	Acceptance or approval
Frown	Anger, confusion, or disappointment
Wide-open eyes	Interest and confidence
Raised brows	Surprise
Wandering eyes	Boredom or distraction

Poise is your ability to act with ease and dignity. When you are poised, you appear self-assured and composed in almost every situation. A poised person appears to be in control of most actions and reactions. Posture is one indicator of poise. Standing or sitting straight and still, without appearing tense or uncomfortable, creates an impression that you are confident about the situation you are in. Think about people you know who are noticeable when entering a room just by the way they hold their body. The way a person carries himself or herself indicates total confidence. Poised people can create energy just by walking into a room.

Each of us has certain mannerisms that either add to or detract from our image. Mannerisms are part of our body language and are formed by habits we have developed. Mannerisms include using your hands a lot to emphasize a point when you speak, tapping your foot while waiting or in a hurry, or rocking back and forth or pacing when standing in front of an audience to make a presentation. While certain mannerisms may have a positive effect, mannerisms like the ones just mentioned may not. Some positive mannerisms that can help you communicate well in most business settings include direct eye contact, a firm handshake, nodding your head to show support or approval, extending your right arm with open hand to let someone go ahead of you or tell them to start first, scanning the entire audience or group with your eyes when making a presentation, or nodding once to acknowledge someone's presence or give them the signal to go ahead with something.

Facial expressions, poise, posture, and mannerisms are all important parts of body language because they influence someone's impression of you before you even speak. By developing appropriate nonverbal responses to situations, you are in better control of the image you portray and have a better chance of making a good long-lasting impression on others.

The Sales Process

Any employer will hire any applicant as long as he or she is *convinced* that the applicant will bring in more value than it costs to hire that person. It has already been well established that knowing yourself and being able to communicate effectively are important to your success. Once you have your own sense of direction and have determined what you want, you need to know how to get it. To successfully compete in tomorrow's workplace, you need to be *convincing*. Knowing yourself and your goals is the first step, but communicating them effectively to the people that count is the key to successfully managing your career.

The person with the hardest job of convincing is the salesperson. The sales process is really the process you will go through on a job interview. Before learning the many specific interviewing techniques that exist, you will want to consider the sales process as an approach to obtaining the jobs you want. In the employment process, think of the *employer as the customer* and *you as the product*. You have a certain set of skills and attributes to bring to the employer, and the employer offers an opportunity for you to use them.

Why are some people with similar skills and attributes hired and others not if their qualifications meet those needed for the job? The difference lies in the candidates' ability to sell themselves. There is a difference between marketing and sales. Both are important in the employment process. *Marketing* involves surveying the market, both employers and potential employers, and assessing their needs and wants.

Selling means convincing! Sales is the formal process of exchanging what you have for what someone else has. In the employment process, your skills are exchanged for a job. Both you and the employer benefit if the match is right. If it is not, neither one of you benefits. So beyond having effective sales ability, you need to be sure you want the job you are going after and that the employer really needs you. Identifying customer needs is one of the keys to effective salesmanship. Let's take a look at why people buy and compare it to why an employer might hire you.

Why People Buy	Employer Interests
To satisfy a need	To fill a job opening
Cost effectiveness	To increase profitability
Comfort and convenience	Employees' professional preparation and ability to "fit in"

It costs a company money to hire you. The company loses money if you don't work out in the job. High company recruiting costs result in competitive candidate selection. The Bank of Boston recently estimated that it costs $80,000 before new managers get through their training program. The bank spends $10,000 on recruiting, $50,000 on training, and $20,000 on relocating and travel expenses. The costly hiring process makes companies highly selective. In a typical year, the Bank of Boston interviewed 1,800 students. They then "cut down" to 1,200 interviews to hire 50 people. The average recruiting cost per new recruit is $1,600. Whether a company visits your school to interview you or runs ads in the newspaper, it costs money to hire someone new.

You stand a good chance of competing for a job if you have the skills to do the job, if you are sure that you want the job before taking it so that replacement costs will not skyrocket for the company, and if you can reinforce the employer's feelings that you've been professionally trained.

GROOMING

A professional appearance is a statement of confidence. People are more apt to listen to you if you look like you take your job seriously. Your professional appearance starts with good grooming.

Good grooming is caring for your body to ensure it is as clean and fit as possible. Good grooming is a way to look and feel good. It includes personal hygiene and your overall wellness.

Personal Hygiene

Cleanliness is important to how you look and to your health. Personal hygiene involves the following practices:

- Bathe or shower daily.
- Be clean shaven. Women should shave the hair on legs and underarms. Men should shave their beards. In certain professions, you will find it necessary to have no beard, while in others it may be acceptable.
- Brush your teeth at least twice a day. It doesn't hurt to carry a travel-size tube of toothpaste and a toothbrush so that you can brush after lunch or dinner if you are away from home.
- Use underarm deodorant after you bathe or shower to avoid possible body odor.
- Keep nails clean and nicely cut.
- Keep hair clean and shaped well by having it cut on a regular basis. Avoid extreme styles or striped colors (green or orange), and be sure hair color or highlights are subtle.
- If you wear makeup, be sure to apply it lightly so that it accentuates your features instead of changing your looks.

Wellness

Proper exercise and diet can help you look and feel brighter, more alert, and more energetic. Diet and exercise are often neglected because of constantly changing work or school schedules. Here are some guidelines for building healthy habits:

- Control total fat and salt intake. It is recommended that total fat intake not exceed 30 percent of total caloric intake. Reading food labels can help you be aware of how much fat and salt are in the foods you eat.
- Avoid substance abuse that can result in overuse or misuse of alcoholic beverages, drugs, or tobacco. Overindulgence of any of these substances can seriously impair your health.
- Drink plenty of water. Drinking eight glasses of water per day helps keep the body in balance. If you find eight glasses excessive for you, be sure to incorporate a good amount of water in your diet every day.
- When restaurant dining, you can follow these same healthy guidelines if you choose the right items on the menu. Most restaurants offer a variety of leaner foods (pasta, chicken, fish, and salads) and a choice of how food is prepared (baked, broiled, poached, steamed, or grilled).
- If you can, exercise moderately every day. You may join a fitness center or a health spa, or you may develop your own routine, such as walking briskly for 20 minutes per day.

DRESS

Developing your own personal style by how you dress can be a lot of fun. The styles, colors, and degree of formality of the clothes you wear can express a lot about your personality. What is important to know as you prepare for your career is the type of dress that will create your best professional image.

Some of the factors that influence your choice of career wardrobe include the type of work situation you will be in every day, the professional look you are trying to achieve, regional differences, and enhancing your own personality and body type. You can enhance your professional image by knowing which colors and fabrics work best for you. Before you begin to plan your business wardrobe, you should know how all of these factors can influence the selections you make.

Work Situations

Different work situations require different styles of dress. The type of work you do and the work setting define your work situation. For example, some jobs require uniforms. Most jobs require a professional look appropriate to the job setting—for example, an office, a store, a bank, or a restaurant. Projecting a good image in "off-the-job" situations is also important.

Uniforms

Jobs in many fields of work require uniforms. This is especially true in the health care, technical, food service, and hospitality industries. If your profession requires you to wear a uniform, don't assume that you can be lazy about your professional attire. When uniforms are required for work or the classroom, treat them as you would any other good clothing you would buy. Keep them clean, pressed, and new looking at all times. Uniforms should not be an excuse "not to have to worry about dressing for work every day." Buy a good number of uniforms to be sure you always have a clean one available. Only wear uniforms that look crisp and clean. Replace a uniform when the fabric or color begins to wear. Wear shoes that are appropriate for the uniform. Do not overaccessorize a uniform with scarves, jewelry, and so on.

Professional Look

You should always strive for a professional look when dressing for the workplace. Carefully choosing the right clothes for work makes you feel better about yourself on the job and tells an employer you care about the image you are projecting for yourself and the company. To help you understand what a professional look is, here are basic dress rules to follow that seem to be universal for both men and women:

- Choose well-coordinated outfits. This means mixing and matching colors and styles tastefully. For example, if you wear a blazer, wear tailored trousers or a skirt to go with it. You wouldn't wear a casual flared skirt or balloon pants with a blazer.
- Suits and dresses are usually worn to conduct business. Don't assume you can dress casually. Even if you are working at your own desk most of the time, your look should always be professional enough to go to an unexpected meeting, greet guests into your area, or represent the company unexpectedly at a social or professional event in the evening. If you are not required to wear a suit, it is always better for women to wear a skirt or dress rather than slacks and for men to wear a sport coat rather than just shirtsleeves.
- Wear long- or short-sleeved blouses or shirts. Avoid sleeveless tops, unless you intend to keep a jacket over them. Do not wear tank tops to work.
- Accessorize tastefully with ties, scarves, or jewelry that are not too gaudy or trendy. For example, even though it is a trend for some men to wear earrings, this is not appropriate in the workplace. A studded belt that might look great with your denim jeans is not fitting for the workplace.
- Wear closed-toe shoes that are new-looking and well polished.

Sound simple? It is easy to begin a business wardrobe with these basic guidelines. Although you may think this sounds boring, having a few outfits that will give you a well-put-together, conservative look is essential for everyone. The chart on page 29 lists basic wardrobe items that are important to building your professional look. Determine which items you have or need, and develop an approximate budget to make any purchases.

There may be some jobs, such as a recreation coordinator, in which very casual attire is common because of comfort, safety, or convenience. However, most research shows that the professional look described is accepted and most often expected. When considering your work situation and how you will dress, keep in mind that you should also use good judgment when dressing for company social events—formal or casual. If you are invited to attend a sporting event or a picnic, choose nice, casual clothing. Try to avoid jeans; wear casual slacks instead. Don't wear T-shirts that have writing or pictures on them; wear polo shirts or short-sleeved shirts or blouses instead. You want to portray a neat yet stylish image and avoid any clothing that might make you look cheap or sloppy. When attending more formal social events, such as a Christmas party or awards dinner, avoid wearing low-cut or sheer outfits, or any type of dress that may be better suited for a school dance.

All of these different work situations require your good judgment when it comes to dress. If you are not sure what is appropriate, observe what other people are wearing or ask ahead of time if there is a preferred dress style for the situation.

Regional Differences

In different parts of the country, professional dress may vary according to a region's culture or climate. The North and Northeast are generally the most conservative in business dress, reflecting the overall conservative attitude in these areas. The colder climate also influences the selection of colors and fabrics. Colors tend to be darker and fabrics heavier (wool, gabardine, polyester blends). The South is not as conservative but is somewhat more formal in its attitude toward dress. In this warmer climate, colors and fabrics tend to be lighter (cotton, linen, silks).

The hotter climates of the West and Southwest tend to dictate less formal attire and certainly lighter fabrics and colors. However, it is important to note some things about this region. Even though the hot climate may be suitable for lighter-weight clothes, it does not give you license to wear low-cut, sheer, or see-through (voile, lace) clothing. These are simply not appropriate at any time in any business setting.

Enhancing Your Look

You can enhance your look by dressing according to your personality and body type. Choose clothes because they complement your figure and not just because

BASIC WARDROBE CHART

Women

	Have	Need	Approximate Cost
Suits			
Blazers			
Blouses			
Sweaters			
Skirts			
Dresses			
Pants			
Coats			
Shoes			
Boots			
Handbags			
Belts			
Scarves			
Gloves			
Total			

Men

	Have	Need	Approximate Cost
Suits			
Blazers			
Shirts			
Sweaters			
Vests			
Slacks			
Pants			
Coats			
Shoes			
Boots			
Hats			
Belts			
Scarves			
Gloves			
Total			

they are the latest style. Remember that dark (black, brown, gray) and cool (blue, green) colors minimize size, while light (white, pink, peach) and warm (red, purple, yellow) colors maximize size. Vertical lines in clothes can help you look taller, while horizontal lines can make you look fuller.

Colors and styles can also reflect your personality. Bold colors (red) or combinations of colors (black and white) often depict an outgoing personality. Cooler colors (beige, light blue) might reflect a calmer or quieter personality or mood. Finally, business accessories can enhance your professional style.

Luggage Discard your outdated and worn bags and invest in some good luggage.

Briefcase Regardless of the position you hold, using a briefcase is the best way to transport your paperwork to and from the office. Briefcases are not limited to use by executives; they are a useful and efficient way to keep important information organized.

Leather-Bound Notebook These are for holding or for attending meetings, keeping daily "to do" lists, or attending conferences and workshops. They look better than a note pad or loose-leaf paper and provide a convenient way to keep papers together.

Calendars Keep one on your desk, one at home, and one in your pocket or handbag. There will be many times you will not be in your work area when you are asked if you are available, and it is very frustrating not to be able to check your schedule immediately. Keeping a calendar at home that records your business schedule is extremely helpful when starting a new week or day.

Watch Wear a watch so you can be on time. Punctuality is an important habit to develop.

Personalized Stationery Two types of personalized stationery can suit your needs—one that you use for personal correspondence and a different one for business. When you use either kind, your correspondence is more personalized.

Subscriptions to Trade Journals Useful information about current trends in your career field is found regularly in trade journals. Make a habit of reading at least one regularly.

These are just a few examples of items that indirectly add to your professional image. These items also make up a terrific gift list for graduation, holiday giving, birthdays, or the start of your first job.

Dress can help you present a positive image of yourself if you choose clothing that is appropriate to your job, the area you live in, and your own body type. Dress is a great form of self-expression which can reflect your individuality. How you dress for work can tell a lot about you and help you project confidence and pride in yourself.

TIME MANAGEMENT

A well-known author once wrote, "Nothing is easier than being busy, and nothing more difficult than being effective." Do you know someone who is constantly busy, has a lot of different activities going on at once, and never seems to get any of them done? Sometimes you are never really sure what that person has done, but he or she displays a sense of urgency about everything. You may eventually view that person as being extremely competent, but not until you have had a chance to see exactly what he or she has accomplished.

Time management is the ability to see a task through from start to finish. To be able to see an *important* task through on time, and with *quality* results, is good time management. The amount of time spent doing something says nothing about the quality of the results or the person's ability. Time management is also defined informally as becoming more efficient at doing things that are important. In this case, *efficient* refers to quality and productivity, while *important* refers to what really needs to be done. Look over the following list of activities for the month of May:

At School	*On the Job*
Term paper	Your performance review
Final exams	Proposal deadline
Counseling session	Monthly statements
Graduation	Train a temporary worker
Oral report	Attend a company function

Either of these scenarios may be familiar to you. If both of them are, chances are you have already had a lot of experience with time management. Read each list carefully. Think about how you would accomplish these activities successfully. List a few of the decisions you need to make.

For School	*For the Job*
Example: Give up one night out a week to work on assignments	*Example:* Work Saturday morning to get caught up
_____	_____
_____	_____
_____	_____
_____	_____

If it were April 1, what actions would you take, knowing your schedule in May?

For School	*For the Job*
Example: Start research now for term paper	*Example:* Start list of things you wish to discuss on your performance review
_____	_____
_____	_____
_____	_____
_____	_____

Did these decisions come easily to you? For many people, there isn't even a decision process, but rather a "do whatever comes next" approach. That approach may even have worked for you up to now, but what will happen when you receive another important school assignment that *must* get done by April 15? When you get sick the second week of May? When your car breaks down on Saturday morning? *Will you still meet your deadlines efficiently?*

Here are some ways to develop time management skills.

- First, and most important, believe that you are in control!
- Learn to say no graciously.
- Delegate appropriately. Don't give the very important work to someone else, yet don't be afraid to ask for help.
- Handle interruptions; don't let them handle you.
- Prioritize. You prioritize by evaluating and asking:
    "How critical is the work?"
    "How long will it take from start to finish?"
    "What do you need to do to get it done?"
    "Who do you need to deal with?"
- Set a timetable to measure how you are doing.
- If the job seems overwhelming, break it down into more easily manageable steps. Finish one at a time.
- Have alternatives for how you will spend your time if you have to wait for someone or something.
- Build in some free time. During very busy times, it is important to take care of your physical and mental health. The quality of your work is easily affected by burnout. Have fun, and don't take yourself too seriously. Instead of becoming consumed with getting things done, enjoy each accomplishment along the way. Take time to pat yourself on the back for a job well done. Look at the challenge in whatever you are doing. When you do, the reward will bring you more satisfaction.

STRESS MANAGEMENT

Stress is a physical, psychological, or performance-related reaction to internal or external events. Symptoms of stress include procrastinating, rushing or skipping meals, difficulty with listening, misplacing things, forgetfulness, lack of energy, lack of social time, frequent lateness, or stifled creativity. Try a few of the following techniques to ward off stress and increase your productivity:

- Build resistance by regular sleep, a moderate exercise plan, healthy eating habits, and participation in outdoor work activities.
- Try to find a 10- to 20-minute period for total body relaxation every day. Tense each set of muscles for a short period, then relax them. With practice, anyone can induce a state of relaxation through muscle control.
- Talk over problems with peers on the job. Social support reduces stress.
- Set clear goals and work toward them at as even a pace as possible; deal with one item at a time.
- Laugh.
- If morning is your high-energy time, tackle jobs that cause you the most stress then.
- Attack problems, not people—including yourself.
- Remember, it's not necessarily *what* happens to you, but how you *interpret* events.[2]

BUSINESS MANNERS

Having business manners means knowing how to move through sometimes awkward situations with ease and grace. Business manners are an essential ingredient to success in today's service industries. With today's emphasis on people in organizations, the art of successful interaction is dependent upon your ability to handle yourself professionally in many different situations. Your ability to do the right thing at the right time or to say the right thing at the right time is not only important in the job interview, but is especially important once you are on the job. Business manners span the whole company from the secretary to the president. Secretaries now have broader responsibilities that require an awareness of proper protocol.

Many meetings between executives occur at luncheons, breakfasts, and dinners, as well as in the boardroom. Salespeople are constantly creating an image for their company with clients. There is no doubt that no matter what your role will be in the organization in which you choose to work, you will play a major role in portraying the company's image. In fact, people really are the

[2]From Carolyn Gold, "Harness Your Stress," *Training Manager,* (company newsletter) The Sheraton Corporation.

company image. In every daily business contact you have, you will be in the powerful position of creating a positive or a negative response in others. Those others will be your superiors, subordinates, associates, and, most important, your customers. How all of these people see you is critical to your own career success. Remember, you have the power to elicit the response you want from them by exercising basic business manners. The following are guidelines to follow that will enhance your social skills as you look for a job and start in your new position. Effective business manners can be exhibited through your conversations with others and telephone skills.

Conversation Is an Art

There is a difference between talking with someone and engaging in interesting conversation with them. A good conversationalist keeps interested and interesting and shows concern for the listener(s). Stay well informed on a wide variety of subjects. Know when to talk business and when not to. Avoid talking about topics that may be too personal, boring, or controversial, such as your health, other people's health, how much things cost, family problems, or harmful gossip. Show interest in what the other person likes to do. Avoid correcting the other person in public. Be excited about others' good news. Don't interrupt. Know how to ask questions that show your interest, but don't pry. Give and accept compliments gracefully. Address everyone within a group, not just one or two people.

When you show through your conversation that you care about other people as well as yourself, you will be received in a more positive way. Balancing your conversations between a focus on yourself and the other person will allow you to express yourself and at the same time make the other person feel good.

Telephone Skills

Telephone skills are an important part of business manners because much of your time in your job search, and even your current part-time job, will be spent on the telephone. Although you are not seen while speaking on the telephone, you are heard and judged by how you handle the call.

Here are some guidelines for making telephone calls.

- Before placing a telephone call, know the name of the person you are calling, his or her title, and the department he or she works in.
- First identify yourself by giving your name and the reason for your call, then ask to be connected to the party you are calling.

- Always refer to the person you are calling by Mr., Ms., or Mrs. and the last name. If you know they have a specific title, such as Dr. or Reverend, use it.
- Learn the proper pronunciation of the person's name before calling.
- If you reach your party, greet them by the proper name and title, introduce yourself, and state the purpose of your call.
- If you cannot reach your party because he or she is unavailable, leave a message that you called and indicate that you will return the call.
- Ask when would be a good time to do so, and then call back when you said you would.
- *Always* remain pleasant and professional, even when your frustration level is high. You don't want the message to read that you were rude.

Here are some rules for receiving telephone calls.

- The telephone should always be answered within three rings. Answering on the first ring is best.
- No one should ever be left on hold for more than one minute. The first call always has priority.
- Transferring a call within a company requires thorough knowledge of the organization, of the different divisions' duties and responsibilities, and of the names of key people who will handle the call properly.

```
        IMPORTANT MESSAGE
FOR   Dr. Smith
DATE  10/5/93   TIME   2:15   A.M.
                              P.M.
        WHILE YOU WERE OUT
M.   Allen Jones
OF  Cartwright Industries
PHONE NO.   (401) 885-6666
TELEPHONE      ✓  PLEASE CALL        ✓
CALLED TO SEE YOU  WILL CALL AGAIN
WANTS TO SEE YOU   RUSH
        RETURNED YOUR CALL
MESSAGE   The contract has been
received and he has some questions.
Please try to call back on
Thursday, 10/7, between 2-4 p.m.
SIGNED  Cheryl Anderson
                        PRINTED IN U.S.A.
```

- If you are not sure where to transfer the call, put the caller on hold briefly, explaining that you are trying to find the proper source to serve the caller's needs, then find out where the call should go. When you are sure you can make the proper transfer, do so.
- If it's your job to screen calls, remember to do so in a professional manner.
- If you are a secretary, you may help an executive return calls by keeping a neat list of calls at your desk and asking the executive if you can place the return call.
- If you must take a message, politely explain that the party being called is unavailable and that you will be sure that the person gets the message.

It is important to remember that the way you handle yourself on the telephone says a lot about you and reflects an image of the company you represent.

THE ART OF TAKING A GOOD MESSAGE

- Name of the caller (correctly spelled).
- Telephone number, including area code if needed, and extension.
- Name of caller's company.
- Date and hour of the call.
- Your name or initials.
- A request to call back immediately, if the call is urgent.
- The message.

ROLE MODELS

A role model is someone you choose to be your frame of reference as you strive to be successful. Your role model usually has qualities you admire and has gone about achieving success in a way you think is admirable. As you set goals for your own personal development, it will be helpful to choose someone who can be your role model. Having a role model is important because you can always have a concrete image of success in mind, even when you are finding it difficult to achieve your goals. Knowing that someone else experienced some obstacles on the path to success and overcame them can be a source of encouragement for overcoming your own obstacles.

AWARENESS OF THE WORLD AROUND YOU

A final step in your personal development is keeping current on what is happening in the world. Develop the habit of either reading the newspaper or watching the news on television every day. It may be helpful to read magazines like *Time* or *Business Week,* or magazines or trade journals specific to your career interest. The point is that being aware of happenings outside of your personal world is important to your ability to hold interesting conversations and relate well to others.

Chapter Three

Career Paths Overview

A career does not limit one's reach. Work tends to be more of an enjoyment because we're satisfying goals that we've set for ourselves. We have a master plan, a life plan, and our current employment is a phase in that.

Edith Jones, *"Do You Know the Difference Between a Job and a Career?"*
The Black Collegian, *September–October 1986.*

One of the best ways to ensure career success is to establish a clear focus on the career path you wish to pursue. When you choose your career path, you understand how you will put your education to work, and you choose jobs and other experiences that will help you reach your career goal. Establishing your career path is important because it allows you to see your career as a progression of many different experiences. A career path is a way of identifying your ultimate career goal and the jobs you may need to succeed in before reaching that goal. Too often, graduates want to be hired into jobs at levels higher than what is realistic in industry. This is because they have established a long-range career goal without a plan for getting there. In this chapter you will learn how to plan the steps to your career by understanding how a job differs from a career, the phases of a career, where the jobs are, types of universal careers, and what the growing career fields are.

JOB VERSUS CAREER

What does work mean to you? By definition, "work is labor—an expenditure of physical energy." In past experience, *work* was something done to earn money. Work has also been defined as a place. To hold a job and to work meant to be at a specific place for specific time periods on specific days because it was required. We therefore lived our lives with *work* as something we did for someone else in some other place. The job, not the person holding it, was important.

The growth of the service industries has changed this perspective dramatically. Personnel officers have become human resource managers as corporations focus on people as key contributors in a struggle for quality, excellence, and innovation. As a result, the workplace has been identified as people-centered. With 80 percent of the work force in service jobs, corporations have become extremely dependent on their human resources for competition and advancement. The difference between a successful company and one that loses its competitive edge relates directly to the quality of its people. Corporations are only as successful as the people who work in them.

Quality performance and true excellence occur only when every individual in the process is committed to them. You will also find that because of these factors, you will determine your own job satisfaction to a large degree. To count only on an employer to ensure your job satisfaction will result in disappointment. In the service industries, your personal, professional, and material rewards will come from your ability to learn and excel at what you are doing. You are very much in control of what happens to you at work.

The phrase *job versus career* is used over and over again while people struggle to define the real differences. Rather than looking at the differences, consider how the terms really complement one another. Since there may be many phases of your career, you may hold many jobs throughout your career. At some point, you will probably stop needing to change jobs and will continue in a key position for a long period of time. It may even be the final job you hold. But the growth you experience in that same job for an extended period of time is also a significant phase in your career.

The difference between a job and a career is not how many jobs you have but rather the meaning that your jobs have for you. To remain in one job for 10 years can be just as successful a career direction as holding a number of jobs. The real determining factors concerning careers are these:

- Your attitude and commitment to what you do goes beyond the tasks you perform every day.
- You have the ability to determine what you want and plan how to get it, as opposed to taking what comes your way.
- Rewards include, but also go beyond, financial rewards.
- Rewards are characterized by growth and change both in you and in the challenges they provide for you.
- Rewards provide a certain degree of psychological and emotional satisfaction.
- Rewards are the result of a planned sequence of related jobs.

Richard Bolles in *What Color Is Your Parachute?* defines a job as "a flexible combination of tasks—which can be arranged in a number of different tantalizing ways."[1] Bolles defines careers as "a flexible combination of skills that can be applied to a wide variety of situations." Flexibility will create job security for you and the confidence that you really are in control of your career.

---

[1]Richard Bolles, *What Color Is Your Parachute?*

A major difference between a job and a career is one's attitude. It is possible for two people to perform the same task, have the same title and similar educational backgrounds, and have very different outlooks on their work. If your job is only what you do to pay the bills, it can quickly become routine drudgery. You may develop the attitude that life begins when the workday ends. You will probably be less willing to look beyond the tasks you need to perform, and you may have less enthusiasm for performing them. In a job that is not part of a career direction, there may be no striving for promotion or planning for the future.

If you see your job in the context of larger career goals, your motivation is different. You see it as a challenge, as an opportunity to gain new skills that will help you in the future. You see a next step. You have goals to achieve. You will probably see the job as part of a lifelong learning process. In Chapter Thirteen, "Career Paths," you will see the many jobs that comprise the career you choose. You will notice that the jobs are all somewhat related; they just vary in degree of responsibility. You may stop at any point along the path to become a member of senior management. *Remember, a career is not determined by where you stop or how far you continue, but rather by the attitude with which you perform the job you have at any point in time.*

CAREER PHASES

As you follow along your particular career path, you will notice changes in the nature of the jobs you hold. Throughout any career, there are three phases that are characterized by different types of jobs: the entry-level phase, the second phase, and the third phase.

In the entry-level phase of your career, you will probably be more of a generalist, being trained in and exposed to a wide variety of company procedures. The purpose of the broad scope of entry-level jobs is to acquaint you with a broad picture of your job and how it fits into the company. This first phase may last anywhere from six months to several years.

The second phase of your career will be characterized by jobs that are more specialized. You can expect to spend many years in mid-management and/or specialist jobs. It is during the second phase of your career that you may change jobs most often as you move through a variety of specializations. In each career path, you will notice that the widest variety of jobs exists in the second phase.

It is important to note that many successful careers revolve around staying in mid-management and specialist jobs. These jobs play a very significant role in the company because senior management relies so heavily on the expertise and specific knowledge of people in those jobs. A significantly rewarding career can result in maintaining jobs within this area due to the tremendous impact they have on the company and the challenge and variety they can offer individuals.

The third phase of your career is management, which moves you back to a more generalist position. If you choose to pursue your career into management at some point, you will find yourself relying on the specialists because your focus will be on many broad areas on a day-to-day basis.

Thus, there are many ways of looking at jobs and careers. The most important point to remember is that you manage your career by the jobs you choose and the attitude with which you perform them. *You* determine those jobs and what you want, and *you* take responsibility for getting there. As John W. Newbern said, *"People are divided into three groups: those who make things happen; those who watch things happen; and those who wonder what happened."*

WHERE THE JOBS ARE

Employment opportunities exist in many different areas. Understanding the options available will help you make a more educated decision about the career path you choose.

The three main avenues for employment are the private sector, the public sector, and the foreign sector. Within the private sector, career opportunities exist with individuals, corporations, and institutions. The public sector deals with government employment, and the foreign sector with business or government agencies conducting transactions overseas. The private and public sectors make up our economy and, with the foreign sector, make up our economy outside of the United States.

Private Sector

Small businesses, large corporations, franchises, entrepreneurial enterprises, and nonprofit corporations are examples of where jobs are in the private sector. Currently, 5 of 6 American employees work in institutions with fewer than 1,000 employees. The share of new jobs created by firms with fewer than 100 employees has increased to 40 percent. Although there are increased employment opportunities with smaller firms, large corporations still employ the majority of American workers.

Franchise opportunities are expanding. A franchise is developed when one company assigns to another the right to supply its product. Kentucky Fried Chicken and McDonald's are examples of successful franchise operations. Individual franchisees are required to put up the capital, with the franchisor providing training, technical assistance, specialized equipment, and advertising and promotion.

Entrepreneurs are people who bring together their product knowledge and business expertise to start their own business and make a profit. The individual takes on the risk associated with the new venture and the responsibility for successfully organizing the company.

Nonprofit corporations are developed to provide a service, usually aimed at helping the human services, supporting environmental projects, or doing other work related to improving the world we live in. Although nonprofit corporations are not established to make a profit, they are usually run like successful businesses and may generate a profit. When they do, the money goes back into the operation rather than to the individuals who run it.

Public Sector

Most opportunities in the public sector are careers with the government. Some federal agencies where employment opportunities exist include:

- Air Force Department
- Army Department
- Department of Health and Human Services
- Housing and Urban Development Department
- Department of the Interior
- Justice Department
- Navy Department
- Department of Transportation
- Treasury Department
- Legislative and Judicial Agencies

All of these offer opportunities with a wide variety of options for professionals.

There are some distinct advantages and disadvantages of working for the government. Some advantages include challenging work, job location throughout the country, considerable responsibility, diversity of career paths, and flexible hours. Some disadvantages may include the extensive paperwork and procedures associated with most jobs, uncompetitive pay, lack of personalization because of vast size, and poor working environments. Many career opportunities also exist in state and local governments. Your state department of personnel can provide you a list of job openings and the qualifications needed.

Foreign Sector

International jobs are becoming more popular as the communication and accessibility among countries throughout the world have increased. When considering an international career, you should determine the reason why you want this experience. Experience with other countries and their cultures can be both a professionally and personally rewarding experience because it broadens your perspective of the world. You may think about an international career in or outside of the United States. Within the United States, there are many foreign-based companies. Abroad, you will find opportunities with American-based companies and companies based within each individual country.

You may find the same variety of private-sector opportunities as available in the United States, as well as many opportunities with the public sector. For example, the Peace Corps is an independent agency of the federal government with career opportunities both in and outside of the United States.

UNIVERSAL CAREERS

In addition to deciding which sector your career path will be in, you may want to think about some career options that exist in almost any field. These *universal careers* can be developed as a result of having expertise in a particular discipline. For example, consulting, teaching, writing, or owning and operating your own business are possible in almost any field. Usually these career paths can be pursued after you have attained a high level of professional experience in your particular field. As you begin thinking about your own career path, it is important to remember that you must gain entry-level, technical experience in your first jobs in order to qualify for the long-range jobs you are thinking about. All entry-level jobs are part of paying your dues so that you can qualify for more responsible positions.

CAREER TRENDS

The most noticeable trend in the kinds of jobs that will be available through the year 2000 is the shift toward service professions.

By the year 2000:

- Manufacturing jobs will decline by 300,000.
- Service jobs will increase by 17 million.
- The number of technicians will increase by 100,000.
- The number of operators and laborers will decline by 700,000.
- Retail jobs will grow by more than 3 million.
- More managers, professionals, and marketing and sales personnel will be needed to develop and sell new competitive products.
- Demand for electronic engineers will increase by more than 40 percent.
- Mechanics and installers and repairers of technology will increase by 13 percent overall, with a 60 percent increase in computer equipment repairers.
- Demand for all computer-related occupations will grow by almost 5 percent a year through the 1990s.[2]

Growing Career Fields

Many new career opportunities are growing as a result of some social and economic trends in the United States and abroad.

---

[2]Anthony P. Carnevale, *America and the New Economy*, U.S. Department of Labor Employment and Training Administration.

Accounting Career opportunities in accounting usually remain high regardless of the state of the economy. When businesses are booming, accountants are needed to manage firms' finances. When business is poor, accountants advise firms on how to maintain their financial stability. The advice that accountants provide is often the most important information for the decision-making process in a business. The fastest-growing jobs within the accounting field include consultants and credit specialists. Consulting services are aimed at assisting companies with applying the factual information they have about their finances to an effective business decision. The need for credit specialists is growing because of the problems plaguing the credit and loan industry. Public accountants, management accountants, government accountants, and internal auditors are always in demand.

Administrative Service Office careers have traditionally encompassed a wide variety of support and management positions from entry-level clerical work to office management. The responsibility of administrative service managers surpasses these traditional roles. They are charged with overseeing the day-to-day operations of a business. In a large company, the scope of responsibility might be for one or more departments. In a small company, duties may include overseeing all of the business's operations. Administrative service managers have the prime responsibility for ensuring cost savings and efficiency while, at the same time, not jeopardizing the quality of work performed.

Computer Aided Drafting and Design (CADD) The use of computer aided drafting and design (CADD) and computer aided manufacturing (CAM) is widespread through U.S. corporations. The efficiency this innovative computer application can generate for drafting technicians is revolutionizing the drafting profession. Basically, drafters use computers to draft layouts, line drawings, and designs. Drafters are able to sketch and modify shapes instantly on their computer screens, allowing time for more creativity, accuracy, and flexibility in the design process. CADD technicians work in such fields as architecture and electronics, and they frequently find employment with auto and aerospace factories. Nearly 1.2 million new jobs will be created in this field.

Computer Security Computer security experts work in major corporations and industries to prevent illegal use of computer resources. This may include preventing an unauthorized user of a system from having access to the equipment. It may also include ensuring against unauthorized release of certain data and/or safeguarding the system from computer viruses. Computer security experts sometimes create guidelines for using the system. Jobs are available in industries where computer usage is high, including the federal government. With computer crime on the rise, this position is extremely valuable to companies storing confidential data on their computer systems.

Computer Systems Computer systems analysts evaluate how computer applications can be used to make business procedures easier. The job includes interviewing the person in need of information from the system to determine how to program the computer to produce that information.

Customer Service This position applies to almost any business whose prime focus is customer satisfaction. The customer service representative's job can take on different meanings. In the past, the term was used more to describe a person who took requests from customers and then tried to find the appropriate person to respond to the request. Today, the customer service representative generates new business through sales calls, and interviews customers with complaints, so as to get to the root of the problem and make recommendations for solving it. Because customer service representatives are the frontline people dealing directly with the customers, they can provide feedback on how well customers' needs are being met. Today, companies value the input of customer service representatives and sometimes alter their course of business based on that input. It is a much more pro-active and critical role today than in the past.

Financial Services Financial planners help individuals and corporations make decisions on how to manage their financial resources. They provide input on changing tax laws and on the many investment options available to their clients. Other financial planners sell financial products such as insurance, stocks, and securities. The trend in this field is for careers to move from larger corporations to smaller firms that specialize in a particular service. This focus may enable these professionals to provide more personalized service to their clients. Other career opportunities include consulting work with financial firms that are reorganizing. As existing firms continue to consolidate and new firms emerge, expert advice is often sought to structure the new firm and effectively market its services.

Food Service By the year 2000, at least 500,000 managerial and administrative positions will exist in the food service industry. Annually, $250 billion is spent on food sales, and over 8 million employees work in the industry. One of the fastest-growing segments of the business, off-premises food service sales, is up 20 percent over business between 1989 and 1991. Off-premises catering involves restaurateurs and other establishments providing food service away from their own sites. This may involve catering at homes, institutions, or other commercial properties, or even selling prepared food items through gourmet sections in large supermarket chains.

Health Service Health care jobs are expected to account for 1 of every 12 jobs in the United States by the year 2000. Part of the growth in jobs is due to an increasing number of outpatient facilities and a higher demand for nursing and personal care facilities. Some of the jobs available include nursing and medical technologist positions. They are most needed in hospitals, nursing homes, and home health agencies. Jobs in hospital sales involve working to recruit patients from the community and from major corporations. Lab technicians' positions are growing in number because they are needed by corporations now testing job candidates and employees for drug use. As the population of elders increases in the United States, there will be expanded career opportunities for geriatric health care workers, which include nurses, rehabilitation specialists, nursing assistants, and home health care workers. Finally, as senior fitness programs become more popular, the need for fitness trainers and advisers with medical backgrounds is growing.

Hospitality Recent acquisitions and mergers of some independent hotels by larger chains has produced many new company structures in the hospitality field. Careers are plentiful in this fast-paced industry; however, the jobs of today are not the same as they were even two years ago. Many major hotel chains have eliminated their formal management training programs and have opted for direct placement instead. This means that instead of being hired into a central training program at corporate headquarters you will be hired to fill available positions and train directly in individual properties in and out of the country. Jobs will continue to be available for hotel managers, assistant managers, and support staff. Tremendous growth in international travel has kept this industry thriving, even during recent times when it seemed to be overbuilt. Trends in the industry include hotels individualizing their marketing strategies to serve the needs of different customers, and a movement toward developing properties as "lifecare" facilities to address the housing and health care needs of the elderly.

Marketing Due to increased competition between businesses in this country and abroad, marketing careers are growing. Businesses must rely on creative marketing strategies to differentiate themselves to customers. One aspect of marketing careers is sales. Sales positions have been the most frequently available opportunities for entering the marketing field. These opportunities still remain strong, especially in advertising and computer sales.

There is a renewed emphasis on market research careers because of new interest on the part of service businesses in measuring quality and customer satisfaction on a regular basis. There is a need for qualified people to develop customer surveys and interpret the results. Professionals with good sales backgrounds will fit best into market research positions because they are already familiar with the needs of the customers. Once the customers' needs are identified, a marketing strategy can be developed to plan the sales, advertising, sales promotion, and public relations efforts needed to fill those needs.

Retail The retail industry has undergone a lot of change in recent years, shifting emphasis from large department stores to specialty, discount, and off-price stores. Career opportunities exist in all of these segments despite the trend from one type of operation to another. However, the quality of the career opportunity varies.

There are some things that you can look for to determine whether or not the company you are considering for employment offers a strong career track. First,

look at companies who have developed almost a total focus on the customer. These firms develop ways to find out what types of products and services their customers want and then think of creative marketing techniques to attract and retain those customers. The retail industry, as a whole, is extremely competitive right now. The companies that are thriving are those that provide a quality product at a competitive price and have reinforced the importance of excellent customer service.

Technical Services   Technical services usually involve repairing, servicing, installing, or inspecting certain types of equipment. For example, CADD technicians, computer service technicians, and electronics technicians are all involved with servicing a variety of computers and other electronic equipment. These opportunities have emerged in recent years in response to the tremendous surge in new technology.

As technical careers continue to grow, new opportunities exist in telecommunications, broadcasting, data communications, and with local area networks. Telecommunications technicians work with voice line switching equipment. Broadcast technicians are hired by stations needing to maintain or improve the quality of their broadcast equipment. Data communications technicians deal with transmitting computer data over telephone lines. Finally, local area network technicians are responsible for working with communication systems that are within limited geographic areas.

Travel/Tourism   The travel/tourism industry employs over 9 million people. The greatest need for professionals is for well-trained travel agents and corporate travel managers. This is because business and personal travel are on the rise. As with the hotel industry, the travel/tourism industry has been positively affected by increased international travel. This creates a need for agents who give advice on destinations, and make arrangements for transportation, hotel accommodations, car rentals, tours, and recreation. For international travel, agents provide information on customs regulations, required papers (passports, visas, and certificates of vaccination), and currency exchange rates. The corporate travel manager is usually employed in-house by a large business firm to work with outside travel agencies on making all travel plans for that company. Although there are many other types of career opportunities in the travel/tourism field, these two jobs are experiencing the fastest growth due to a more global business and social climate.

Career Opportunities for Women

Many fields provide wide-open career opportunities for women. Recently, women have found employment in the fields of communications, sales, marketing, and finance readily available to them. This is in addition to the careers more traditionally pursued by women, such as the areas of health, education, office technology, and human resources. Women are beginning to assume more positions as computer specialists, paralegals, electronic technicians, financial consultants, and business managers. Finally, many women enjoy successful entrepreneurial careers in a variety of industries, including travel, child care, financial consulting, employment agencies, and food service.

Career Opportunities for Minorities

Overall, career opportunities for minorities are growing in most fields. Minorities provide the right qualifications for many jobs, as the number of minorities enrolled in career education programs increases. Some fields tend to hire more minorities than others. These include the hospitality industry and health services. Minority candidates are also actively sought, along with other qualified candidates, in the technical fields. There has been substantial improvement in the recruitment of minority candidates, but work still needs to be done in this area. The best way for minority candidates to sustain a competitive edge in the hiring process is to complete the educational training necessary to do the job, sharpen communication skills, and gain work experience while in school.

Understanding the career phases you will go through, where the jobs are, and career trends is the beginning of establishing your own career path. Your career path is the sequence of jobs you plan to take to build your professional experience. These jobs can lead you to the job in your career field that you think matches your interests and abilities. For example, if your career goal is to be a retail store manager, you may first work as a sales associate, department manager, and assistant store manager. This series of jobs is your career path.

To build your career path, you should start by choosing the job you would like to have in the future, for example, store manager. Then you should strive to obtain the jobs that will give you the experience you need to get there.

Using the information in Chapter Thirteen, "Career Paths," you will be able to build your own career path. Reviewing the many options available to you in your career field and considering what you have learned about your own values, interests, personality, and skills in self-assessment, you can create your own plan for a successful career.

JOB SEARCH TECHNIQUES

Chapter Four

Résumés and Job Applications

Before attempting to apply for any job, you should be able to prepare a professional résumé and a concise job application. Both documents are very often the first impression an employer has of you. Remember, you never get a second chance to make a first impression, whether on paper or in person! So take the time to do the best job you can.

RÉSUMÉS

A résumé is a factual presentation of yourself and an opportunity for self-promotion. Employers use résumés to determine your eligibility for the job. Employers can quickly see whether you have the right educational background, previous work experience, and professional objectives needed to be successful in the job for which you are applying. Employers like to be able to scan the résumé quickly to find this out. Your résumé should be brief, to the point, and formatted for easy reading. The length and style of your résumé will depend on how much work experience you have. Even for someone with a lot of experience, no more than two pages is recommended. A résumé should be a one-page, error-free, concise, and attractive outline of relevant job experiences, skills, accomplishments, and academic credentials. It should be personalized to reflect each individual's qualifications and professional interests. Differences in style distinguish the functional résumé from the chronological résumé.

Types of Résumés

Two basic types of résumés are used most frequently in a job search. Here is what they are and when they are used.

Chronological Résumés The chronological résumé lists your work experience and educational history in chronological order, that is, by date. This type of résumé is excellent for individuals entering the job market for the first time or for individuals who are exchanging jobs within a given career field, because it helps to highlight the education and work experience you have in your field. Sometimes your education is more important than unrelated work experience when you are seeking a new job, because your education emphasizes for the employer the career direction you wish to take despite the work experience you have or do not have up to now.

Functional Résumés The functional résumé organizes your experience according to specific skills or functions. This format is appropriate for the individual who is changing careers or for a person who is reentering the work force after a period of absence, because it emphasizes your skills and abilities and downplays any gaps in employment or unrelated work experience. This résumé is especially effective for the individual with a lengthy work history.

Most employers value previous work experience, both in and out of the field. This is thought to reflect a person's work ethic and commitment to improving professional skills. The résumé is viewed as your sales tool for attracting an employer's attention.

Tips for Preparing a Résumé

Identification Print your first name, middle initial, and last name at the top of the page.

Address A correct address is critical information. A potential employer may want to send you an offer letter or communicate with you for some other reason. In any case, receiving that information will be extremely important to you. If you are not currently living at your permanent address, list both your temporary address and permanent address.

Telephone Numbers Your telephone number is a critically important item. Always include your area code. Do not assume the caller will know it. If you have no telephone or have an unlisted number that you prefer not to give out, leave the telephone number of a very reliable person who is home much of the time and can take messages for you without damaging your credibility. During your job search, check with that person regularly for messages. If you use an answering machine, be sure your greeting is professional and positive.

Personal Data The listing of personal information such as weight, height, sex, age, marital status, and so forth, is optional. You may wish to make a general statement such as: "single, excellent health." Some employers feel that certain jobs, such as sales, which require a lot of traveling, are more suited to single people and thus may be looking for someone who is single. If you know that there is certain personal data that is specifically related to the particular job for which you are sending your résumé, then it would be wise to give that information.

Professional Objective   Some suggest that a professional objective is not required on a résumé because it may limit the applicant's possibilities for being considered for a wide range of jobs. On the other hand, there are those who feel your professional objective is an important part of your résumé and should be included whether you are just starting out or making a next step in your career. If properly done, a professional objective indicates direction to an employer. You've gone to the trouble of trying to decide what you want to do; now you want to show the employer that you *know* what you want. A professional objective can be stated most clearly in one sentence, or no more than two sentences. Your professional objective should reflect your short- and long-term career goals and a realistic attitude. It should be stated so that it is broad enough to give you some flexibility but specific enough not to appear that you are floundering with your career direction.

The following are examples of good professional objectives:

- An entry-level job as informations coordinator leading to a career doing market research in the travel industry.
- An entry-level job as a store manager trainee leading to a career in retail operations.

These are examples of poor professional objectives:

- An entry-level job as a store manager trainee leading to a retail buying career. [This is inappropriate because it is not a correct career path. If a buying track is what you want, you must start off on a buying track, as opposed to a management track.]
- An entry-level position with a growing company with an opportunity for advancement. [This is too general; it does not indicate that real direction has been thought through.]

Use the short-term and long-term goals you developed in Chapter One, "Self-Assessment," to develop an effective professional objective.

Education   Don't leave anything out. You want to account the best you can for how you have spent your time. If you attended a school but did not complete a diploma, certificate, or degree, then list it as a place you attended.

Courses   These are especially helpful to list for entry-level applicants without a lot of work experience and for those people having taken highly specialized courses that will help them on the job.

Special Skills   You should list any special skills you have that are relevant to the job you are seeking. Typing speed and computer skills are some examples.

You don't want to list more personal characteristics in this area. Save talking about your personality for the cover letter.

Work Experience   Don't make assumptions for employers and leave out certain experiences because you think they won't be valuable. Chances are if you think this way, an employer won't value them either. It is important not to leave big gaps of time on your résumé. You should list most of the experiences you have had and be prepared to convince an employer that you have learned from each one of them. This is a very important point. Whether these experiences have been part-time or full-time jobs, it is very important for you to examine what you might have gained from each experience. So many times an employer sees someone who has worked as a waitperson for three summers and subsequently asks about the job. The employer then waits for the applicant to talk about his or her experiences as a waitperson—working with the public, working under pressure, working nights, weekends, and holidays, only to find the applicant apologizing for lack of work experience related to his or her chosen career. Certainly if you worked to support your college education, that should be noted on your résumé.

Example: Earned 80 percent of college tuition through part-time employment.

This spells initiative, determination, and responsibility.

Extracurricular Activities/Hobbies   Your extracurricular activities and hobbies demonstrate leadership potential, interpersonal skills, initiative, creativity, and ability to plan and organize. They also show that when there's nothing to do, you choose to make valuable use of your time rather than seeing it as an opportunity to do nothing. This may be an important characteristic to the manager who wants a secretary who will take initiative when he or she is away.

References   You should always be prepared to list references. Have the courtesy to call and ask or write to the person you'd like to be a reference for you. It is not essential to actually list references on your résumé, but you should at least indicate: "References available upon request." When you do this, type up your list of references on a separate sheet of paper headed: **REFERENCES** for *Your Name*. This does not have to be mailed out with your résumé, but you should take it with you on a job interview.

On page 55 is a list of power words that will help you prepare your résumé. Note that they are all active verbs that will describe your accomplishments in a lively and specific way. The following pages give formats and samples for both chronological and formal résumés.

POWER WORDS FOR RÉSUMÉS

Accompanied	Composed	Employed	Insured	Outlined	Regulated
Accumulated	Computed	Encouraged	Integrated	Overcame	Related
Achieved	Conferred	Engineered	Interpreted	Packaged	Relayed
Administered	Constructed	Entertained	Interviewed	Packed	Renewed
Admitted	Consulted	Established	Introduced	Paid	Reorganized
Advised	Contacted	Estimated	Inventoried	Participated	Repaired
Aided	Contracted	Evaluated	Investigated	Patrolled	Replaced
Allowed	Contrasted	Examined	Invoiced	Perfected	Reported
Analyzed	Controlled	Exchanged	Issued	Performed	Requested
Answered	Converted	Experienced	Judged	Piloted	Researched
Applied	Convinced	Fabricated	Kept	Placed	Reserved
Appointed	Coordinated	Facilitated	Learned	Planned	Responsible for
Appraised	Copied	Fed	Lectured	Posted	Retrieved
Arranged	Corrected	Figured	Led	Prepared	Revised
Assembled	Corresponded	Filed	Licensed	Prescribed	Routed
Assessed	Counseled	Filled	Listed	Presented	Scheduled
Assigned	Counted	Financed	Listened	Priced	Secured
Assisted	Created	Finished	Loaded	Printed	Selected
Attached	Credited	Fired	Located	Processed	Sent
Attended	Debated	Fitted	Logged	Produced	Separated
Authorized	Decided	Fixed	Mailed	Programmed	Served
Balanced	Delivered	Formulated	Maintained	Promoted	Serviced
Billed	Demonstrated	Founded	Managed	Prompted	Set up
Bought	Deposited	Governed	Manufactured	Proofread	Showed
Budgeted	Described	Graded	Marked	Proposed	Sold
Built	Designed	Graphed	Marketed	Proved	Solicited
Calculated	Detailed	Greeted	Measured	Provided	Sorted
Cashed	Determined	Handled	Met	Published	Stocked
Catalogued	Developed	Headed	Modified	Purchased	Stored
Changed	Devised	Helped	Monitored	Ran	Straightened
Charged	Diagnosed	Hired	Motivated	Rated	Summarized
Charted	Discovered	Identified	Negotiated	Read	Supervised
Checked	Dismantled	Implemented	Nominated	Rearranged	Supplied
Classified	Dispatched	Improved	Noted	Rebuilt	Tallied
Cleaned	Dispensed	Improvised	Notified	Recalled	Taught
Cleared	Displayed	Increased	Numbered	Received	Telephoned
Closed	Directed	Indexed	Observed	Recommended	Tested
Coded	Distributed	Indicated	Obtained	Reconciled	Transferred
Collected	Documented	Informed	Opened	Recorded	Transported
Commanded	Drew	Initiated	Operated	Reduced	Tutored
Communicated	Drove	Inspected	Ordered	Referred	Typed
Compiled	Earned	Installed	Organized	Registered	Verified
Completed	Educated	Instructed			

Format for a Chronological Résumé

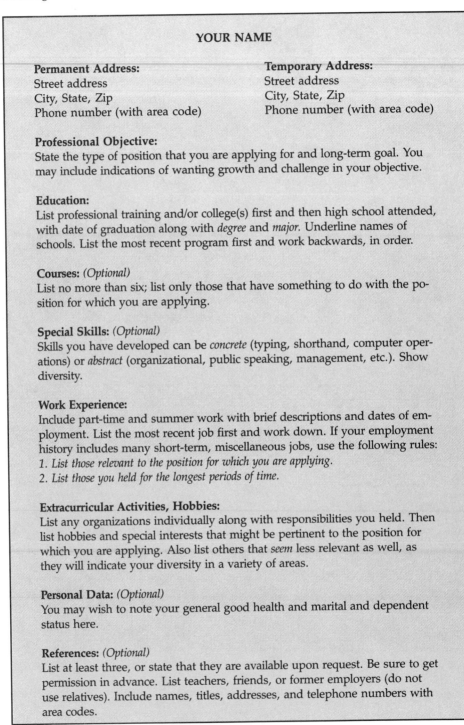

YOUR NAME

Permanent Address:
Street address
City, State, Zip
Phone number (with area code)

Temporary Address:
Street address
City, State, Zip
Phone number (with area code)

Professional Objective:
State the type of position that you are applying for and long-term goal. You may include indications of wanting growth and challenge in your objective.

Education:
List professional training and/or college(s) first and then high school attended, with date of graduation along with *degree* and *major.* Underline names of schools. List the most recent program first and work backwards, in order.

Courses: *(Optional)*
List no more than six; list only those that have something to do with the position for which you are applying.

Special Skills: *(Optional)*
Skills you have developed can be *concrete* (typing, shorthand, computer operations) or *abstract* (organizational, public speaking, management, etc.). Show diversity.

Work Experience:
Include part-time and summer work with brief descriptions and dates of employment. List the most recent job first and work down. If your employment history includes many short-term, miscellaneous jobs, use the following rules:
1. List those relevant to the position for which you are applying.
2. List those you held for the longest periods of time.

Extracurricular Activities, Hobbies:
List any organizations individually along with responsibilities you held. Then list hobbies and special interests that might be pertinent to the position for which you are applying. Also list others that *seem* less relevant as well, as they will indicate your diversity in a variety of areas.

Personal Data: *(Optional)*
You may wish to note your general good health and marital and dependent status here.

References: *(Optional)*
List at least three, or state that they are available upon request. Be sure to get permission in advance. List teachers, friends, or former employers (do not use relatives). Include names, titles, addresses, and telephone numbers with area codes.

Sample Chronological Résumé

LAUREL A. STARK

64 Potter Street
Sodus, NY 14551
(315) 585–6609

Professional Objective:
To obtain a challenging culinary position in the hospitality industry which will allow for personal and professional growth.

Education:
Johnson & Wales University, Providence, RI 02905 A.O.S. Culinary Arts Degree, May 1989

Sodus Central High School, Sodus, NY 14551 High School Diploma, June 1987

Wayne Area Vocation Center, Williamson, NY 14589 Completion of two-year food service certificate, June 1987

Achievements:
* Experience in public speaking
* Obtained catering experience
* Trained and supervised employees in food production
* Assisted in purchasing, receiving, and storing in various food service establishments

Work Experience:

9/88–Present *Johnson & Wales University,* Providence, RI 02905
Career Development Work Study
Assisting both the Director of Placement and Cooperative Education Director with various clerical duties: typing, filing, answering phones. Updating job listings and maintaining resource library.

6/88–8/88 *Alton Coffee Shop,* Alton, NY 14551
Waitress. Controlled personal cash register receipts.

4/87–8/87 *Sodus Point Fish and Crab House,* Sodus Point, NY 14551
Line Cook. Participated in receiving goods to the storeroom. Assisted Sous Chef in sauté and fry station and with grilling and broiling.

9/86–3/87 *Perkins Restaurant,* Newark, NY 14513
Line Cook. Operated broiler station. Trained and supervised all new employees in various stations in the kitchen.

Honors and Awards:
4/88 Distinguished Visiting Chef award.
12/87 Student of the Month award, Wayne Area Vocational Center.

References upon request

Format for a Functional Résumé

YOUR NAME

ADDRESS
Street address
City, State, Zip Code
Phone number (with area code)

PROFESSIONAL OBJECTIVE:
State the type of position that you are applying for and long-term goal.
You may include indications of wanting growth and challenge in your
objective.

QUALIFICATIONS:
List (and discuss if necessary) all of the professional skills you can bring to
an employer as a result of the different work experiences you have had.
These may include personal and interpersonal skills that are helpful to
your career but should also stress your technical skills. Think about *all* of
the skills you have acquired and focus on those you think are transferable
to other jobs.

EMPLOYMENT HISTORY:
List the jobs you have had, including your present position, in order by
date, starting with your most recent job. You may omit any jobs held for
just a few months or any that are completely unrelated to the job you are
seeking. It is not necessary to provide a detailed description of the jobs
you held, but do list your job titles and place of employment along with
the dates employed. (Remember, the information should be presented in
such a way that the reader can focus first on your qualifications.)

EDUCATION:
List professional training and/or college(s) first and then high school
attended, with date of graduation along with *degree* and *major.* Underline
names of schools. List the most recent program first and work backwards,
in order.

REFERENCES:
List at least three references, or state that they are available upon request.
Be sure to get permission in advance. List teachers, friends, or former
employers (do not use relatives). Include names, titles, addresses, and
telephone numbers with area codes.

Sample Functional Résumé

ROSE MARTINSON
43 Racine Avenue
Skokie, Illinois 60076
(312) 546-7898

PROFESSIONAL OBJECTIVE:
To obtain an executive secretarial position within a major corporation which will benefit from my administrative, communication, and interpersonal skills.

QUALIFICATIONS:
Production
Generated all personal and business correspondence via IBM word processor.
Processed over 25,000 full- and part-time job opportunities annually.
Arranged hotel and travel accommodations for executive staff.
Typing 75 wpm.
Shorthand 120 wpm.
Knowledge of IBM DisplayWriter, WordPerfect, and Lotus 1-2-3.

Planning/Promotion
Coordinated daily schedules of management staff.
Supervised four clerical assistants.
Initiated and implemented new filing system and interoffice communication procedural manual.
Assisted in formulation of marketing strategies.
Aided in generation of promotional materials serving as liaison among professional photographers, printers, and media personnel.
Coordinated the planning and execution of a one-day conference on stress management.

EMPLOYMENT HISTORY:

1992–present	Northwestern University, Chicago, IL Administrative Assistant to Placement
1990–92	The Field Foundation, Chicago, IL Administrative Assistant to Director of Office Services
1988–90	Howard T. Mack, Inc., Skokie, IL Administrative Assistant to Associate Personnel Director

EDUCATION:

1988	Bryant & Stratton Business Institute, Buffalo, NY A. S. Administrative Management

REFERENCES: Available upon request

PORTFOLIOS

Portfolios are an option to using only your résumé as a way to present yourself to a potential employer. A portfolio may be considered your own "professional scrapbook." It is a promotional package that you assemble to give an employer examples of your unique qualifications and accomplishments. Certain fields, such as advertising and public relations, may require a portfolio because samples of work provide evidence of the skill level of the candidate. A portfolio can be used in most career fields as a different way to present yourself as a job candidate. Advantages of using a portfolio include providing a more detailed description and samples of your skills, highlighting your individual accomplishments and unique qualifications as a job candidate, and consolidating the paperwork important to a prospective employer into a neat and concise package that can be easily reviewed and kept together for future use. Your portfolio may contain some or all of the following:

- Samples of your writings or publications.
- Certifications you have received.
- Letters or certificates documenting special honors or awards.
- Transcripts.
- Description of your school and your program.
- Letters of recommendation.
- Letters of commendation.
- Photographs of projects, products, or events that you developed or implemented.

Samples of your writings demonstrate your aptitude for written communication. This is a weakness in many job candidates today. If you are a good writer, you should emphasize that skill in this unique way to a prospective employer. Whether the job includes actually writing articles or promotional literature or writing routine letters, reports, and proposals, good writing skills are an asset you should promote.

Certifications may be a requirement in your field. Examples of such professions include certified public accountants, court reporters, and positions in the medical field. Evidence that you have passed the necessary tests to become certified in your field is extremely important.

Documentation of awards or honors are best displayed in a portfolio. Often, listing such recognitions on the résumé does not provide the opportunity for someone to learn what you did to receive the recognition. Usually letters or certificates that go with the honor or award tell a little about the criteria or the outstanding accomplishment that led to you receiving the award or honor.

A short description of your school and the program you are in might be very useful in promoting your qualifications. This is especially true in cases where your school does not have a high profile. Being able to promote your school and the education you have received from it is an important part of your job search. Often this information can be extracted from your school's admissions catalog. Transcripts are sometimes required by some employers. Be prepared to show them upon request.

Letters of recommendation can be included in your portfolio so that you complement your own promotional material with someone else's promotion of you. Letters of commendation are usually written to thank you or to congratulate you on a job well done. These are another valuable source of external support of you as a job candidate.

Anytime you can illustrate an accomplishment with a photograph, do it! Pictures add your personal touch to the portfolio and break up the traditional written information you have included.

A portfolio can be assembled into a handsome scrapbook available at many card shops, in a three-ring binder, or in any other format you think is original and professional. By developing your portfolio at the same time as your résumé, you can package the material to support and demonstrate the accomplishments you have cited on your résumé. A portfolio is a terrific tool for marketing your uniqueness in a job search.

JOB APPLICATIONS

Completed job applications are commonly required by employers as part of the job application process. Job applications are used by human resource departments for candidates who apply for a job in person at a company. Job applications are often used during interviews conducted at your school. When you are asked to complete a job application prior to an interview, you should submit your résumé along with it. This is because one purpose of the job application is to obtain factual information about you (for example, social security number, emergency information, family relationships) that can be used for payroll or health insurance. Although the other purpose of the job application is to obtain information about your employment history, your professional qualifications are usually expressed better in your résumé. By providing the employer with both a job application and a résumé, you can be sure that your qualifications are presented in the best light to an employer.

On a job application you are simply presenting information an employer needs to see in order to determine whether you should be considered for a particular job. The job application is a screening device. It does not get you the job. Sometimes you will be asked to complete a job application after you've been hired so that the factual information about you needed by the human resources department can be recorded and used to process the necessary paperwork to start you as a new employee. You will want to ensure that your job application is the best one an employer sees.

PARTS OF A JOB APPLICATION

Identification   Position desired
Family relationships   Experience
Health   Miscellaneous
Education

Identification:
Name
Social security number
Address
Telephone number
Physical traits
Date and place of birth
Proof of age
Citizenship
Emergency information

Family relationships:
Marital status
Dependents
Family names and occupations

Health:
General health
Disabilities and physical limitations
Emotional and mental disorders
Family illness
Workers' compensation
Attendance

Education:
Education and formal training
Future schooling

Position desired:
Position desired
Salary desired
Availability
Transportation

Experience:
Work experience
Military experience
Volunteer activities
Certification, registration, and licenses

Professional associations
Clubs and organizations
Hobbies, interests, and leisure-time activities
Other skills

Miscellaneous:
Future plans
References
Arrest, jail, and conviction record

Points to Remember When Completing a Job Application

Name Be sure to *print* your name where asked on the application and *sign* neatly on the signature line. You should carefully read and verify all statements on the application before signing it. Never list a nickname. Always use your complete legal name.

Social Security Number Be sure to print your social security number so that it is readable and *correct*! Many companies use their employees' social security numbers in filing and computer systems. An error in your social security number could cause problems with your payments, benefits, taxes, retirement, and unemployment account. If you do not have a social security number, you should apply now at the nearest social security office or post office.

Address Before you list your address, read instructions. Then be prepared to put all your data in the correct spaces. If the application does not ask for a certain order, list in the following order: your street address, rural route or box number, city, state, and zip code. Consider your answer when asked how long you have lived at a certain address. This information will give employers an impression of your stability.

Telephone Number A source of frustration for an employer is wanting to reach a good candidate and not being able to do so because the candidate has either forgotten to leave a telephone number or has left an incorrect one. List a phone number that is likely to be answered during the day. If no one will be answering your phone, or if you do not have a phone, list the number of someone who can accept messages for you. Choose someone who will be polite, take your message accurately, and get the message to you very quickly.

Physical Traits Some employers need this information for insurance or security reasons. Certain jobs have specific height and weight requirements (police officer, fire fighter).

Date and Place of Birth You may be asked to give the date of your birth on some applications. It is important that you give the right information. This date is used to compute your insurance and retirement plans after you are hired. You can be fired for falsifying information on a job application. Remember that the law will be on your side if you are *denied* a job because of your age.

Proof of Age   You may be asked to prove your age for some employers. Most employers accept a driver's license as proof of age. If you do not have a driver's license, get a copy of your birth certificate or any other legal document that shows your age.

Citizenship   You may be asked to indicate whether or not you are a citizen of the United States. Noncitizens are usually asked to list their visa type and number.

Emergency Information   There are two reasons why this question is asked. The first is obvious—to be sure your family will be notified of any emergencies that may arise. The second is to show your stability. Employers might think of you as a "drifter," and thus unreliable, if you do not list the name of someone who would be concerned about you.

Marital Status   On all applications list your marital status as either *married* or *single*. Other terms invite employers to pry into your social life. *Single* best describes your status even if you are engaged, living with someone, or divorced. *Married* best describes your status even if you are separated.

Dependents   A *dependent* is anyone who relies on you as a source of support. Most dependents are family members (spouse, children, elderly parents). When listing your number of dependents, do not list yourself. If you have no dependents, put a dash in the space.

General Health   It will benefit you the most if you can list your health as excellent. You may have a health problem that will *not* affect your ability to do the job you want. If so, do not note any negative information on your application. Leave the health sections blank if necessary and be prepared to discuss during an interview. If you have a health problem, ask your doctor if it will in any way impair your ability to perform your job. If your doctor thinks the problem would be limiting, ask for advice on how to handle this on a job application.

Attendance   The best person for the job is the one who will be there every day. The fewer days you have missed in your previous employment, the more dependable you will seem to new employers.

Education and Formal Training   You should be able to account for all the time you spent in school or in training. This information could be important in explaining gaps in your employment history. It will also clearly indicate to employers whether or not you meet one of the primary requirements for the job that is available.

Salary Desired   If you have not recently researched the job market, be careful how you answer this question. You do not want to undersell yourself or ask for such a high salary that you rule yourself out of the competition! You can research the job market by following these suggestions:

Read want ads that list salaries for similar positions.
Call your local employment office or job placement office and ask the salary range for the type of job you are seeking.
Talk with people who do the kind of work you want.

You may list a specific salary, give a high-low range, or leave the space blank. Another alternative is to respond with the word *open*. This is a positive word. It will not commit you to a future either too low or too high. When considering a salary offer, don't forget to consider the benefits as well as the base salary. Added benefits can make one salary more valuable than a slightly higher one without benefits. Mentally adjust your desired salary according to the benefits, then state the salary you want.

Work Experience   You should be well prepared to list your work history. List the data for your most recent job first. List your next most recent job in the next form, and so on. If you have no work experience, leave the spaces blank and be prepared to offset this during an interview.

Professional Organizations   Employers may be interested in the professional organizations to which you belong. Such a membership is especially important if the organization and job are directly related.

Hobbies, Interests, and Leisure-Time Activities   What you do with your free time tells an employer much about your interests and drive. An employer may have a special interest in you if your hobby relates closely to your job.

References   Consider the following people to be your references:

Former employers, supervisors, and co-workers.

Former teachers, instructors, and professors.

Your minister, priest, or rabbi.

Acquaintances who have job titles indicating responsibility.

Long-time acquaintances.

Many job-seekers think that employers do *not* contact references. This is a myth. Employers *often* contact references—especially when the job includes significant responsibility.

How to Complete a Job Application

You Will Need a Pen   Do not use a pencil; only use a black or blue pen. Your pen should let you print neatly without blobs, smudges, or smears. You may want to use a fine-point pen. This kind of pen makes it easier to print small when you must write in small blanks or boxes. It is wise to carry a spare pen with the same ink color and line width as your first pen.

Bring Your Résumé   If you prefer, you may carry an extra résumé with you to use as a reminder of important information as well. In fact, it is wise to be prepared to present a résumé should you obtain an immediate interview.

Follow Instructions   Be sure to read all of the instructions before writing anything on an application. Many applications begin with general instructions, such as "Print in ink," or "To be handprinted in ink," or "Typewritten." Separate instructions may tell you not to put any data in certain spaces.

Following instructions is important. Employers want to hire people who can follow instructions on the job! Employers will not have a high regard for your dependability and skill if you cannot follow instructions on an application.

The Dash Some application questions *will not apply to you.* Make a short dash (—) after each of these questions. The dash is simple; it tells the employer you have read the question but it does not apply to you.

Blank Spaces It is sometimes better to leave a blank space on your application. An application will not get you a job. However, it can keep you from being considered for a job. If an honest answer to an application question is negative or can easily be misunderstood, leave this item blank. Do not even make a dash in this space. You can explain the blank in the interview if necessary. In this way, the blank will not automatically be used to screen you from a job for which you might otherwise qualify.

Expect employers to ask you questions about blank spaces. If a blank space is not mentioned in the interview, be sure to mention it after you are offered the job. This will prevent the possibility of your being accused later of withholding information. An alternative to leaving a space blank is to write "will explain in interview." Decide for yourself which way is better for you. But *do* be prepared to explain it!

Sample Job Application

Review the following job application for employment to get an idea of what a typical job application looks like. Review the questions you are required to answer, and be sure you feel comfortable with each response.

APPLICATION FOR EMPLOYMENT

Name _____ Social Security Number _____

Address _____

City _____ State _____ Zip _____

Home Phone _____ Work Phone _____

If your educational or work records are listed under another name, please indicate _____

List previous address if changed during the past five years _____

Position Desired _____ Salary Expected _____

For the following questions please circle the appropriate response.

Location Desired   *New York   Boston   Either*   Date Available _____ Hours Desired _____

What prompted you to come to our company? *Newspaper Employment Agency School Employee Community Agency*
   Other _____ Source Name _____

Have you ever applied to or interviewed at our company? *Yes   No*   If *yes*, when? _____

Have you ever been employed by our company?   *Yes   No*   If *yes*, when? _____

Are you related to an employee of our company?   *Yes   No*   Relationship _____

   If *yes*, name of employee and department _____

Do you know of anything that may prevent our company from obtaining a Fidelity Bond for you?   *Yes   No*
   If *yes*, what? _____

Have you ever been *convicted* of a felony or misdemeanor?*   *Yes   No*   If *yes*, explain _____

_____

Have you ever been *convicted* of a criminal offense involving dishonesty or breach of trust; including, but not limited to robbery, embezzlement, forgery, perjury, tax evasion, etc.?*   *Yes   No*   If *yes*, explain _____

_____

Are you lawfully authorized to work in the United States?   *Yes   No*

*Federal law requires that all applicants must furnish information concerning conviction of any criminal offense involving dishonesty or breach of trust. If the conviction did not involve dishonesty or breach of trust, the following rules should guide your explanation of any conviction:
A. An applicant for employment with a sealed record on file with the Commissioner of Probation may answer "no record" with respect to an inquiry herein relative to prior arrests, criminal court appearances or convictions; B. An applicant must report a conviction for any felony; C. A first conviction for any of the following misdemeanors may be omitted: drunkenness, simple assault, minor traffic violations, affray, disturbance of the peace; D. An applicant may omit any misdemeanor where the resultant incarceration or confinement terminated more than five years ago.

Chapter Five

Letters

During your job search, letter writing is an important form of communicating with an employer. By corresponding directly with an employer throughout your job search, you demonstrate a sustained interest in the job and reveal something about your personality and professional goals.

The prime reason for writing a letter as you initiate your job search is to secure a job interview. If your background and work experience are comparable to other candidates', it is your cover letter that really distinguishes you from everyone else. This is because the cover letter reveals the reason you want to work for the company and gives you an opportunity to talk about your positive traits and what you can bring to the employer. The clarity, conciseness, and professionalism of your letter can make a positive first impression on an employer who has not yet met you.

GUIDELINES FOR WRITING JOB SEARCH LETTERS

Writing letters as part of the job search can be one of your most valuable efforts. It can also be one of the most difficult. These are some basic guidelines to remember:

- Be brief and to the point.
- Use standard business letter writing formats.
- Make sure you address the letter to the proper individual and use his or her proper title.
- Make absolutely *no* errors in grammar, punctuation, spelling, or typing. An error could automatically rule you out of consideration.

SEVEN LETTERS YOU MAY WRITE DURING YOUR JOB SEARCH

Cover Letters

A cover letter is a letter that accompanies your résumé. It is the main letter used in a job search. The purpose of the cover letter is to promote your qualifications to an employer so that you will obtain an interview. Employers can receive hundreds of résumés for a single job opening, depending on the type of job it is and on how many people are unemployed or looking to change their current jobs. When many of the résumés received show similar backgrounds among many candidates, employers look for some way to narrow down the number of applicants to be interviewed. A well-prepared cover letter can make you stand out favorably among other applicants and lead to your being selected for an interview.

There are two types of cover letters. They are the letter of application for a specific position and the letter of inquiry. The first is used when sending your résumé in response to a specific position you know is available through the classified ads, through a job posting system at work, or by word of mouth. The second type of cover letter is used when you are inquiring about the availability of employment at a firm. In both cases, the cover letter is your tool for promoting your qualifications for employment. Here is how you would approach writing these letters in slightly different ways.

Letter of Application for Specific Position   This letter states your specific qualifications for the job for which you are applying. You should always begin by addressing the letter to a specific person, using his or her full title. Be sure to enclose a typed copy of your résumé and say in the letter that you did so. State the position for which you are applying and mention where you found out about the job (placement office, newspaper, etc.). You should try to relate how your education has made you qualified for this position. Go on to state what you can offer rather than what you hope to gain. Do not mention a salary requirement in your letter because by being too high, or even too low, you can eliminate yourself from an interview. Request an interview at the employer's convenience, and follow up in approximately one week with a telephone call.

Letter of Inquiry   This letter may be used if a mass-mailing campaign is part of your job search. It is a letter that is similar to a "cold call" in sales. You are writing to inquire whether or not the company has a need for someone with your background. To your knowledge, there is not a specific position available. Begin by addressing your letter to a specific person and use his or her full title. This may mean that you will need to actually call the company in order to know the correct person's name and title. Enclose a typed copy of your résumé and say that you did so in the letter. Go on to state your interest in the company. Be sure to refer to the company by name. Briefly state how your background may benefit the company, including mention of your education and skills gained through outside activities or part-time jobs. State that you would like the opportunity to discuss your qualifications in person, at the employer's convenience. It might be useful to incorporate some of the tangible benefits you offer the employer by using some of the information from the Proof by Example exercise you completed in Chapter One.

Letter to Request a Recommendation

This letter is written to persons who you feel will be able to recommend you satisfactorily for a position. A personal call should be made in addition to a letter. Choose people you are sure will recommend you favorably. Identify yourself by name and make reference to how you know the person. If your name has changed since the time you first knew this person, mention the name by which they knew you. Ask permission to use this person's name as a reference in your job search. Make the contact friendly, but convince the person that this is important to you. You may want to follow the letter up with a phone call if that is possible. You should always send a brief thank-you letter if the reference is given.

Thank-You Letter Following an Interview

This letter is written after the interview to acknowledge the interviewer's time and cooperation. This is a good way to ensure your interviewer will remember you. Be sure to send the letter right after the interview and thank the interviewer for his or her time. Restate the position for which you applied, and give the date and/or place of the interview. Express your interest in the opportunities offered in an enthusiastic way. Be sure to include your telephone number and return address. Without this information, an employer may not be able to contact you and you could lose out on a job offer.

Letter Accepting a Position

This letter is written after you have agreed to accept a specific position. Whether a job offer comes to you verbally or in writing, answer the offer immediately. Be direct about accepting and restate the specific position you have accepted. Be sure to express your appreciation for the opportunity your employer has given you and express your eagerness to begin your new job.

Letter Refusing a Position

This letter is written after you have definitely decided not to accept the particular position offered. You should always write this letter to an employer, because by doing so you make a favorable impression. Someday you may again be applying for a job at that company, and it is good to be remembered as a professional person. Answer the offer immediately. Don't be embarrassed to tell the employer that you have decided not to accept the job offer. Be direct with the answer, but soften your tone to show appreciation for the offer. Be brief and concise and make the letter simple. Express your thanks, remembering that you may want to reapply for a future position with the same company.

Thank You Letter for a Plant Visit or an Office Visit

Address these letters to the specific person or people who hosted you. State your appreciation for their valuable time. Comment on what impressed you the most and on what you learned from the visit.

Application Letter for Cooperative Education/Internship Program

Address the letter to the hiring authority and/or person involved in the selection process. Enclose a typed copy of your résumé and include references if typed separately. State why you would like to be considered for the program. State the kind of professional experience you hope to gain and how you will use this experience to reach your career goal. Finally, state what qualifications you can bring to the employer.

FORMAT FOR COVER LETTERS

Return Address ➤

Inside Address ➤ Mary Jones, Vice President
American Insurers
2500 Brook Avenue
Boston, MA 00215

Salutation ➤ Dear Ms. Jones:

First Paragraph:
Your reason for
writing. ➤ In your initial paragraph, state the reason for the letter, name the specific position or type of work for which you are applying, and indicate from which resource (placement office, news media, friend, employment service) you learned of the opening.

Second
Paragraph:
Your
qualifications. ➤ Indicate why you are interested in the position, the company, its products or services—above all, what you can do for the employer. If you are a recent graduate, explain how your academic background makes you a qualified candidate for the position. If you have some practical work experience, point out your specific achievements or unique qualifications. Try not to repeat the same information the reader will find in the résumé.

Third Paragraph:
Refer to enclosed
résumé or
application. ➤ Refer the reader to the enclosed résumé or application form which summarizes your qualifications, training, and experiences.

Final Paragraph:
Indicate your
plan for
follow-up. ➤ In the closing paragraph, indicate your desire for a personal interview and your flexibility as to the time and place. Repeat your phone number in the letter and offer any assistance to help in a speedy response. Finally, close your letter with a statement or question that will encourage a response. For example, state that you will be in the city where the company is located on a certain date and would like to set up an interview. Or, state that you will call on a certain date to set up an interview. Or, ask if the company will be recruiting in your area, or if it desires additional information or references.

Closing ➤ Sincerely,

Your written ➤
signature
Your name typed ➤ Thomas L. Smith

SAMPLE LETTERS YOU MAY WRITE DURING YOUR JOB SEARCH
Letter of Application for a Specific Position

Your address

Date

Inside address
(If possible, use individual's name.)

Dear _____ :

I am writing in response to your ad in the *Boston Globe* on Sunday, February 3, 19__ , for an administrative assistant for your executive offices.

Your company interests me because of your worldwide reputation and excellent history of stability. I have read about your plans to expand your business into the Southeast, and those plans for growth convince me that XYZ Corporation is a progressive company.

Enclosed is my résumé. My typing speed is 75 wpm, shorthand 120, and I am proficient with machine transcription. I ranked second among the secretarial graduates in my class and completed an internship with your firm last year.

I look forward to an interview and will call you shortly to arrange a convenient time.

Sincerely,

(written signature)

Your name typed

Sample Letter of Inquiry

Your address

Date

Inside address
(If possible, use individual's name.)

Dear _____ :

I am writing to inquire about a career opportunity in marketing with your company.

At a recent career day held on my campus, I learned that XYZ Bank is expanding its branches throughout the Northeast. I have read about your profits over the past five years and see that XYZ Bank is a growth-oriented organization with a solid history.

My résumé is enclosed for your information and highlights my work experience in the marketing field. My phone number is also listed.

I look forward to an interview with you to further discuss how I think I can contribute to XYZ Bank.

Sincerely,

(written signature)

Your name typed

Sample Letter to Request a Recommendation

Your address

Date

Inside address
(Always use individual's name.)

Dear _____ :

I am currently conducting a job search and would like permission to give your name as a reference to some prospective employers.

I value the experience I gained when working for you last summer. Since you were my direct supervisor, you have first-hand knowledge of my skills, dependability, and ability to work well with others. Would you be willing to share your thoughts about my work performance with another employer by telephone or by writing a letter of reference for me to present on my interviews?

I can be reached at (telephone number, including area code). My current address is _____. Thank you in advance for your cooperation.

Sincerely,

(written signature)

Your name typed

Sample Thank You Letter Following an Interview

Your address

Date

Inside address
(Always use individual's name.)

Dear _____ :

I appreciate the opportunity to talk with you on (date). The information
you shared with me about (company name) was excellent, and I am
excited about the possibility of applying my education and experience to
the position we discussed.

If I can provide you with any additional information, please let me know. I
look forward to hearing from you soon.

Sincerely,

(written signature)

Your name typed

*Make sure you keep current and accurate records of every interview: the date, time,
location, interviewer, and any special information concerning the company or job itself.*

Sample Letter Accepting a Position

> Your address
>
> Date
>
> Inside address
> (Always use individual's name.)
>
> Dear _____ :
>
> I am very pleased to accept your offer (state offer) as outlined in your letter of (date). (Include all details of offer—location, starting salary, starting date.)
>
> (Mention enclosures—application, résumé, employee forms, or other information—and any related commentary.)
>
> I look forward to meeting the challenges of the job, and I shall make every attempt to fulfill your expectations.
>
> Sincerely,
>
> (written signature)
>
> Your name typed

Resist the temptation to sound either overly grateful or reticent about your abilities to fulfill the job requirement. A straightforward, pleasant but confident response is all that is needed.

Sample Letter Refusing a Position

Your address

Date

Inside address
(Always use individual's name.)

Dear _____ :

Thank you for your letter of (date) offering me the position of (state
position).

After considerable thought, I have decided not to accept your offer of
employment as outlined in your letter. This has been a very difficult
decision for me. However, I feel I have made the correct one for this point
in my career.

Thank you for your time, effort, and consideration. Your confidence in me
is sincerely appreciated.

Sincerely,

(written signature)

Your name typed

Sample Thank You Letter for Plant Visit

Your address

Date

Inside address
(Always use individual's name.)

Dear _____ :

Thank you for the time you took yesterday to show me (name of company)'s distribution center.

I was extremely impressed by the efficiency of the operation and the positive attitude of your employees. As a result of the visit, I am considering a career in distribution once I complete my business administration program. Please thank Mr. _____ as well for the time he spent with me.

Perhaps I will contact you again when I am about to graduate to see if there is a position available at (name of company).

Sincerely,

(written signature)

Your name typed

Sample Thank You Letter for an Office Visit

Your address

Date

Inside address
(Always use individual's name.)

Dear _____ :

Thank you for the tour you provided to our typing class on Wednesday.

It was interesting to see how some of the new word processing equipment is being used at a large company like yours. I was impressed by the teamwork among the office staff in your customer service department. This must be a real asset to your customers.

While I was there, Ms. _____ mentioned that there was a part-time job open for a typist in your human resources department. I am interested in the job and have enclosed a copy of my résumé for your consideration.

Sincerely,

(written signature)

Your name typed

Sample Application Letter for a Cooperative Education/Internship Program

Your address

Date

Inside address
(If possible, use individual's name.)

Dear _____ :

I am writing this letter to apply to the (name of school's cooperative education or internship program).

This program offers me an opportunity to strengthen my current work history by giving me more focused experience in my career field. I feel this would give me an advantage over other students when I seek full-time employment.

Enclosed is my résumé. I am available for an interview at your request. I look forward to the opportunity to meet with you.

Sincerely,

(written signature)

Your name typed

Chapter Six

Interviewing Techniques

Job interviews are a critical step in your job search because they provide you an opportunity to actually meet with a prospective employer and convince that employer you are the best candidate for the job. Interviews also give you time to evaluate whether or not the job or company is right for you.

You can take several steps, ranging from preparing properly for interviews to following up your interviews in a professional manner, to make the interviewing process easier and more effective for you. In addition, you should learn how to secure your own job interviews. Even if your school arranges interviews for you, there will be companies you will want to seek out on your own. Learning how to secure your own interviews will also be important to you once you are established in your career but wish to move on to a new job.

SECURING A JOB INTERVIEW

You may secure a job interview with the assistance of your school's placement office or through contacts you initiate on your own through a variety of channels.

Your School's Placement Office

JOHNSON & WALES UNIVERSITY
BUSINESS CAREER DEVELOPMENT

JOB OPPORTUNITY

FULL TIME: **XX**   DATE POSTED: 09/31/92
PART TIME:
TEMPORARY:
SEASONAL:

JOB TITLE: **Micro Computer Specialist**

START DATE: **A.S.A.P.**

SALARY: **$22,500 to start**

BENEFITS:

HOURS: **Flex**

RELOCATION:

BUSINESS NAME: **Fuller Memorial Hospital**

STREET ADDRESS: **231 Washington Street**

CITY, STATE, ZIP: **South Attleboro, MA 02703-5599**

TELEPHONE NUMBER: **(508) 761-6500**   FAX: **(508) 761-4240**

CONTACT PERSON: **Kurt Ganter**

TITLE: **VP Employee Services**

DESCRIPTION OF JOB: **Hardware selection, maintenance & installation. Assist w/ software problems of clients. System analysis. Software installation.**

QUALIFICATIONS: **Technical Training. 2 year preference. Self motivated & willing to learn. Service oriented attitude.**

GENERAL INFORMATION: **Maintain 25 PC systems, multiple computers and printers. Microsoft Word for Windows, Lotus 123 used.**

In most postsecondary schools, the services of a job placement office are available to the school's students and graduates. The range of services available will vary from school to school. Although no school can guarantee the placement of its graduates, most schools make every effort to assist their graduates with finding a job in their chosen field of study. Some of the most common sources of job interviews through your school's placement office include:

- *Job postings:* Whether on bulletin boards or in job books maintained in the placement office, job opportunities that are currently available are usually posted by the placement office.
- *Career days:* Many schools hold some type of career day to bring employers and students together. Although career days are mostly aimed at providing career information to students, the contacts you make with

industry representatives during these programs are another source of job interviews for you.

- *On-campus interviews:* Some schools invite companies to conduct job interviews for graduates at the school. This type of on-campus recruiting program is one of the most direct ways to secure an interview through your placement office.
- *Company visits:* Many other types of company visits may occur at your school besides career days and on-campus interviews. These may include industry guest speakers' programs, industry advisory board meetings, or employer recognition programs. The contacts you may make with industry representatives through these situations are all great sources for job interviews as well.

Your school's placement office is one source of job interviews. You should find out exactly what resources are available to you through the placement office and make full use of those services.

Beyond the Placement Office

If there is anything true about finding a job, it is that you should not depend on any one source for results. Even if your school boasts a high placement rate for its graduates, you always need to explore all of your options before making a final decision. The placement office may be the source of several good job offers, but the job you take may be one that came from somewhere else. Many, many good jobs are never advertised in the newspaper and never called into your school's placement office. You can find out about these jobs by the means described in the sections that follow.

Networking Spread the word that you are job hunting. Talk to friends, relatives, teachers, current employers (if appropriate), employees at different companies that you think you would like to work for, and your school's alumni. Many people will be able to let you know about jobs at their own company because of internal job posting systems.

Professional Associations Some of the professional associations in your career field are listed in Chapter Thirteen, "Career Paths." They can be an extremely valuable source of information to you throughout your career. For more contacts like this refer to the *Encyclopedia of Associations* in the reference area at your local library. Some professional associations publish job bulletins, some actually provide placement services, some do not. The only way you will know is to write and ask. If you are a member of the Future Business Leaders of America or the Distributive Education Clubs of America, write and ask for advice and any career literature they may have.

Independent Mass-Mailing Campaigns At first, you may think they are a waste of time, but your chances of unearthing the job you want at a company you really never thought of are good through this method. Visit your placement office, go to the library, use the Yellow Pages—find lists of potential employers. First identify at least 20 that you may really be interested in, and from there, it's up to you. Mailing out 200 résumés and cover letters is not a bad idea if your field is especially competitive. When using the mass-mailing campaign, you may want to adjust your cover letter to suit particular types of employers.

For example, when applying for a job as a chef in a large hotel, you may use a different approach than if you were applying to a small fine-dining establishment. The menus will be different, the clients will be different, and the employers' needs will be different, even though both are in need of the same type of professional. If you receive a lot of rejection letters, don't panic. If many of the companies you write to don't reply right away, *don't get discouraged*! It is not a reflection on you. The employer hasn't even met you! It is an indication that your background is not appropriate at the current time. Pay attention to the positives. One of the few answers you get might be just what you're looking for. When a company sets up an interview with an unsolicited candidate, there is a good chance that either there is an opening suited to your background or one may be coming soon.

Employment Agencies Agencies are especially helpful to you once you have a few years of work experience. Some agencies are able to assist with entry-level positions, but most deal with advanced positions requiring at least two to three years' experience. It won't hurt to select one or two reputable employment agencies to submit résumés to during an entry-level job search. If you do have a lot of experience, use them more heavily. Just do not fall into the trap of depending solely on the agency to find you a job. And remember, be sure to ask if the employer will pay the placement fee if you are hired.

Telemarketing Campaigns Get on the telephone and do some preliminary work for your job search. Call companies directly to see if they are actively seeking applicants in any particular area of the company. Find out the name, title, and address of the person who may be responsible for hiring. You can create a job for yourself over the telephone if you are smart! When you call, know what you are going to say, and be prepared to announce your qualifications and what you have to offer the company, rather than just asking if there are any jobs available. Many times employers will call a candidate in for an informational interview if it sounds like the candidate might fit into the company somewhere. When you speak to someone on the telephone, you have an opportunity to create an impression that you cannot produce on a résumé or a job application.

Job interviews are an important part of your job search. They provide you the opportunity to convince an employer you are the best candidate for the job and to evaluate whether or not the job or company is right for you.

PREPARING FOR A JOB INTERVIEW

Successful interviews are the result of good preparation. Preparation not only gives you the information and the appearance you need to succeed, but more important, it gives you the confidence to succeed.

Think of preparing for an interview like preparing for a final exam. If you start studying well in advance, it helps. If you get enough of a head start on studying, you may not have to cram the night before. What this means is that you can get to sleep on time, and you can probably get up in time to have breakfast and freshen up properly so that you will arrive on time and feel good when you sit down for the exam. There will be an air of calmness and confidence that will help you think straight throughout the exam. You will leave knowing that regardless of the outcome, you gave it your best shot—you did the best you could. If you give the same preparation to an interview, you will gain the same satisfaction.

PREPARING FOR AN INTERVIEW

The three keys to interviewing success

1. Preparation	→	Know yourself
2. Preparation	→	Know your career goals
3. Preparation	→	Know your employer

How to Research a Company

Company Standings Look at the company's annual financial report and determine the following: Private or publicly owned? What information can I obtain

from privately owned companies? Growth rate? Expansion? Analyze the competition: Who's the leader? How much competition? Reputations?

Organizational Framework Look at the company's organizational chart thoroughly and determine: Degree of individual responsibility? Centralized or decentralized? What is the chain of command? What is the system for promotions within the company?

Philosophies and Policies Consider the philosophies of the company: Are they practiced as stated? Do you agree with what is practiced? Is the company production- or people-oriented? Is the management traditional or progressive? Are you allowed to read the company's policies? Do you agree with them?

Geographic   Where is the company's market (international/national)? Direction and rate of expansion? Do you know where you will be located? How often is relocation required for promotion? How much travel is involved?

Management Development   How much training is provided by the company? Is continuing education endorsed? Does the company have a human resources program? What support groups are available?

Salary and Benefits   How open is the company about salary? How does it compare with the industry average? How are raises determined? What is the maximum earning potential?

Read the company's benefits and consider the following: insurance package (reputation of insurance company), travel pay, sick leave, training pay, overtime, vacation, pregnancy leave, relocation fee, holidays, continuing education, profit sharing, and retirement. On the average, benefits will equal about 25–30 percent of the salary. Remember, benefits are nontaxable.

Miscellaneous Advice   Talk to someone employed by the company who is where you would like to be in two years, and ask:

How honest has the company been?

How strictly are policies followed?

Any questions your interviewer avoided or was unable to answer.

References and Resources   You may obtain information from the company's:

Financial reports

Charts of corporate structure

Company literature

and from other sources, including:

Professors

Employees of the company

Alumni

Journals

One of the best ways to learn about a company is to thoroughly read their annual report. That is often easier said than done. The following guidelines should enable you to read and understand a typical annual report.

How to Decipher Annual Reports

The following step-by-step guide offers insight and explains business and technical jargon.

To many employees and shareholders, reading an annual report is about as enlightening as hieroglyphics.

The average shareholder or company employee spends only 5 to 10 minutes looking at an annual report, according to an article in *The Courier,* employee magazine at First Citizen Bank & Trust Company, Raleigh, NC. The article, "Reading Your Annual Report: Beyond the Pictures," appeared in conjunction with the mailing of First Citizens' 1981 annual report.[1]

The reason for this is simple: Most people don't know what to look for when they read an annual report. Yet, for many companies, the annual report is the only document concerning the firm's financial health that is distributed widely on a regular basis.

To help employees (and others) make sense out of First Citizens' or any company's annual report, *The Courier* offered these tips:[2]

- If you do nothing else, look at the "Highlights" section, usually outlined on the first page of the report. These numbers tell at a glance how the company did for the year and offer some comparisons to the prior year.
- The first thing to look for is net income, often called "the bottom line." Earnings per share tell how much profit is earned by each share of stock and is of particular interest to shareholders. Shareholders' equity tells what the company is worth. This number is produced simply by subtracting liabilities (what the company owes) from assets (what the company owns). "Be wary if liabilities ever exceed assets—it means your company is bankrupt."
- After reading the highlights, read the chairman's message to shareholders. It's a good summary of how the company did and why, and it gives the general outlook for the coming year.
- Now you're ready for more financial details, so turn to the page in the financial section entitled "Analysis of Earnings." This section analyzes in detail the company's performance for the year. Charts, graphs, and tables usually accompany a narrative discussion.
- Finally, unless your brain has overheated from the strain, you're ready to study the most significant part of the report . . . the audited financial statements. Each of the audited financial statements previews current period information along with comparable data for the prior year.

---

[1] Danita Morgan, editor, *The Courier,* First Citizens Bank & Trust Company, P.O. Box 151, Raleigh, NC 27602.

[2] Reprinted with permission from *Communication World*—a monthly publication of the International Association of Business Communicators.

- The Balance Sheet gives a detailed look at the company's financial position at the end of the year.
- The Statement of Income is a more detailed report of revenues, expenses, taxes, gains and losses on sales of securities, and the amount of money earmarked for retained earnings.
- The Statement of Changes in Shareholders' Equity provides a summary of changes in stock, surplus, undivided profits, and shareholders' equity.
- The Statement of Changes in Financial Position provides a summary of the sources of funds and how they were spent during the year.
- An integral part of the audited financial statements are the footnotes, which present more details and explain information contained in the basic financial statements.

"The annual report is a specialized publication which talks the language of stockbrokers and business executives," the article concludes. "But that doesn't mean you have to be left in the dark."

Possible Sources for Researching a Company

Write for information
Research information
Know the sources that are available to you

Reference Volumes

American Men of Science
College Placement Annual
Dictionary of Corporate Affiliations (National Register Publishing Company, Inc.)
Dun & Bradstreet Directories (Million Dollar Directory, Middle Market Directory)
Encyclopedia of Associations, Vol. 1 (National Organizations, Gale Research Company)
Encyclopedia of Business Information Sources (two volumes)
Fitch Corporation Manuals
Fortune Magazine's Directories
Foundation Directory
Investor Banker, Broker Almanac
Mac Rae's Blue Book
Moody Manuals
Research Centers Directory
Register of Manufacturers (For different states, e.g., *California Manufacturers' Register*)

Standard & Poor's
Standard Register of Advertisers
Thomas' Register of American Manufacturers
Walker's Manual of Far Western Corporations and Securities

Periodicals

Advertising Age
Business Week
Dun's Review
Forbes magazine
Fortune magazine
The Wall Street Journal
New York Times

Self-Preparation

The various forms of preparation for your interview are situational knowledge, mental preparation, physical preparation, and written preparation.

Situational Knowledge

- Do you know where the company is located?
- Do you know how long it will take you to get there?
- Do you know where you will park?
- Do you know what office to go to?
- Do you know the name and title of the person with whom you will be interviewing?
  - Do you have the phone number of the company so that you can call if you are going to be late for any reason?
  - Do you know if you will be interviewing with more than one person?

Mental Preparation Mental preparation for a job interview involves several areas. It involves your knowledge of the company, the position for which you are applying, and the career path you wish to follow, as well as your mental attitude about work in general, your expectations about the job, and your confidence in your ability to do the job.

You have seen the kind of information you should research about the company with which you are to interview. Knowledge about the company serves many purposes on a job interview. *First,* it confirms your real interest in working for the company. *Second,* it provides you with a frame of reference for the interview. For example, if you are extremely nervous about your interview, you may want to jot down some questions about the information you read. Maybe it is to clarify something you did not really understand, or maybe it is to find out something you want to know that could not be found in the literature. By having a frame of reference from which to ask questions on the interview, you will feel more relaxed. You will be able to pick up the ball when there is a lag in conversation during the interview or have something to respond to if the interviewer asks you if you have any questions. The interview should be a *conversation* between two people. You shouldn't let yourself be talked at because you are too shy to ask questions. Remember, this is an investment for both you and the company. You have as much right to evaluate the opportunities being discussed as the interviewer has to evaluate you.

Third, knowledge of the company before the interview puts you in a convincing position that shows the employer you really want to work with that company. Equipped with the proper knowledge, you can bring the company name into your responses and conversations. You can clearly and specifically state the reasons you want to work for that company and the reasons you would be an asset to the company. This is most difficult to do without being able to incorporate specific information about the company. You already learned how to use the sales process on a job interview. *Convincing* is the key word. *Genuinely convincing* is most important.

Part of mental preparation for an interview is having a clear understanding about the job for which you are interviewing. Time after time, interviewers comment that applicants don't really understand the nature of the job for which they are applying. Typically, the employer may ask, "What do you see yourself doing every day as a (*title of the job*)?" The one area in which applicants fall short is lack of specific information available to really answer questions effectively. And yet, isn't it critical to know what you are getting into when you choose a career field? The information provided in Chapters Thirteen and Fifteen should give you the information you need about the job for which you are interviewing. You used this information once in deciding on your career goal; use it again to make yourself more convincing on your job interview. Be able to speak comfortably about the job you are applying for as it relates to your career field and the professional objectives you have developed. Let the interviewer know that you have thought about the big picture and that the decisions you are making are a part of an overall plan. Employers like to see applicants who have *career direction.*

Next, your mental attitude about work will be evaluated in your interview. You should be enthusiastic about the challenges your career presents to you, as opposed to the person who does not see the value of work beyond the paycheck. Emanating motivation and enthusiasm about work relates a work ethic and a belief on the part of the employer that you might be able to make some valuable contributions to the company. Your attitude about work is important.

The employer will evaluate your expectations about the job as well. Demonstrate realistic attitudes about the responsibilities and authority you hope for as well as the starting salary you expect to earn. Be confident in your ability to do the job.

Physical Preparation   Physical preparation for a job interview reinforces your mental preparation. You could have spent a lot of time thinking through all you will be discussing on the interview, but if you feel sick, tired, or sloppy, your mental attitude and alertness will be diminished.

Some important guidelines include:

- Start with good hygiene and good grooming.
- Get proper rest the night before.
- Eat breakfast.
- Wear a professional outfit that still relates your own personal style.
- Present a professional image—enhance it! Along with the clothing you wear, bring your résumé and references in a leather-bound folder. Properly arrange your portfolio if this is part of your presentation; have a pen with you and bring extra copies of your résumé along. Also have with you the small index card you prepared earlier with all pertinent dates and salaries so that you can quickly and efficiently complete a job application if you are required to do so.
- Wear little jewelry, perfume, or cologne—just enough to enhance your presentation of yourself but not so much that it becomes the focus of attention. The same applies to makeup.
- Remember to have clean hair, neatly and stylishly groomed.
- Arrive 10 minutes early.
- Relax.
- Smile.
- Be energetic.

Written Preparation   Make sure you have the proper street directions to the company. It is not inappropriate to bring notes with you on an interview. Bring notes from your company research in case you need them. Prepare a brief list of questions to have with you. Write down any miscellaneous information that does not appear on your résumé that you feel might be worth bringing up at the interview. Summarize the details of the job as you perceive them from the ad you read or the information you researched. This information should not prove to be a distraction during the interview, but rather a help should you need it. Remember how important eye contact is as an indicator of listening and interest level.

Finally, as a wrap-up to preparation in general, review the Proof by Example Exercise in Chapter One. The information you have outlined through this simple exercise is the most valuable information you can impart during your interview.

Study it.

Review it.

Rehearse it mentally.

Rehearse the information in a conversational style that is clear, confident, and convincing.

Self-Preparation Summary

- Is my **goal** clear to me? If not, it will not be clear to an employer! **Repeat the steps in the career planning process** until you can answer this question comfortably.
- Have I decided if and **where** I am willing to relocate?
- Have I decided **how much** I need to earn to meet my living expenses?
- Have I **researched** the company so that I know the company's:
  Relative size.
  Plans or potential for growth.
  Array of product lines or services.
  Potential new products, services, location.
  Competition. What makes this company different?
  Age and style of management.
  Number of plants and stores or properties.
  Geographic locations, including location of home office.
  Parent company or subsidiaries.
  Structure of the training program.
  Recruiter's or department manager's name.
- Can I now explain to an employer why I want to work for **them?**
- Can I also explain to an employer why they should **hire me?**
- Do I have the proper **outfits** to wear on my interviews?
- Will I be **well-groomed, alert, and on time** for my interview?
- Is my **résumé** ready?
- Have I developed a **positive attitude** so that the interview will be successful?
- Have I remembered the key to the sales process—why people buy, how to sell—the features and benefits way!

THE INITIAL INTERVIEW

Following is a summary of the five stages of an initial interview, detailing the topics the interviewer will cover in each and what the interviewer will be looking for from you.

Stages and Topics	Stages	Interviewer Topics	Interviewer Looks for
Covered during the Initial Interview	First impressions	Introduction and greeting Small talk about traffic conditions, the weather, the record of the basketball team	Firm handshake, eye contact Appearance and dress appropriate to the business, not college setting Ease in social situations, good manners, poise
	Your record	*Education*	
		Reasons for choice of school and major Grades, effort required for them Special areas of interest Courses enjoyed most and least, reasons Special achievements, toughest problems Value of education as career preparation Interaction with instructors High school record, important test scores	Intellectual abilities Breadth and depth of knowledge Relevance of course work to career interests Special or general interest Value placed on achievement Willingness to work hard Relation between ability and achievement Reaction to authority Ability to cope with problems Sensible use of resources (time, energy, money)
		Work Experience	
		Nature of jobs held Why undertaken Level of responsibility reached Duties liked most and least Supervisory experience Relations with others	High energy level, vitality, enthusiasm Leadership, interest in responsibility Willingness to follow directions Ability to get along with others Seriousness of purpose Ability to motivate oneself to make things happen Positive "can do" attitude
		Activities and Interests	
		Role in extracurricular, athletic, community, and social service activities Personal interests—hobbies, cultural interests, sports	Diversity of interests Awareness of world outside the lab Social conscience, good citizenship

Stages and Topics	Stages	Interviewer Topics	Interviewer Looks for
Covered during the Initial Interview (concluded)	Your career goals	Type of work desired Immediate objectives Long-term objectives Interest in this company Other companies being considered Desire for further education, training Geographical preferences and limitations Attitude toward relocation Health factors that might affect job performance	Realistic knowledge of strengths and weaknesses Preparation for employment Knowledge of opportunities Seriousness of purpose: career-oriented rather than job-oriented Knowledge of the company Real interest in the company Work interests in line with talents Company's chance to get and keep you
	The company	Company opportunities Where you might fit in Current and future projects Major divisions and departments Training programs, educational and other benefits	Informed and relevant questions Indicators of interest in answers Appropriate, but not undue, interest in salary or benefits
	Conclusion	Further steps you should take (application form, transcript, references) Further steps company will take, outline how application handled, to which departments it will be sent, time of notification of decision Cordial farewell	Candidate's attention to information as a sign of continued interest

Twenty Questions Typically Asked by Interviewers

- What kind of company or work environment are you looking for?
- What kind of job or duties/responsibilities are you looking for?
- Tell me a little bit about professional training and/or your college experience.
- Describe some of the part-time/summer jobs you've had in the past.
- What is your academic/school record up until now?
- Describe some of your extracurricular/student activities.
- What do you consider some of your strong points?
- What are some of your short- and long-term job goals?
- Tell me about your past employers.

- What do you know about this company?
- What led you to choose your major field of study?
- Why did you select your institution for your education?
- What are the three most important accomplishments thus far in your life?
- What is the most difficult assignment you have tackled, and how did you resolve it?
- Why should I hire you?
- How would a friend/former employer/instructor describe you?
- Will you relocate/does relocation bother you?
- Are you willing to travel?
- What are your salary expectations?
- Are you willing to spend at least six months as a trainee?

You should also be aware that there are some questions that are not appropriate for an employer to ask on an interview. The table on pages 97–99 summarizes what is appropriate and inappropriate for an employer to ask in a preemployment interview regarding a number of personal subjects.

Interview Strategies

When you meet the recruiter:
> Shake his or her hand firmly, maintaining eye contact with the person, offer a pleasant but professional smile and say, "Hello, I'm (*your name*). It's good to meet you (*Mr., Ms., or Mrs. recruiter's name*)." Wait for the recruiter to indicate you should sit down or wait for him or her to sit down before you do so.

During the interview maintain:
> A positive attitude.
> Good posture.
> An interested manner.
> A good appearance.
> A pleasant look on your face.
> Eye contact with the recruiter.
> Confidence.
> Be yourself. This is what recruiters look for!

Make the interview a two-way conversation:
> Ask questions, as well as answering them!

The recruiter will be assessing:
> Why this kind of employment?
> Ultimate goal.
> Relocation.

Guide to	Subject	Acceptable	Unacceptable
Appropriate Preemployment Inquiries	Name	"Have you worked for this company under a different name?" "Have you ever been convicted of a crime under another name?"	Former name of applicant whose name has been changed by court order or otherwise.
	Address or duration of residence	Applicant's place of residence. How long applicant has been resident of this state or city?	
	Birthplace		Birthplace of applicant. Birthplace of applicant's parents, spouse, or other relatives. Requirements that applicant submit a birth certificate, naturalization or baptismal record.
	Age	"Can you, after employment, submit a work permit if under 18?" "Are you over 18 years of age?" "If hired, can you furnish proof of age?" or Statement that hire is subject to verification that applicant's age meets legal requirements.	Questions which tend to identify applicants 40 to 64 years of age.
	Religious		Applicant's religious denomination or affiliation, church, parish, pastor, or religious holidays observed. "Do you attend religious services or a house of worship?" Applicant may not be told "This is a Catholic/ Protestant/Jewish/atheist organization."
	Work days and shifts	Statement by employer of regular days, hours, or shift to be worked.	

Guide to Appropriate Preemployment Inquiries	Subject	Acceptable	Unacceptable
	Race or color		Complexion, color of skin, or other questions directly or indirectly indicating race or color.
	Photograph	Statement that photograph may be required after employment.	Requirement that applicant affix a photograph to his application form. Request applicant, at his option, to submit photograph. Requirement of photograph after interview but before hiring.
	Citizenship	Statement by employer that if hired, applicant may be required to submit proof of citizenship.	Whether applicant or his parents or spouse are naturalized or native-born U.S. citizens. Date when applicant or parents or spouse acquired U.S. citizenship. Requirement that applicant produce his naturalization papers or first papers. Whether applicant's parents or spouse are citizens of the United States.
	National origin or ancestry	Languages applicant reads, speaks, or writes fluently.	Applicant's nationality, lineage, ancestry, national origin, descent, or parentage. Date of arrival in United States or port of entry; how long a resident. Nationality of applicant's parents or spouse; maiden name of applicant's wife or mother. Language commonly used by applicant, "What is your mother tongue?" How applicant acquired ability to read, write, or speak a foreign language.
	Education	Applicant's academic, vocational, or professional education; schools attended.	Date last attended high school.

Guide to Appropriate Preemployment Inquiries	Subject	Acceptable	Unacceptable
	Experience	Applicant's work experience. Applicant's military experience in armed forces of United States, in a state militia (U.S.), or in a particular branch of U.S. armed forces.	Applicant's military experience (general). Type of military discharge.
	Character	"Have you ever been convicted of any crime?" If so, when, where, and disposition of case?	"Have you ever been arrested?"
	Relatives	Names of applicant's relatives already employed by this company. Name and address of parent or guardian if applicant is a minor.	Marital status or number of dependents. Name or address of relative, spouse, or children of adult applicant. "With whom do you reside?" "Do you live with your parents?"
	Notice in case of emergency	Name and address of person to be notified in case of accident or emergency.	Name and address of relative to be notified in case of accident or emergency.
	Organizations	Organizations, clubs, professional societies, or other associations of which applicant is a member, excluding any names the character of which indicates the race, religious creed, color, national origin, or ancestry of its members.	List all organizations, clubs, societies, and lodges to which you belong.
	References	"By whom were you referred for a position here?"	Requirement of submission of a religious reference.
	Physical condition	"Do you have any physical condition which may limit your ability to perform the job applied for?" Statement by employer that offer may be made contingent on passing a physical examination.	"Do you have any physical disabilities?" Questions on general medical condition. Inquiries as to receipt of workers' compensation.
	Miscellaneous	Notice to applicant that any misstatements or omissions of material facts in his application may be cause for dismissal.	Any inquiry that is not job-related or necessary for determining an applicant's eligibility for employment.

Social, civic activities.
Future career goals.
Job or career.
Reason for wanting to work for the company.
Quality of professional training.
Past experiences.
How you heard about this company.

What to Find Out during an Interview

- The exact job: its title, responsibilities, and department in which you would work.
- The fit of the department into the company structure: its purpose, its budget, and other departments with which it works.
- Reporting structure: one or more bosses.
- Type of formal or informal training you would be given.
- Working on your own or as a member of a team.
- Will skills you learn on this job prepare you for higher-level jobs?
- How job performance is measured.
- What your opportunities for advancement are and where those who previously held your position are now.
- What the salary for this position is.

There are two ways to sharpen your interviewing skills: mock interviews and informational interviews.

Mock Interviews

A mock interview is simply a practice interview. It is conducted by someone other than a potential employer. You can ask several people to give you a mock interview: an instructor, a friend, a relative or, of course, a member of your school's placement office. First, go through the following steps:

- Review "Twenty Questions."
- Rehearse the answers mentally.
- Review the Proof by Example exercise in Chapter One.
- Look over your résumé.

Give the person who will interview you the list of questions most frequently asked on an interview. Let them conduct the interview and evaluate you by using the following Mock Interview Evaluation form. Go through as many mock interviews as you think necessary to master the interviewing process.

MOCK INTERVIEW EVALUATION

	Out-standing	Very Good	Good	Needs Improvement	Unsatisfactory
Communication skills					
Appearance					
Proof by Example					
Enthusiasm					
Initial impression/clothing					
Poise/confidence					
Preparation					
Comments and evaluation					

Interviewed by:

Date:

Informational Interviews

An informational interview is one in which you interview someone who is already working in your chosen career. Preferably it is someone who actually has the same type of job that you are seeking. The following list of questions for informational interviews will give you an idea of the kind of information you can obtain. You can actually use this form to collect information when conducting the interview.

Questions for Informational Interviews

Occupation: _____

Person to be interviewed: _____

Write comments and additional interview questions in the spaces provided.

What do you like about your occupation? Why?

_____

_____

_____

What are the activities and responsibilities connected with your job? Could you describe your job routine for a typical day or week?

_____   _____

_____

_____

Do the activities and responsibilities of your occupation vary depending on the employer, or are they generally the same? In what ways could your job situation be different from those of others in your occupation?

_____

_____

_____

Do the number of responsibilities in your occupation remain constant or increase over time?

_____

_____

_____

What skills are necessary to perform your job activities?

_____

_____

What training and education does your occupation require?

_____

_____

_____

Do the training requirements for your occupation vary from employer to employer?

_____

_____

_____

How much variety is connected with your work routine?

_____

_____

_____

How would you describe your actual work setting or workplace?

_____

_____

_____

What opportunities are there in your job for sharing ideas, acquiring new skills, and learning from your co-workers or supervisors?

_____

_____

_____

How competitive is entry into your field? What is the outlook for openings in your field over the next few years?

_____

_____

_____

What is the usual progression of jobs and assignments for people in your occupation? What career paths can people follow?

_____

_____

_____

Is yours considered a staff (management) or a line (support) position? If a line position, what other people do you supervise?

_____

_____

_____

What qualities do employers look for in job applicants who want to enter your occupation?

_____

_____

_____

What are the goals of your organization? How would you describe its overall philosophy and objectives?

_____

_____

_____

This interview began with the question, "What do you like about your occupation?" What do you _not_ like about your occupation? What job frustrations and negative points should I know about before deciding whether to enter this field?

_____

_____

_____

To what extent are the advantages and disadvantages of your particular job attributable to your particular place of employment?

_____

_____

_____

Do you know the names of employers other than your own who hire people in your occupation? Do you know of any sources I could consult to locate still more employers?

_____

_____

_____

Can you recommend the names of other people I can consult to find out more about your field? May I use your name to introduce myself?

_____

_____

_____

Procedures for Arranging and Conducting Informational Interviews

- Compile a list of employers for the occupations in your career field. Use business directories, the *Encyclopedia of Associations*, the Yellow Pages of cities across the United States, the *College Placement Annual*, or other sources. Note employers' locations, phone numbers, types of businesses, product lines, and other relevant information that you discover. Include alumni from your school on your list. Check with your alumni or placement office for names of past graduates who would be willing to help you out.
- Review your list of employers and mark those you consider the most attractive.
- If possible, compare employer locations with other members of your class. Coordinating trips to visit the same city with a classmate may reduce travel costs.
- Mark those employers on your list located where you are able to travel and visit.

- Draft a separate list of employers to contact for arranging interviews. Base your new list on the occupations you are considering the most seriously, the new employers that appear the most attractive to you, and your ability to travel.
- Before contacting employing organizations, consider the following issues:

    When can the interviews be conducted? Other commitments may conflict or need to be rescheduled. Interviews should be scheduled to allow more than adequate time to locate destinations, accommodate delays, conduct the interviews, and take advantage of invitations to extend your visit or tour employers' facilities.

    What people are available for interviews? This can be checked by telephoning the employer to explain your needs. Public relations or personnel offices are good sources of this information.

    How can you know if the person you ask for an interview is able to give you the kind of information you are seeking? Verify that the person you contact actually works in the occupation you are assessing. Clearly explain your needs and objectives before requesting an interview.

    Where should the interviews be conducted? Request that interviews be conducted in locations allowing privacy and freedom from distraction. The people you interview may agree to provide tours of their work-places. Your interviews should be conducted close enough to actual work settings for you to be able to observe them at some point during your visits.

- Schedule your informational interviews. Whenever possible make your arrangements directly with the people you plan to interview. Explain the nature of this class and your reasons for requesting an interview. You should find most people open to talking with you about their occupation.
- Leave your phone number or address so your interview subjects are able to contact you if rescheduling becomes necessary.
- If you have not had experience in interviewing for information, you may want to practice mock interviewing with a classmate, friend, or relative.
- Review the information you want to obtain about your interview subjects' occupations. You can use the previous interview, Questions for Informational Interviews, or draft questions of your own. You should be familiar enough with the questions you want to ask so that you will not continually need to refer to a list during the interviews. This will help achieve a more natural, relaxed, and spontaneous conversation with your interview subjects. This style of interview is likely to provide more honest, candid, and complete information than a straight question-and-answer interview format.

- Reconfirm interview times, dates, and locations on the day before each scheduled interview.
- At the conclusion of each visit, ask your subject for the names of other people who can provide information about the occupations in your targeted range of occupations. Obtaining permission to use your subjects' names can help in arranging future interviews.
- After each interview, take time to send a thank-you letter to your subject. Courtesy is a good habit, and you may want to be remembered favorably by your subjects' organizations.

©1982. National Computer Systems, Inc.

SECOND AND THIRD INTERVIEWS

Second and third interviews are sometimes conducted by a prospective employer in order to become more familiar with which candidates best fit the job.

Second interviews are conducted to allow the candidate and prospective employer the opportunity to discuss in greater detail the available job and whether or not the candidate's qualifications and career goals match the job opportunity. A second interview helps both the employer and the candidate to determine if they are the right match for each other. Second interviews are conducted in different ways. As the job candidate, you may be asked back to speak with your first interviewer again or to interview with others in the company. For example, if your first interviewer was from the human resources department, your second interview may be with the head of the department in which you would be working. Very often, the human resources department screens potential candidates for department heads to interview, and the department head actually makes the hiring decision.

On your second interview you may be interviewed both one-on-one and with a group of other candidates. This method is sometimes used to determine how well you interact with others. Bringing in a group of applicants is also a way for some companies to show the candidates the company and talk about its history or future. During the second interview, you should be prepared to ask a lot of the more detailed questions you didn't discuss the first time. It is more appropriate to discuss salary and benefits during a second interview than during the first interview.

Third interviews are not the norm, but many companies conduct them with the one or two top candidates for the job in order to make a final decision. By the third interview, many employers feel familiar enough with the candidate to extend a job offer. Benefits and salary are almost always discussed in detail during a third interview because by this time the employer is only dealing with the most serious candidates.

POSTINTERVIEW EVALUATION

HOW COMPANIES RATE APPLICANTS

Evidence of ability	→	Grades
Desire to work	→	Part-time and summer jobs
Ambition	→	Future career plans
Ability to communicate	→	Interview
Acceptable personality	→	Interview

HOW EMPLOYERS RATE APPLICANTS

Appearance and manner	→	Well-groomed
		Professional presence
		Considerate
		Polite
Personality	→	Warm and friendly
		Attract or repel
		Attentive
		Responsive
		Enthusiastic
Intelligence	→	Mental organization
		Alertness
		Judgment
		Understanding
		Imagination
Attitude	→	Loyal
		Tactful
		Constructive
		Cooperative
		Reasonable
Self-expression	→	Clear and interesting
		Convincing
		Pleasant voice
Effectiveness	→	Reliable
		Trustworthy
		Industrious

EMPLOYER'S INTERVIEW EVALUATION

Appearance

Grooming	__ A __ B __ C
Posture	__ A __ B __ C
Dress	__ A __ B __ C
Manners	__ A __ B __ C

Preparation for Interview

Asked pertinent questions	__ A __ B __ C
Résumé	__ A __ B __ C

Verbal Communication

Conversational ability	__ A __ B __ C
Expression	__ A __ B __ C

Direction

Well-defined goals	__ A __ B __ C
Confidence level	__ A __ B __ C
Realistic and practical	__ A __ B __ C

Maturity

Responsible	__ A __ B __ C
Self-reliant	__ A __ B __ C
Decisive	__ A __ B __ C
Leader—school	__ A __ B __ C
Leader—work	__ A __ B __ C

Sincerity

Genuine attitude	__ A __ B __ C
Artificial attitude	__ A __ B __ C

Personality

Enthusiastic	__ A __ B __ C
Extrovert	__ A __ B __ C
Motivation	__ A __ B __ C
Aggressive	__ A __ B __ C
Unresponsive	__ A __ B __ C
Noncommittal	__ A __ B __ C

Qualifications

Academic preparation	__ A __ B __ C
Work experience	__ A __ B __ C
Position match	__ A __ B __ C

Overall Evaluation

Long-range potential	__ A __ B __ C
Drive and ambition	__ A __ B __ C
Ability and qualifications	__ A __ B __ C

A - Outstanding
B - Average
C - Below Average

POSTINTERVIEW COMPANY EVALUATION

Company name _____

Company Standing	Yes	No	Comments
Is the company public?	_____	_____	_____
Is the company private?	_____	_____	_____
Is the company an industry leader?	_____	_____	_____
Is the company growing?	_____	_____	_____
Does the company have a positive reputation?	_____	_____	_____

Organizational Framework	Yes	No	Comments
Is the company mainly centralized management?	_____	_____	_____
Is the company mainly decentralized management?	_____	_____	_____
Is the company's advancement Vertical?	_____	_____	_____
Horizontal?	_____	_____	_____
Frequent?	_____	_____	_____

Philosophies and Policies	Yes	No	Comments
Do I agree with the company philosophy?	_____	_____	_____
Is the company production-oriented?	_____	_____	_____
Is the company people-oriented?	_____	_____	_____
Is the company's management traditional?	_____	_____	_____
Is the company's management progressive?	_____	_____	_____

Geography	Yes	No	Comments
Is the job in a desired location?	_____	_____	_____
Is relocation required?	_____	_____	_____
Is travel required?	_____	_____	_____

Management Development	Yes	No	Comments
Is there a formal training program?	_____	_____	_____
Is the majority of training "hands on"?	_____	_____	_____
Is there a continuing education program?	_____	_____	_____
Is there a remedial training program?	_____	_____	_____
Is the evaluation system used as a management tool?	_____	_____	_____
Are there criteria to be met before salary increases are given?	_____	_____	_____
Are salary increases given on the basis of merit?	_____	_____	_____
Is there a maximum earning level?	_____	_____	_____
Does the company provide Health insurance?	_____	_____	_____
Dental insurance?	_____	_____	_____
Sick leave?	_____	_____	_____

FOLLOW-UP AFTER AN INTERVIEW

Your evaluation by the employer doesn't stop when you leave your interview. How you follow up after the interview is just as important as the preparation you did beforehand.

Follow-up begins as you end your interview with the employer. If it is unclear to you what will happen next, *ask.* The employer may indicate that he or she will get back to you in two or three weeks or by a certain date. If that is the case, you may want to ask whether you will be contacted by telephone or in writing. If by telephone, you will want to be sure to leave a number where you can be easily reached.

If the employer says that he or she would like you to get back to him or her after thinking about the interview and indicate if you would like to pursue things further, *do it!* They are not giving you the runaround but may be testing your initiative and your genuine interest in the company. The employer may even ask that you visit one of the company's locations before pursuing a second interview if you have not done so already. This is to be sure that you will understand the company style and the type of environment in which you may be working. If you are unsure of your interest in the company, this visit could be a deciding factor for you. In that case, it is a benefit to both you and the employer.

If an employer asks you to take initiative in any way, *do it!* If you are absolutely sure the job or the company is not right for you, don't waste their time by taking the next step, but *do* send a thank-you letter acknowledging the time given to your first meeting. You do not want to burn any bridges as you move through your career. If an employer says nothing about follow-up, *ask* what you should do or expect next. If an employer does not get back to you in the time indicated, call. Be sure to wait for the designated amount of time to go by before calling.

Always send a thank-you letter immediately after an interview. If you are interested in the job, the letter will jog the employer's mind about you as an applicant and will relate your interest in the job. If you are not interested in the job, still send a thank-you letter for the time the employer took with you. A few years from now, that employer may be one that you want to work for, and you would not want to have created a negative first impression of your professionalism.

Follow-up after an interview is part of your evaluation process as a candidate. Be conscientious in this area. It will benefit you in the long run.

THE INTERVIEW HALL OF FAME . . . AND SHAME

The Interview Hall of Fame and Shame depicts examples of some interviews that were successful and some that were not so successful.

These stories demonstrate that certain things, when taken to an extreme, can hurt your chances of leaving an employer with a favorable impression. On the other hand, given the right balance between creativity and professionalism, you can develop some unique ways to stand out in a positive way when interviewing for a job.

For the best results, check first with your placement office to see if your strategies to impress an employer on your interview have a good chance of working.

Hall of Fame Case 1: John—Sous Chef

John was about to graduate from a two-year culinary arts program. He loved his profession, and it showed in the quality of his work. John had received good grades in school, had four years of part-time work experience in the food service industry, and had represented his school well by earning several gold and silver medals in national food competitions. At graduation, John was interviewing with many companies visiting his campus for his first full-time job. For one interview, John came to the placement office, properly dressed and résumé in hand. He also carried with him a black box. The placement director offered to store the box for John while he went on his interview. He declined the offer, stating he needed to bring it with him on his interview.

John was the last interviewee of the day. He went into the interviewing room, introduced himself, and before the interviewer could begin to ask questions, John opened the black box, producing the makings for a flaming dessert coffee. He said to the interviewer, "I know you've had a long day and that I am your last interview. I thought you'd like to sit back and relax a moment. While I prepare you some coffee, feel free to begin my interview." The interviewer smiled and immediately said, "You're hired."

Hall of Fame Case 2: Susan—Advertising Assistant

Susan was about to graduate from a two-year program in advertising and public relations. In addition to the job interviews she secured through her school's placement office, Susan arranged her own interview with a top advertising firm in Manhattan. Susan realized the competition would be stiff because there were many applicants.

Susan decided to use her expertise in her field to create a unique approach for her interview. Two weeks before her scheduled interview, Susan sent a portfolio by mail to her prospective interviewer, asking that it be reviewed prior to her interview. Her portfolio contained samples of two promotional brochures she had designed for her advertising class. Also enclosed were a copy of an ad she had created for the company where she had completed her internship and other samples of her writing.

That same week, Susan remembered the name of a graduate of her school who worked for the company with which she would be interviewing. Susan telephoned that person, introduced herself, and informally acquired some information about the company. Finally, one week before her interview, Susan had a classmate videotape her class presentation on how to design an effective promotional brochure and mailed it to her prospective employer. By the time Susan arrived for her interview, she felt comfortable because she knew a little about the company and her interviewer knew something about her.

Susan's preparation allowed more time during the interview to discuss the details of the job. The originality Susan demonstrated in her job search, combined with her qualifications, led to a job offer which she accepted. Employers appreciate creativity that is professional yet different from everyone else. This approach told the employer that Susan really wanted the job and that she had initiative and creative skills to bring to the company.

Hall of Fame Case 3: Kirsten—Corporate Travel Agent

After receiving her diploma in Travel/Tourism from a local travel school, Kirsten decided to continue at her job as a receptionist for a travel agency where she had worked while in school. After working there full-time for two months, Kirsten was fired. Because of a personality conflict she had with a co-worker, Kirsten refused to work on several projects with her. Before interviewing for her next job, Kirsten sought advice from her school's placement office on how to explain the fact that she had been fired from her job.

When her next interviewer asked Kirsten why she had left her job, Kirsten said that she had been fired because she had had differences with a co-worker and that she had responded by being uncooperative several times. Kirsten explained that there were no problems with her individual work performance but that she hadn't yet learned to be a good team worker.

Kirsten went on to discuss the positive side of the job she had and emphasized her accomplishments. She stated that she had sought advice from her school's placement office and now realized that despite her individual talents, she could not be successful until she learned how to work well with others. Kirsten expressed sincere interest in the corporate travel agent's position and said she was ready to learn how to work better with others.

After a second interview with the company's department manager, Kirsten was hired as a corporate travel agent, with a three-month probationary period. The department manager explained that she liked Kirsten's qualifications very much. She said that she was also impressed with Kirsten's honest and mature approach to discussing her problems with her previous job, that her commitment to improving her relations with others seemed sincere, and that she thought Kirsten could succeed in the job.

Kirsten started her new job and consciously worked at being a team player, even with a co-worker who was a lot different from herself. Kirsten passed the probationary period and developed a successful career with her new employer.

Hall of Shame Case 1: Dennis—Computer Systems Analyst

The placement director at XYZ Business School was successful in getting Digital Corporation to recruit XYZ graduates for the first time. Five of the top students from the Computer program were selected to interview with Digital Corporation.

Dennis, one of the candidates, appeared to have the best qualifications. He was in his last year of the program, was academically one of the top five graduates in his major, had part-time job experience as a computer systems analyst, successfully completed a computer internship, and was a lab assistant on campus. Dennis was articulate and also had a professional image. On the interview, the interviewer asked Dennis, "What type of environment do you like to work in?" The question was intended to determine how much supervision Dennis needed and if he could work well in a fast-paced environment. Dennis responded to the question as follows: "See this suit I have on? I never wear these. I program best in my jeans with a six pack of beer." The interviewer was thoroughly confused, commenting that Dennis seemed to have the appearance of one person and the personality of another. She decided he was not a match for their company because he did not appear ready to adapt to the corporate environment at Digital Corporation.

When the placement director asked Dennis why he responded this way, he answered, "I went to your professional development seminar, and you said to always be honest on an interview." Four years later, Dennis was hired to work at Digital, after realizing that portraying a professional image is necessary in most corporate environments.

Hall of Shame Case 2: Larry—Retail Management

Larry was a Retail Management major from Brooklyn. He came to the placement office with a request to interview with Abraham & Straus department store for a buying position in their jewelry department. Larry first came to the placement office wearing a ring on every finger, expressing his desire to be a jewelry buyer because he liked jewelry. The placement director advised Larry to investigate the role of a buyer, explaining that it entailed excellent quantitative skills and business management expertise. She told Larry that if he tried to promote himself on the basis of his interest in jewelry, he would not be perceived as someone who really understood what the job entailed. Larry convinced the placement director that he understood and was scheduled for an interview.

On the day of the interview, Larry came to the placement office dressed professionally and seemingly well prepared for his interview. When the interview ended, the interviewer came to the placement director to tell her that Larry would not be called back for a second interview. The reason was that Larry had an unrealistic viewpoint of what a retail buyer does. In fact, before entering the interviewing office, Larry slipped his rings onto every finger and proceeded to tell the interviewer he liked jewelry and wanted to be a jewelry buyer. Larry did not get a job in the retail field that year. After trying two or three jobs, Larry established a career as a sales representative for a local manufacturing company. Having a clear understanding of what a job entails day to day is critical.

Hall of Shame Case 3: Cheryl—Administrative Assistant

Cheryl saw a job posting in the placement office for an administrative assistant. Since this is what she trained to do at her school, Cheryl saw this job as a good opportunity to launch her career. Cheryl was a good student. She received A's and B's in almost all her classes. She really did not have much part-time job experience. The only jobs she had had for the past two summers were as a waitress and a retail sales clerk.

When Cheryl began preparing for her interview, she reviewed the checklist given to her in her professional development class. The checklist reminded her to wear her best dress or suit. Cheryl selected the new dress she had worn just once at her class formal the previous week. It was a straight, black dress with a low V back and sheer, long sleeves. She wore black hose and shoes and added a pearl necklace to complete her outfit.

When Cheryl went on her interview at the bank, she felt confident she would get the job. When she did not, she went to discuss with the placement director what might have gone wrong. The placement director called the personnel representative at the bank who interviewed Cheryl and asked for her feedback on Cheryl's interview. The interviewer thought that Cheryl had interviewed well, but they were looking for a "different type" of person, one who would fit into the professional environment at their company. Cheryl made the mistake of thinking that her best dress for a social occasion was also best for her interview. The message we give by our appearance is powerful on an interview.

Chapter Seven

Accepting a Job

Congratulations! You have received one or more job offers. You now need to decide whether or not you will accept one of them. Accepting a job is a big step. It is a commitment. You must decide whether or not this opportunity is the right match between you and your prospective employer. This decision involves evaluating what you offer the employer, what the employer offers you, and how well this opportunity fits into your personal lifestyle and career plan.

WHAT YOU OFFER THE EMPLOYER

When you receive a job offer, it is always good to review what you can bring to this job. This step is important because if you don't feel that what you have to offer matches what the employer is looking for, you probably will not be happy in your job.

A review of what you offer the employer will help you decide which job offer is right for you. You should review the skills you have that can benefit the company. You will want to be sure that you have the opportunity to use at least some of your skills on the job. This will help you practice and improve your skills so that you become more valuable to your company and better prepared to accept new responsibilities throughout your career. You may also offer the company a positive and realistic attitude about the level of responsibility you will have in the job. Being realistic about what you expect in your job is important to your employer because it means you can be focused on and satisfied with your current job for a period of time. This means you will not be overly concerned with a promotion or salary increase before the appropriate time for these changes. Consider whether the job offered can be a stepping-stone to more responsibility in that job or in your next job. You should also offer your employer the reassurance that you can be committed to this job for at least a one- to two-year period.

Finally, in considering your job offer, you can express to an employer that this job offers you the chance to learn new skills and techniques and contribute to the company those you already have. Your willingness to learn from as well as contribute to the company is important to an employer because it means you are willing to grow to become a more valuable asset to the company. By thinking about what you offer the employer and the job, you can make a better decision about whether or not this opportunity is the right one for you.

WHAT THE EMPLOYER OFFERS YOU

Among the things to consider when deciding on a job offer is what the employer can offer you. To determine if this is the right career opportunity for you, consider how much you can learn and grow professionally (professional development), the current standing of the company (how is it doing?), and the compensation package.

Professional Development

The very first thing you should think about is what you can learn in your new job. This is especially true when accepting your first job, because you will want this job to prepare you for future career opportunities. Many students underestimate the value of selecting a job based on the learning it can offer. You should consider the first job a stepping-stone in your career and focus primarily on how it will help you grow professionally. You can learn directly on the job or through training programs offered by the company. On the job, you will learn new skills and techniques, how to work better with others, and how to work better independently. By observing your co-workers and those in management or leadership positions, you can learn how the company operates and how certain situations are handled.

Training Programs

Training programs vary from company to company. Before accepting a job, find out about any formal training the company may have. You should know the duration of the program, salary during the training phase, location of the training (on site, home office, etc.), and what type of ongoing training will occur.

If training is done on the job, as opposed to in a formal program, this is fine in most cases. Just be sure to ask enough questions to get the feel of whether or not the training will be structured enough for your needs. If an employer offers you a lower salary to begin training on the job and says that it will increase to a certain amount after your training period, ask how long that will be. If you are accepting this as a condition of employment, you should be able to measure the time frame within which the change should occur. This will be important to you from a financial standpoint. You will then have an idea as to how long you will be working within a particular budget and be able to plan your personal and financial responsibilities based on that knowledge. On-the-job training and formal training programs can help you do a better job and will better prepare you for new opportunities that may interest you later on.

Promotional Opportunity

Some companies have more predictable promotional routes than others. Some move employees through different grades or levels of jobs based on their seniority with the company. Others base promotions strictly on performance. The large ones may offer many employees the chance to move up, while other, smaller companies have less room at the top. There are those that have a formal, internal job posting system to which employees may respond by applying for posted positions. Other companies go directly to employees selected on the basis of good performance to fill positions. Knowing promotional procedures at a company before you accept a job will help you understand your chances for advancement within that company. Whether available daily on the job or through formal training programs, a company that makes learning opportunities available to you provides you with the tools you need to enhance your professional development.

Company Standing

Before you accept a job, you should feel comfortable about the company's current status. This means knowing such things as the financial stability of the company, plans for growth or expansion, reputation and standing with the competition, involvement with employees, and stability of the work force.

Financial Stability   Financial stability means knowing enough about the company to be reasonably sure it is financially healthy and will be in business in the future. When you've started your new job, you don't want to have to worry about whether your company will be around in a few years.

Growth or Expansion   A company that is growing or expanding may have a wider offering of long-term career opportunities than one that is stagnant. You want to know that the position you take will be made interesting and challenging because the company is active and growing. If the company is expanding, this may raise questions in your mind about possible future relocation or changes in responsibilities.

Reputation and Standing with the Competition   Knowing if the company has a reputation for good business practices is important because you want to be proud to be associated with your employer. Knowing how well the company stands with its competition may tell you something about its ability to stay in business despite competition from other companies. If the company continues to perform well in comparison to its competitors, you may feel more secure about the company's ability to stay in business and about your ability to keep your job!

Involvement with Employees and Stability of the Work Force   Some companies communicate with and involve employees in the company more than others.

Employees may be involved in providing ideas to improve the work environment or customer service, to cut costs, or to implement a new program. Working in a company that encourages employee participation can be more interesting and more professionally rewarding. Knowing that a company's employee turnover is low may tell you that employees are generally happy with their jobs.

These are some examples of how knowing some things about the company's standing can help you decide if the company is right for you.

Benefits

The first thing to be aware of is that compensation does not consist of salary alone, but is *the combination of both the salary and benefits offered to you.*

This is important because if you are tempted to accept a job that pays a high salary and has few benefits, you may be required to pay a substantial amount of money for the benefits you need. You may find it better to understand what the value of the benefits offered to you are, and then, by relating that to the salary, you can determine if this is the best compensation package for you. For example, if you need a health insurance plan, the average cost paid by a company for this benefit is approximately $3,000 per employee. So if you were offered a job that paid $23,000 per year at a company that did not pay for your health insurance, instead of $20,000 elsewhere, that extra $3,000 would not be an advantage to you. Not only would you have to pay your own health insurance with it, but you would also be taxed more on the higher salary. There are many other types of benefits. Some are financially beneficial, some provide you personal or professional assistance, while others simply offer a convenience or enjoyment of some kind.

Health Benefits   Health benefits vary from company to company. Some firms pay this benefit in full; others provide partial payment, with the employee contributing the remaining portion; and some companies offer no health care coverage. Be sure to ask what is available and how extensive the coverage is so that you will know if you need to plan for any of this expense on your own.

Life Insurance   Life insurance is usually available in most companies. The purpose of life insurance is to provide your dependents financial support in the event of your death.

Education and Training   Education and training benefits may be available through a variety of programs. *Formal* training programs for new hires or for retraining current workers usually consist of planned sessions aimed at teaching the employee the company's systems and any specific skills needed to do the job. *Informal* training may occur in a less structured approach through on-the-job instruction. *Tuition reimbursement* is frequently available from many firms. This is a great benefit for employees who wish to continue their formal education while working. The economic value of this benefit is tremendous as the cost of education remains relatively high.

Seminars or *conferences* are also popular forms of education and training in many companies. Offered for periods from as little as a few hours in one day to sessions lasting a week or more, these are good vehicles for providing new skills to staff or keeping them updated in current issues and techniques in their field.

Bonuses Some companies have a bonus system in addition to the regular salary plan. If you earn a bonus, it is usually in addition to an annual salary increase. A bonus is usually a monetary reward paid to an individual for outstanding performance.

Housing, Meals, and Transportation Housing, meals, and transportation are often referred to as "living expenses." These costs are frequently covered in full for employees who must relocate temporarily or travel regularly for their jobs.

Travel opportunities are often presented as benefits to employees. When travel is required for the job, companies usually reimburse employees for these expenses. Sometimes trips are given away as a bonus or reward for top performance.

Financial Counseling Financial counseling provides employees the opportunity to learn how to better manage their own personal finances. For example, advice may be given on budgeting, investing, or computing personal income tax returns. In some companies, employees have the option of buying stock in the company which earns a monetary return for the individual based on how well the company does financially.

Time Off Time off with pay is usually available through paid vacations. Most companies also allow a certain amount of sick leave, which is to be used in times of illness. Generally, sick days are not to be used to supplement vacation time, because they have the exclusive purpose of being available only if needed for sickness. Paid holidays are another form of time off with pay. Although you should not seem primarily interested in time off, it is good to ask enough questions to be sure you thoroughly understand the company's position on time off before accepting a job. This will allow you to plan your time well and not overextend yourself with more time off than is acceptable to the company.

Family Care   Family care assistance is often available to support employees in caring for children or older family members.

Other Benefits   Fitness and wellness programs may be available on the company's premises, or support for participating in off-site programs may be provided.

Additional types of benefits may include a company car, club memberships, or discounts on products or services. These are usually referred to as "perks." Perks are benefits offered to provide a convenience, entertainment, or comfort of some kind. Although these are usually not as important to your final decision as the other benefits listed, when they exist, these extras may entice you to take the job.

Keep in mind that although this variety of benefits may be available to you, you must consider which ones you need at this point in your life to determine if the compensation package is for you. For example, when accepting your first job, health insurance, education, and training will probably be more important to you than club memberships or a company car.

Salary

The salary offered you is certainly important; everyone likes to know they are paid what they are worth in the marketplace. In addition to benefits, geographic location of the job can affect the total value of that salary, because in each area of the country, living expenses (cost of living) vary. This means the same salary does not always have the same worth in different parts of the country. You may decide to take a job because it pays more than another and be willing to relocate. The American Chamber of Commerce Researchers Association recommends: Don't jump at a high salary unless you know what it is really worth!

COST OF LIVING

The following information will help you weigh the value of the salary you've been offered in a particular geographic area. The chart will enable you to do your own city-by-city comparisons of national cost-of-living differences. All index numbers are based on the composite prices of groceries, housing, utilities, transportation, health care, clothing, and entertainment in each city listed, with 100.0 as the national average. To calculate your approximate purchasing power in various areas, use the salary comparison equation.

SALARY COMPARISON EQUATION

$$\frac{(City \#1)}{(City \#2)} \times Salary = \$_____$$

- What is the San Diego equivalent of a $35,000 salary in Lincoln, Nebraska?

$$\frac{San\ Diego\quad 129.2}{Lincoln\quad 93.2} \times \$35,000 = \$48,519$$

- What is the Lincoln, Nebraska equivalent of a $35,000 salary in San Diego:

$$\frac{Lincoln\quad 93.2}{San\ Diego\quad 129.2} \times \$35,000 = \$25,248$$

EEO Bimonthly

CITY-BY-CITY INDEX

Average City, USA	100.0	Denver	103.9	Chicago	123.4
Alabama		Ft. Collins	96.3	Naperville	124.3
Birmingham	98.3			Quad Cities	92.5
Mobile	97.3	**Connecticut**		Rockford	103.6
		Hartford	125.8	Schaumburg	120.3
Alaska		Stamford	132.5	Springfield	98.9
Anchorage	122.6				
Fairbanks	124.9	**Delaware**		**Indiana**	
		Dover	107.1	Evansville	95.3
Arizona		Wilmington	119.1	Ft. Wayne	98.0
Phoenix	104.6			Indianapolis	100.1
Tucson	102.5	**District of Columbia**		South Bend	94.8
		Washington, DC	129.8		
Arkansas				**Iowa**	
Fayetteville	88.4	**Florida**		Cedar Rapids	98.7
Jonesboro	90.1	Jacksonville	95.6	Des Moines	104.9
		Miami	109.9		
California		Orlando	99.6	**Kansas**	
Fresno	109.0	Tampa	98.1	Lawrence	99.0
Los Angeles County	124.4	West Palm Beach	110.3	Wichita	96.7
Orange County	129.0				
Palm Springs	116.6	**Georgia**		**Kentucky**	
Riverside	108.3	Atlanta	106.5	Bowling Green	91.8
Sacramento	112.6	Macon	94.5	Lexington	101.3
San Diego	129.2	Savannah	96.9	Louisville	98.3
San Francisco	125.6				
San Jose	123.0	**Idaho**		**Louisiana**	
		Boise	95.1	Baton Rouge	94.5
Colorado				New Orleans	96.8
Boulder	101.3	**Illinois**			
Colorado Springs	91.2	Champaign/Urbana	101.5		

CITY-BY-CITY INDEX (CONCLUDED)

Maine
Portland — 120.8

Maryland
Baltimore — 109.5

Massachusetts
Boston — 157.6
Springfield — 119.8
Worcester — 121.1

Michigan
Benton Harbor — 108.3
Jackson — 109.2
Traverse City — 109.9

Minnesota
Minneapolis — 100.7
Rochester — 100.1

Mississippi
Gulfport — 89.4

Missouri
Columbia — 92.8
Kansas City — 96.7
St. Louis — 98.7

Nebraska
Lincoln — 93.4
Omaha — 92.2

Nevada
Reno — 103.4

New Hampshire
Manchester — 122.9

New Jersey
Ridgewood — 113.9

New Mexico
Albuquerque — 101.5
Santa Fe — 106.6

New York
Albany — 106.6
Binghamton — 102.2
Buffalo — 109.6
Nassau/Suffolk — 157.9
Syracuse — 95.8

North Carolina
Chapel Hill — 106.1
Charlotte — 101.1
Raleigh — 102.2
Winston-Salem — 96.2

Ohio
Akron — 94.7
Cincinnati — 100.8
Cleveland — 110.9
Columbus — 104.1
Dayton — 104.3
Toledo — 107.2

Oklahoma
Oklahoma City — 96.5
Tulsa — 97.2

Oregon
Eugene — 99.4
Portland — 103.3

Pennsylvania
Erie — 104.9
Harrisburg — 110.2
Lancaster — 103.2
Philadelphia — 127.2
Pittsburgh — 104.7
Wilkes-Barre — 98.8

Rhode Island
Providence — 102.2

South Carolina
Columbia — 98.8
Greenville — 97.2

South Dakota
Rapid City — 96.9

Tennessee
Chattanooga — 90.2
Knoxville — 96.0
Memphis — 94.6
Nashville — 99.1

Texas
Amarillo — 92.6
Austin — 95.6
Brownsville — 92.0
Dallas — 102.6
El Paso — 96.8
Houston — 102.8
Midland — 101.0
San Antonio — 95.9
Waco — 95.6

Utah
Salt Lake City — 95.6

Vermont
Montpelier/Barre — 127.6

Virginia
Richmond — 108.3
Roanoke — 97.5

Washington
Seattle — 108.5
Spokane — 91.6
Tacoma — 102.7
Yakima — 97.7

West Virginia
Charleston — 96.4
Huntington — 91.7

Wisconsin
Fond du Lac — 98.0
Green Bay — 96.5
Janesville — 95.9
La Crosse — 97.5
Milwaukee — 103.4

Wyoming
Casper — 91.2

Reprinted with the permission of the American Chamber of Commerce Research Association, P.O. Box 6749, Louisville, KY 40206.

After you have viewed your salary offer with respect to the cost of living, you may want to actually calculate your potential budget based on that salary. After reviewing this model budget, you will be able to see how your salary might be allocated to suit your individual financial needs.

BUDGETING YOUR FIRST SALARY

Savings Plans

Put yourself at the top of the list. Charles Lefkowitz, Chairman of the *International Association for Financial Planning* recommends that "You should put away . . . 5 percent to 20 percent of every paycheck before you do anything else. If you can learn that discipline early on, you'll be way ahead." Payroll deduction plans are a great way to do this. Because the money never touches your hands, the temptation to spend it is not there. Also, some employers offer special benefits, such as IRAs, 401ks, or matching programs, to savers by means of payroll deductions.

Reserve Funds

Have your own slush fund. Having at least a month's salary in a liquid, money-market-type account works well.

Avoiding Debt

Get out of debt as soon as possible after you graduate. Student loans that are paid off early give you the opportunity to invest your money. Be moderate with other debts you might incur. Never incur any debt unless you are sure you can afford to do so.

Tax Planning

Plan a good tax strategy. Seeking professional help in this area may pay off. Keeping track of what is and is not fully deductible is the job of a professional. The key for you is to find out what deductions you are entitled to as well as the limitations involved. A free information packet, including a state-by-state directory of certified financial planners, is available from the *International Association of Financial Planning (IAFP), 2 Concourse Parkway, Suite 800, Atlanta, GA 30328.* A typical consultant's fee is $250. Depending on your needs and interests, the fee may be well worth the return.

Investments

Invest early in your career. Investments in the stock market, mutual funds, or other sources won't be as important as your initial basic investments such as clothing and a car. Exercise discipline and pay off these debts as soon as possible. A working wardrobe and a vehicle are investments because they will get you to the job on time, looking good—leverage that you will need at the beginning of your career.

COMPUTE YOUR NET CASH FLOW

Monthly Income

Wages and salary   _____

Interest on savings, CDs, bonds   _____

Other   _____

    Total monthly income   _____

Monthly Expenses

Rent   _____

Automobile loans   _____

Personal loans (student loans)   _____

Charge accounts   _____

Income taxes   _____

Social Security   _____

Savings and investments   _____

Contributions   _____

Household maintenance   _____

Furniture   _____

Gas   _____

Electricity   _____

Telephone   _____

Water   _____

Transportation   _____

Food   _____

Clothing   _____

Medical   _____

Entertainment   _____

Other expenses   _____

    Total monthly expenses   _____

    Total monthly income   _____

    Total monthly expenses   _____

    Discretionary monthly income   _____

    (Subtract your expenses from your income.)

Source: International Association of Financial Planning.

When considering a job offer, you need to evaluate how well the compensation offered meets your needs. Understanding the many different types of compensation programs that exist will help you make a good career decision. Understanding the compensation package offered you is important in the process of accepting a job, because you want to have a sense of financial security and know that your personal needs are being met. This sense of security will leave you free to concentrate on your job performance and professional development.

MANAGING YOUR CAREER

Chapter Eight

Your First Months on the Job

When you begin your new job, there will be a period of adjustment to your work and to your new environment. Most companies will assist you with that adjustment through company orientation or training programs and periodic assessments of how well you are doing. The purpose of these programs is for you to become better acquainted with the company; to learn how you, in your new role, fit into that company; to sharpen your skills; and to receive feedback early on how well you are doing on the job.

BEFORE ARRIVAL ON THE JOB

Your orientation actually begins with your pre-arrival period. Use the time between acceptance of the job offer and the first day of employment to maintain contact with the company. Be sure you have taken care of as many final arrangements as you can before your first day. For example, ask if any benefit forms can be completed, and be sure to ask if there are any organizational procedures you should be aware of before you start your job. Most often the company will provide you with literature to describe the company's benefits or with an employee manual or handbook designed to welcome you to the company. Read all of this material carefully, and ask any questions you may have so there will be fewer questions on your first day. Know where and to whom to report on your first day.

YOUR FIRST DAY

You can relieve the anxiety usually associated with your first day on the job by following some basic guidelines. Arrive a little early so that you are sure you are reporting to the right place. You may still have some paperwork to fill out before you start work, and an early arrival can give you more time to do this properly. Someone in the company will probably be responsible for guiding you through the day. While you should focus more on listening the first day, don't be afraid to ask any questions you may have.

Part of your day will probably be spent touring the area you are working in and meeting people in the organization. Focus on remembering the names of the people you will be working with most often. You may also be shown your work area and where and how to access the resources and supplies you need to get your job done. Someone may offer to take you to lunch as part of your welcome. If so, be sure to stick to your scheduled lunch time and avoid overindulging in food or drinks, so that you will still feel alert throughout the afternoon. You will probably get a feeling for the company and the people who work there by the end of the first day. If something left you feeling unsure or uncomfortable, don't panic. This is normal. There is so much to get used to in a new job that you certainly won't feel totally adjusted after your first day. You should feel excited about all that lies ahead!

ORIENTATION PROGRAMS (FIRST FEW DAYS, WEEKS)

After your first day, your orientation may last anywhere from a couple of days to a few weeks, depending on the company. Some examples of information provided during these extended orientation periods include on-the-job safety instructions, an overview of the company's background, present operations, products or services, and how to get involved with employee programs (employee of the month, recognition programs, contests). Remember that your orientation period is mostly focused on getting you acquainted with your new environment and how it works. This differs from actual training programs, which may be longer (30–90 days) and aimed at giving you the tools to actually perform your job better.

TRAINING PROGRAMS (ONE TO THREE MONTHS)

Training programs may be administered individually for new employees as they are hired or may be conducted periodically for small groups of employees who begin their new jobs at approximately the same time. Training may be hands-on to teach or refine technical skills (drafting, machine operations), or classroom style to reinforce interpersonal skills (teamwork, customer service). The box on page 131 is a sample of a basic retail training program.

PROBATIONARY PERIODS (ONE TO THREE MONTHS)

Some companies have a period of formal probation for new employees. A probationary period is meant to give you the opportunity to demonstrate your skills, abilities, and overall fit with the company. Probationary periods may range from 30 to 90 days, depending on company policy. If your job involves this testing period, use it as an opportunity to demonstrate your abilities and positive attitude.

PERIODIC REVIEW AND ASSESSMENTS

During your first three to six months on the job, it would be helpful to you for your employer to conduct periodic reviews and assessments of your job performance. This will help you know whether or not you are on the right track and give both you and the employer a chance to discuss your strengths and weak-

TRAINING PROGRAM

Designed to help our Management Trainees achieve company objectives and identify individual store needs, our eight-month, three-phase Training Program is comprised of the following:

- Phase I, II, and III Participant Manual
- Product Knowledge Manuals
- Supplemental Videos
- Management Resource Books
- Support Materials (Tests and Evaluations)
- Graduation Certificate

PHASE I

This 30- to 60-day intensive program trains participants in the fundamentals of salesmanship, customer service, in-depth product knowledge, and basic store operating procedures. Trainees will learn skills ranging from the proper methods of Greeting Customers, Determining Customer Needs, and Overcoming Objections to Footwear Fitting Techniques.

PHASE II

Reinforcing the basics begun in Phase I, this 90-day period gives the trainee hands-on experience in various aspects of retail store operations. During this phase most trainees will attain the position of Assistant Store Manager and will take an active role in Sales Floor Management. Skills covered include: Recruiting and Hiring Techniques, Coaching for Improved Sales Productivity, Visual Merchandising, Training Techniques, and Advanced Store Operating Procedures, including Loss Prevention, Bookkeeping, and Accounting.

PHASE III

Under the guidance of our most experienced Store Leader—the Manager-Trainer—trainees receive 90 to 120 days of hands-on experience in managing a total retail store operation. The skills taught during this phase are designed to fine-tune the MIT (Manager-in-Training) in the areas of communication, customer relations, delegation skills, recruiting and training, leadership, marketing, merchandising, and maximizing profits.

This program is divided into weekly lessons, each with clearly defined goals, discussion questions, and practice assignments. The objective of each lesson is reached through daily interaction on the sales floor and through one-on-one training with the Store Manager. The lessons are outlined in the *Management Training Development Manuals.*

Upon successful completion of this program, trainees can expect to attain a Store Management position in the near future.

nesses so that you can set immediate goals for improvement. Periodic reviews and assessments can help you adjust to your job during the first few months by setting and keeping you on a successful course. If these are not formally planned by your employer, you might want to ask your immediate supervisor to conduct these sessions because you think they may be helpful to both of you.

Getting off to the right start can make a big difference to both you and your employer. If you learn early what is important to functioning well in your organization, the chances of your feeling comfortable and doing well may be greater. For example, Corning is a company that has successfully implemented an employee orientation program. Corning's primary objectives were to reduce early career turnover by 17 percent and to shorten by one month the time it takes a new person to learn the job.

Chapter Nine

Growing with Your Job

Once you have completed your adjustment period to your new job and company, you can focus more on your professional development. Professional development is the process of establishing yourself in your career. This may include building your professional relationships, changing job responsibilities, improving your effectiveness on the job, and building job skills that can survive economic swings.

BUILDING PROFESSIONAL RELATIONSHIPS

Throughout your career, you will be required to interact with people at different levels in your organization and with those outside the company. This interaction will range from dealing with your boss and associates to dealing with customers. Each of these situations always requires professionalism, but each requires a slightly different approach.

Your Relationship with Your Boss

Your relationship with your boss can enhance your personal development as well as your professional growth. You have the ability to create a positive and productive working relationship with your boss. The following should help you:

- *Loyalty* sets the stage for trust. You can be loyal to your boss and to yourself even when you don't both agree. Be upfront and discuss the issue honestly with him or her only.
- Don't talk negatively about your boss or the company you work for to other people.
- Don't waste your boss's time.
- Be aware of your boss's priorities.
- Help your boss get promoted. It may help you in the same way.
- Incorporate the boss's point of view in your decision making. Try to see his or her point of view, and you may make better decisions.

- Take criticism from your boss as a learning experience. Criticism should not be interpreted as a threat. It should be seen as a desirable challenge.
- Admit your mistakes.
- Ask for feedback.
- Don't ever upstage your boss.
- Avoid bad news early or late in the day or week.
- No surprises—keep your boss informed.

Remember you are part of the management team regardless of what position you hold. Your relationship with your boss should be mutually beneficial. You should foster an environment of cooperation so that you help each other achieve personal and company goals. Being a team player with your boss makes both of your jobs more productive and meaningful.

Your Relationship with Your Associates

When you are at the top of your graduating class, you are used to being number one. You've earned the job you have now, but something is different. You've been hired along with a lot of other "number ones," and suddenly the skills and talents that once put you on top now put you in competition. Yes, there are other people who are smarter, who can do it better, and who will challenge you. Learning to work with others and respect their opinions, talents, and contributions to your organization can be a difficult adjustment. Perhaps one of the hardest things you will face in your career is having to work with people you really don't like. Learn to separate your personal feelings and preferences about people and situations from professional life. The person you dislike the most might be an important link in your team. Tomorrow's jobs require the ability to get things done with other people. You will actually be measured on team efforts as well as your individual accomplishments. You will be treated the way you treat other people. The following tips should help you as you learn to become part of a team:

- Be a team player.
- Build working relationships with those at your level and in other departments.
- Realize the power of praise. Compliment people for a job well done.
- Say "Thank you."
- Listen to what other people have to say.
- Respect other people the way you want them to respect you.
- Be objective; if there is a problem, ask yourself, "What's wrong? Am I part of the problem? What can I do about it?"
- Deal with pressure. Control your temper and emotions and remain level-headed when the going gets rough. You may say or do something you'll be sorry about.

- Look at competition as an opportunity to do the best job you can. Above all, play fair as you compete to reach whatever goal you have set for yourself.
- Use common sense.
- Develop a genuine interest in other people. Show that you are sensitive to their individual needs.
- Be courteous.
- Cooperate. Work is more difficult when the climate is tense. Cooperation builds spirit and is often more productive than individual effort.
- Be humble. If you are humble, you will still receive the credit you deserve. Don't be caught up in always having to win, to have the best idea, or to be number one. You have a long career ahead of you, and if these are your goals, you will be disappointed many times.

Your Role as a Leader

If you are in the position to lead a team, then your human relations skills will determine your success. People want to be led, not managed. You manage projects, things, and your time. You lead people.

Leadership can be developed if you know its essential ingredients and have a real desire to lead. The strong desire is important, because leadership requires much time, energy, commitment, and skill; and if you really don't want the responsibility, you will give up easily. If you really don't want a leadership role, don't accept it. You won't do yourself justice, nor will it be fair to the people looking for leadership. If you do think the leadership challenge is for you, here are some qualities of a good leader that you should master:

LEADERSHIP QUALITIES

- Vision
- Self-starting
- Positive attitude
- Intelligence
- Character
- Integrity
- Courage
- Risk-taking
- Energy level
- Enthusiasm
- Ability to motivate others
- Ability to plan and organize

Leaders create an atmosphere in which others can grow and develop their abilities. Effective leadership focuses on putting the people in your responsibility area first. Here are some guidelines for leaders:

- Recognize the power of people in your area.
- Empower commitment and loyalty by example.
- Recognize individual accomplishments as well as team efforts.
- Combine monetary rewards with other benefits such as free time, a new opportunity, or additional authority.

Your Relationship with Customers

Good customer service is a major factor in allowing a company to remain competitive and stay in business. To provide good customer service, employees need to think about what the customer wants and how the customer wants to be treated. Being responsive to customers requires excellent communication skills (listening and speaking). Being able to talk with customers about their needs and preferences is helpful to the company in developing programs and products. If you are in a position that involves contact with customers, keep in mind that your reputation and your company's reputation are largely based on the customers' impression of you!

Teamwork

More and more companies are encouraging teamwork, as well as individual performance, as a means of professional development and as a technique for achieving company goals. As a member of a team, you are usually responsible for performing a specific role to help the team be successful. For example, the team's goal may be to win the perfect attendance award for its department during the month of September. For that to happen, everyone must have perfect attendance. If one person on the team does not fulfill his or her role, the team will not succeed. Teamwork is important because it is a way of bringing together individual ideas and opinions to create new ideas or solve a problem. In some cases, teamwork is more effective than an individual effort. Teamwork is also intended to foster relationships among the team members by opening their minds to different perspectives.

Total Quality Management (TQM)

You might find that your company has a total quality management (TQM) program of which you are a part. TQM programs are designed to deliver superior performance to the customer by giving employees more ownership in the day-to-day operations of the company. This means that if a customer has a particular problem with a product or service, employees at many different levels are able to take action to resolve that customer's problem or make recommendations to the company on how to improve something so the problem will not recur. TQM programs bring employees together to solve customer problems and provide input to the company on how to do things better. Being part of a TQM program can give you the opportunity to demonstrate your initiative, creativity, and problem-solving skills.

Cultural Diversity

Cultural diversity is the coming together of people from different races and ethnic backgrounds. Cultural diversity in the workplace is increasing as the number of people with varied backgrounds increases rapidly throughout the United States. Building relationships with people from diverse backgrounds may take an understanding of their culture and require different communication skills or motivational techniques based on those differences. In the workplace, we cannot communicate with everyone the same way and expect the same results. Sensitivity to differences helps to foster positive relationships between diverse groups. You need to become familiar with the people in your workplace and develop an understanding of how to relate to them. Many of the relationships you build throughout your career are important because the people you interact with form impressions about you and the company by how you deal with them. Relating to others in a positive way helps them build a positive image of you, which is important to your credibility as a professional person.

IMPROVING YOUR EFFECTIVENESS

You can be more effective in your job if you have good planning and presentation skills, exercise good meeting behavior, and focus your performance on results.

Planning Skills

Planning is preparing for what lies ahead. If you know that you will assist with showing the company's office procedures to the new secretarial staff, you may set a goal now to prepare a procedures manual for that purpose. As an assistant sales manager, you may be required to help project the next year's sales in your area and establish strategies for reaching those goals. Being a good planner helps you set direction for your job and keep yourself focused.

Presentation Skills

Good presentation skills help you to be convincing about your ideas because they help the listener(s) be attentive to what you are saying. Many people feel nervous at the thought of making a presentation even to a small group. You can reduce your anxiety about making a presentation and increase your effectiveness by following these guidelines. Decide on the main point you wish to convey. Develop convincing information (articles, statistics, etc.) to use to illustrate your point. This will help you address any questions. Prepare a brief outline on index cards. Do your homework. Spending enough time preparing your presentation will help you be more confident about what you say. Look confident. Dress professionally, look alert and well groomed, and show enthusiasm for what you say.

Proper Meeting Behavior

How you interact at company meetings reflects an image of you to others. There are actions you can take to help to create a positive image:

- Arrive on time. It is wise to arrive 10 to 15 minutes before the start of any meeting. This will give you time to become oriented to the room and the meeting agenda, and to avoid having to sit on the perimeter of the room because all the best seats are taken.

- Introduce yourself to participants you may not know prior to the beginning of the meeting. Also, introduce yourself when you speak at the meeting if there are some attendees who may not know you.

- If the meeting is delayed, turn to someone and begin an informal conversation. You should be relaxed and prepared enough not to have to worry about any last-minute details by this time. This may give you an opportunity to communicate with someone you don't see on a regular basis.

- Arrive prepared for the meeting. Don't count on being able to make last-minute copies or notes within 10 or 15 minutes before the meeting. Be prepared when you leave your own office.

- Rehearse your remarks well if you are to make a presentation. Bring a one-page list of key points you want to make at the meeting so you will be sure not to leave any out.

- Sit straight. Look interested, alert, and ready to participate.

- Pay attention, even when topics don't relate directly to you; don't shift to converse with others when the topic shifts. You should always listen to everyone who is speaking. Not only is this professional courtesy, but you may learn something important.

- Avoid interrupting. If you have questions or comments when someone else is speaking, try to wait until he or she has finished making the main point.

- Don't monopolize the time. Be concise and to the point with your remarks. You will be more effective this way and will leave others the opportunity to speak.

- Ask for clarification if you don't understand. Don't be afraid of appearing stupid. If you don't ask for clarification, you may make an important decision based on the wrong facts.
- Be positive and tactful when disagreeing. Even though it is right for you to express your disagreement with someone, make sure you make it clear that you are attacking the issue, not the person.
- Use *we* instead of *I* when talking to a group; *we* signifies being part of the group.
- Think before you speak. It is more important to focus on the quality of what you say at meetings than on the frequency of times you speak.
- Don't smoke in a room where it is not permitted. Not only would you violate a company policy, but you also may alienate some participants who may be bothered by smoking.
- Pour soft drinks into a cup. Never drink from a can at a business meeting; it looks unprofessional.
- Say "Thank you" quietly and leave at the end of the meeting or when the chairperson indicates you should leave.
- After the meeting, congratulate anyone who performed exceptionally well in his or her presentation.

Focus on Results

In every job you have, you can increase your effectiveness by knowing what's important for you to do. Jobs exist because certain functions need to be performed and certain results are expected. For example, your job as a telemarketer involves selling TV cable service by telephone. You decide that you want to do better today than you did yesterday. Yesterday you made 25 calls and convinced eight clients to buy the service, and so you decide to make 35 calls today. However, what's really important is not making more calls but selling more cable subscriptions than you did yesterday.

There will be many times during your daily job routine when the hectic pace and multitude of tasks that need to get done become overwhelming. By using good planning and presentation skills, exercising proper meeting behavior, and keeping focused on results, you can get things done independently and with others.

PROMOTIONS

As you progress in your job, you may demonstrate the ability to take on other responsibilities in the company. This is a great way to build your career, because assuming new roles makes you more versatile and more valuable to your company. These growth opportunities can involve a new job or more responsibilities than you have in your current job. There are a few things to think about before accepting your new role.

Job Enlargement versus Job Enrichment

You may be asked to perform more tasks at the same level of difficulty. This is job enlargement. Or you may be asked to assume more responsibility (for example, supervising other people). This is job enrichment. Either of these two instances could be described as a promotion.

The reason it is important to be aware of these two different types of promotion is that at some point you need to decide what type of growth opportunity is best for you. If you enjoy the hands-on work you do and would be challenged by doing more of it, you may choose this as a way to grow professionally. Sometimes people who prefer to continue in their same job but expand upon it a little more don't see these additional responsibilities as a promotion. A promotion does not always have to involve supervising others or moving up to the next-higher job title and level of responsibility. For some people this works very well, while others do better growing in the existing job. What is most important about either of these forms of promotion is that you feel properly challenged in a job that suits your skills and personality. You and your employer are the best judges of which route suits you best.

Mentors

A mentor is someone with more experience than you who is willing to provide helpful advice for your professional development. If at all possible, find a mentor early in your career. This person can be a big help in setting and achieving your professional goals.

Performance Reviews

Although you may have a three- or six-month assessment on your first job, performance reviews are conducted once a year in most companies. You should view your performance review as a chance to assess your professional strengths and weaknesses and to set goals for improvement. It is helpful to do your own pre-performance review prior to the actual scheduled time for your meeting with your supervisor. You should review the major responsibilities of your job, evaluate how many of those responsibilities you have met, evaluate the quality of the work involved, and think about why you were not able to fulfill some of your job responsibilities if this applies. You should also jot down a list of any of your unplanned accomplishments; these may range from winning an award to being asked to take charge of a special project. Be honest with yourself. By taking the time to reflect on your performance prior to your formal review, you accomplish two things: you reduce the chances of there being any surprises with your performance review, and you prepare yourself to discuss action steps for improvement. Even when your performance is satisfactory to both you and your employer, there is always room for improvement.

RECESSION-PROOFING YOUR JOB

In tough economic times, many businesses are faced with the decision to reduce their work forces. If you are properly prepared, you can handle these times should you become unemployed.

The key is to try to remain marketable to an employer. You can do this by having experience with a broad scope of responsibilities in your field, by being willing to take on many tasks, and by remaining flexible. You should also become comfortable with a little risk or uncertainty, because in a job transition you cannot be sure where you will end up or how long it will take to get there. Many times, a company may be willing to work at finding you a new role within the company, but there may be a long period of uncertainty in the process. Be patient and be open to a variety of job options.

Build an account of all the transferable skills you have. Transferable skills are those that are acquired in one set of circumstances (job) that can also be applied to a new set of circumstances (job). Examples of some transferable skills include organizational, budgeting, or interpersonal skills. Being able to show that you have talents to bring to a new situation and that you are willing to do so can help you keep your current employment or be hired by a new employer. If you are laid off or fired from a company due to an overall staff reduction and have maintained a positive relationship with your employer, the company may provide you with outplacement assistance.

FACTORS THAT ENABLE YOU TO RECESSION-PROOF YOUR CAREER

- Broad responsibilities
- Many skills
- Flexibility
- Ability to deal with risk or uncertainty
- Transferable skills
- Positive attitude

SUCCESSFUL CAREER MOVES

There are points in your career when you need to evaluate your position within the company, to determine if it is where you should be at this time in your professional development. If you decide that you are not receiving the challenge, compensation, or recognition you really need, it may be time to leave the company and pursue a new career opportunity. When you decide to do this, do it right. Give proper notice to your employer that you are leaving. Depending on your job and the company, anywhere from two weeks' to two months' notice may be appropriate. It is better not to leave your job until you have a new one. Not only does this ensure a steady source of income for you, but, in general, prospective employers would rather interview candidates who are currently employed. This is because employed people tend to be more current with their skills and active in their profession. Always leave your job on good terms with your employer. Hopefully, both you and your employer have gained something from your professional relationship, causing your departure to be amicable. Remember that the company you leave may serve as a reference for you later on, so you want to leave a positive image of yourself. Every career change can be a new beginning for you if you approach it professionally and with a positive attitude.

CONTEMPORARY ISSUES IN THE WORKPLACE

The world of work is changing toward increasing integration between personal and professional lifestyles. The overlap of personal interests affecting the workplace is a result of changing personal value systems. For example, there is a trend for workers to value free time more than ever before. Personal problems such as alcoholism or drug addiction affect a person's performance in the workplace. Career women who want to raise families are now faced with conflicts in priorities.

Changes in society also influence contemporary issues in the workplace. For example, the onset of drug testing and AIDS testing and a renewed emphasis on ethics in the workplace are a direct response to these topics as larger societal concerns, resulting in some behavioral problems in the work force. These contemporary issues in the workplace affect the way we live and work. You should be aware of some of the issues that will affect you during your career. In the following chapters are updates on health-related, family, and ethical issues, including discussions of:

- Substance abuse
- AIDS
- Health education
- Smoke-free workplace
- Accommodations for special-needs employees
- Family care
- Equal Employment Opportunity (EEO)
- Sexual harassment

Chapter Ten

Health-Related Issues

Health-related issues affect employees in the workplace in many ways. Substance abuse may affect an employee's productivity and attitude and can result in increased absenteeism. Health issues, such as AIDS, have employees concerned about learning the facts about ways the disease can be transmitted and how to relate well to a co-worker who has contracted AIDS.

Laws requiring more accommodations for special-needs employees are opening up new career opportunities for these workers. And companies that have implemented a "smoke-free" workplace are encouraging some smokers to become nonsmokers and all employees to become more conscious of their personal health habits. As a result of the emergence of these health-related issues, more companies are committed to formal health education programs for their employees.

SUBSTANCE ABUSE

Overuse of some drugs and alcohol can produce behavioral problems for employees that disrupt either their own productivity or the environment they work in. An increasing number of employers—including the U.S. Postal Service, General Motors, Alcoa, the New York Times, and American Airlines—are requiring pre-employment urine or blood tests to screen for the presence of cocaine, barbiturates, amphetamines, marijuana, and opiates.

The effects of substance abuse problems are profound on both the employer and the employee, and that is why they have become a major focus of attention. Employers report higher incidence of problems with productivity, accidents, medical claims, absenteeism, and employee theft among employees with substance abuse problems. These all result in higher costs to the employer. As a job candidate or an actual employee, you can be affected by these problems whether you are a substance abuser or not.

In fact, 64 percent of recovering drug abusers admitted that drugs adversely affected their performance, while 44 percent of them admitted selling drugs to employees. If you test positive for drugs when looking for a job, you will almost certainly not be hired. Once you are employed, detection of drug or alcohol use

WORKPLACE ISSUES

	All Organizations	Number of Employees				
		100-499	500-999	1,000-2,499	2,500-9,999	10,000 or More
Drugs						
Test employees for drug use (with probable cause)	32%	30%	33%	40%	49%	47%
Test employees for drug use (without probable cause)	10	8	13	18	20	23
Test job applicants for drug use	32	29	37	45	57	63
Have a formal policy on substance abuse	81	81	82	83	88	87
Conduct or sponsor training about substance abuse	37	35	40	43	51	59
Have an Employee Assistance Program (EAP) that handles substance abuse problems	53	51	63	59	70	78
AIDS						
Do AIDS antibody testing of employees	1	1	1	1	1	3
Do AIDS antibody testing of job applicants	1	1	0	1	6	3
Have a formal AIDS policy	20	18	23	28	27	27
Have an AIDS education program	22	20	25	26	29	38
Smoking						
Have a policy limiting smoking at work	73	73	73	67	80	77
Have a policy that bans smoking at work	32	31	39	32	43	32
Do not hire smokers	1	1	0	4	3	3
Miscellaneous						
Have a formal policy on sexual harassment	74	73	77	76	81	86
Have a formal affirmative action plan	65	62	71	71	76	87
Have a formal code of ethics	55	54	54	55	60	72

can cause you to be fired if you show any kind of work-related problem because of it.

Some companies attempt to help an experienced employee overcome the problem. It is often more cost effective for the company to do that because there really is no guarantee that a new worker won't have the same problem. Through Employee Assistance Programs (EAPs), companies offer on-site confidential counseling and treatment. Other companies' insurance plans cover drug programs, and some offer paid leaves of absence. When AT&T evaluated its EAP after three years, it found that 86 percent of those who had been treated were completely rehabilitated.

THE REALITIES OF SUBSTANCE ABUSE IN THE WORKPLACE

- Alcohol and drug abuse is estimated to raise insurance costs $50 billion annually.
- Nearly 30 percent of employers are said to test college recruits for drug use.
- One employer's decision not to promote an employee because the employee's husband was a drug abuser has been upheld.
- An Attorney General has called on employers to conduct "surveillance" of areas where employees may be using drugs.

AIDS

The prevalence of the AIDS (Acquired Immune Deficiency Syndrome) virus has led to much discussion about the potential effects of being HIV-positive on the employee's productivity and on attitudes of co-workers. Most companies have weighed these issues and developed company policies regarding the employment of HIV-positive workers and job candidates. In most companies, guidelines state that physical disabilities and chronic health conditions are not to be considered in hiring and promotion decisions unless they interfere directly with performance. This means that HIV-positive workers are no less productive than other employees because of the infection. An infected worker's chance of being productive is the same as for anyone not infected with the virus.

A different concern regarding this issue may be transmission. The question among fellow employees and the employer may be whether or not workers will be safe. Except for professions involving exposure to blood, there should be no concern for transmission due to exposure in the work environment. Despite this truth, many HIV-positive workers today face fear and prejudice from colleagues, friends, and even family, and as a result can lose their jobs, their insurance, and other work-related benefits. Education of the work force is the answer to this problem; and many companies, such as Levi Strauss & Co., offer education on this workplace issue to their employees.

HEALTH EDUCATION

As a result of some of these health-related issues, there is an increased effort to provide health education in the workplace. Many employers have implemented such programs to familiarize employees with how their substance abuse or that of their co-workers can affect them on the job. The programs are also aimed at prevention. Health education programs can inform workers how to interact with co-workers who have tested HIV-positive and help to correct misconceptions about the virus.

Another major component of health education involves wellness programs, which promote overall good nutrition and exercise as a way of life. These wellness programs instruct employees on how to keep fit and may recommend individual fitness programs as well. For companies, the major reasons for offering wellness programs are that they are cost effective (their cost often is outweighed by savings in health care costs), responsive to employees' demand, and offer a sense of social responsibility. For the employee, participation can result in reduced absenteeism because of improved physical health and mental attitude, reduced expenses from joining outside fitness programs, stress reduction, and assurance that one's work life can be a positive factor contributing to an overall healthy lifestyle.

SMOKE-FREE WORKPLACE

The predominance of the smoke-free workplace is a direct result of health hazards caused from smoking and pollutants in the work environment. Heavy pressure to forbid smoking in more and more work sites continues. Local ordinances continue to be enacted that require employers to provide a smoke-free workplace. When executives were asked to choose between two job candidates with equal qualifications, and only one smoked, they were 15 times more likely to hire the nonsmoker. Accountemps, a temporary service for the accounting industry, surveyed 100 corporate vice presidents and human resources managers. Results indicated that smoking during a job interview may reduce your chances of being hired. Employees who smoke cost their companies a substantial amount of money. In addition, negative social reactions are attached to smoking in the workplace.

HIRE A NONSMOKER

- Nonsmokers . . . are more likely to make a better impression with the general public. Receptionists, salespeople, and executives present a better image if they don't smoke. They smell better, look better, and don't risk offending nonsmokers who don't like smoke.

- Nonsmokers . . . tend not to offend fellow workers. No need to elaborate on this! Any nonsmoker who has had to work with smokers will tell you what it's like.

- Nonsmokers . . . have less absenteeism than smokers. The U.S. Public Health Service studies show that smokers are absent from work because of illness 30 percent more often than nonsmokers.

- Nonsmokers . . . are less subject to many occupational health hazards. When an industrial condition such as airborne contaminants already exists, nonsmokers do not further endanger their health with tobacco smoke.

Source: William L. Weis, "No Ifs, Ands, or Butts—Why Workplace Smoking Should Be Banned," Management World, *September 1981 (from* Best of Business Quarterly, *Summer 1986).*

ACCOMMODATIONS FOR SPECIAL-NEEDS EMPLOYEES

The Americans with Disabilities Act (ADA) has required employers to make accommodations for employees with special needs. The act bars employment discrimination against the disabled and mandates access for the disabled to public spaces. Companies that fail to meet these standards are subject to civil actions for noncompliance. The Americans with Disabilities Act makes it easier for job candidates and employees to get to and from work and move about safely in the workplace.

Substance abuse, AIDS, the smoke-free workplace, wellness and health education programs, and the Americans with Disabilities Act are some of the health-related issues you should know about. By being better informed on these issues, you can understand why certain company policies are in place and what assistance is available to you to help you deal with these issues personally or with co-workers.

Chapter Eleven

Family Care Issues

Parental leave for child care and leave for elder care are the two fastest-growing work–family conflicts that are emerging. Responsibility for caring for the family often means taking care of older parents as well as children. This, coupled with job demands, puts tremendous pressure on many workers, who often experience stress trying to keep everything balanced.

Employees Reporting Stress Due to Work-Family Conflict

	All Employees	Men	Women
Due to job	71%	69%	74%
Due to elder care	52%	42%	63%
Due to child care	43%	38%	49%

PARENTAL LEAVE

According to a survey by the Catalyst Career and Family Center in New York, barely half of the nation's firms offer even unpaid maternity leaves. Catalyst also reports that 36.8 percent of American corporations participating in a recent survey offer paternity leave. Yet of these, only 2.7 percent give men even partial pay for their time off. Although the number of companies offering parental leave is on the rise, most leaves are nonpaid. Despite the strong interest many men and women have in staying home to care for their children, many of them simply cannot afford to. Some studies interpret the low number of men taking leave as a lack of interest, when it appears likely that the absence of pay is the real issue. In Sweden, a parent-insurance benefit program was established by law in 1974. Men are paid up to 90 percent of their salaries during their leaves. Today, according to Sheila Kamerman, Ph.D., a professor at the Columbia University of Social Work, about 25 percent of eligible men make some use of the parent insurance. Perhaps if American men knew that their jobs would not be threatened and they could be paid for their time off, more would ask for leave.

CHILD CARE

"Seventy-seven percent of women and 73 percent of men surveyed report that they take time away from work attending to their children—making phone calls or ducking out for a long lunch to go to a school play. That alone translates into hundreds of millions of dollars in lost output for U.S. corporations," says John P. Fernandez, manager of personnel services at AT&T. Dana Friedman, senior research associate at the Conference Board, says, "Child care is likely to be the fringe benefit of the 1990s because what's good for employees becomes good for business."

The quality of day care varies enormously. States license and monitor the private for-profit and not-for-profit centers. In some states, important matters such as learning activities or the teacher–child ratio are ignored. The tremendous amount of time being spent by workers on child care and the inconsistent quality of day care centers are creating a new push toward the corporate on-site day care center. There are advantages to such centers. Parents can drop in any time. Companies benefit in the recruitment and retention of employees. One of the most innovative efforts recently made was by Levi Strauss & Co. When children get sick, traditional day care centers are not the answer for working parents, because sick children are not allowed in day care centers. To enable parents of sick children not to miss work, Levi Strauss & Co. funded a 17-bed children's infirmary that is attached to an independent day care center in San Jose, California.

Chicken Soup is a sick-child day care operation in Minneapolis. First Bank System, a Minneapolis bank holding company, pays 75 percent of the $26.26 a day for each employee's child who checks into Chicken Soup. First Bank loses $154 a day if a $40,000-a-year middle manager misses work to take care of a sick child. Chicken Soup saves the company 87 percent, or almost $135 a day.

Companies are realizing the advantages of day care centers. About 3,000 companies offer subsidized day care centers, financial assistance for child care, or child care referral services.

WHAT WORKING PARENTS SAY ABOUT CHILD CARE

	Men	Women
Report that both spouses share equally in child care responsibility	55.1%	51.9%
Say the job interferes with family life	37.2	40.9
Sought less demanding job to get more family time	20.5	26.5
Refused a job, promotion, or transfer because it would mean less family time	29.6	25.7
Felt nervous or under stress in past three months	49.2	70.2
Missed at least one workday in the past three months due to family obligations	37.8	58.6
Think children of working parents benefit by having interesting role models for parents	77.5	86.3
Think children of working parents suffer by not being given enough time and attention	55.4	58.2
Would like their companies to provide a subsidized child care center	38.5	54.1
Would like their companies to offer flexible working hours	34.8	54.1
Think companies can do more to help manage work/family responsibilities	34.5	30.9

Though working fathers and mothers pretty much agree that they share equally in child care responsibilities and that their jobs interfere with family life, more fathers say they have refused a new job, promotion, or transfer that would take away from family time. Mothers are more likely to report that they feel stress. Only 30.9% of the women polled in *Fortune*'s nationwide survey of 400 working parents wanted more child care help from their companies. But over half said they would like their employers to offer flexible working hours and provide subsidized day care centers. *Source: From* Fortune, *February 16, 1987.*

ELDER CARE

Elder care (caring for older parents or relatives) is an issue affecting the workplace because, with more women working and not at home on a full-time basis to respond to elders' needs, employers need to make accommodations for workers faced with this responsibility. Employers can offer them reduced work hours, time off without pay, or rearranged work schedules as needed so that employees do not have to quit their jobs. Although, to date, more women than men have been affected by the elder care issue, it is expected that men may share this responsibility to the same degree as child care responsibilities as the need develops.

You should be aware that most companies are willing to accommodate some of your special needs, especially the need for a more flexible work schedule, to properly care for elderly family members. As child care and elder care become a concern for you, you should plan on meeting with your employer to discuss your unique situation and make arrangements that will satisfy both of you. The fact that these options are available to you demonstrates companies' commitment to attracting and retaining competent workers by assisting them with family issues that may directly impact their work life. This should reduce the number of workers who need to quit working for extended periods of time to care for their family responsibilities.

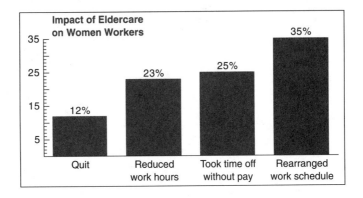

Chapter Twelve

Ethics

Although the practice of good business ethics has always been important, as we look to the 21st century, there needs to be a stronger commitment not only to the practice of ethics but also to its enforcement. The prevalence of unethical behavior in the workplace, and in society, requires stricter enforcement of laws against such behavior in order to stop it. Many individuals or companies have become comfortable with behavior with which they should be uncomfortable. Theft, fraud, discrimination, and harassment are a few examples of unethical behavior that exist in today's workplace.

EQUAL EMPLOYMENT OPPORTUNITY (EEO)

Fairness in hiring practices is the goal of the Equal Employment Opportunity policy. This is intended to reduce discrimination in hiring. However, few U.S. corporations can be proud of their minority hiring and promotion records to date. This is because issues not related to performance keep entering the hiring process and prevent us from realizing equal employment opportunity. As the number of available minority workers will be increasing over the years, measures must be taken now to revisit this issue and set the law in practice. Minority workers may find more attention given to this effort in future years as the potential work force is comprised of more minority candidates.

SEXUAL HARASSMENT

Awareness of sexual harassment in the workplace has been heightened by recently reported incidents that have been publicized nationally. As a result, companies are reviewing their policies on sexual harassment and setting in place programs to teach people what it is and the toll it can take.

Sexual harassment is defined by many companies as follows: "All unwelcome sexual advances, requests for sexual favors, and other such verbal or physical conduct. It is prohibited by the company."

These policies exist so that all employees can share a work environment free of potentially harmful comments or actions. Employees who feel they have been harassed usually have the option of complaining to someone in the company (human resources department, supervisor's boss, etc.) other than the harasser. This provides them a more comfortable form of communication.

In addition to Equal Employment Opportunity and sexual harassment, the most commonly known issues, other ethical issues affect the workplace on a regular basis, such as abuse of privilege, conflict of interest, and preferential treatment.

ABUSE OF PRIVILEGE

Abuse of privilege occurs when someone takes a privilege that is given them, such as a company expense account, and extends its use beyond what is acceptable or expected by the company. In this case, an individual may use a company expense account to be reimbursed for personal expenses that are not company related.

CONFLICT OF INTEREST

Conflicts of interest sometimes occur between company and personal interests or goals. A drafter who has a private consulting business outside of the job with his or her employer may experience a conflict of interest if trying to consult during the employer's work hours.

PREFERENTIAL TREATMENT

Preferential treatment is when an employee shows special treatment of certain groups of people or takes short-cuts for one person and not another. An example would be an account representative at a bank who processes a loan for a friend without following the prescribed waiting period for approval or without checking all of the necessary references.

These are just some examples of how day-to-day work activities can lead an individual into an ethical dilemma. When faced with an ethical decision, most people follow their own personal code of behavior, as opposed to the behavior of others or any formal company policy. Ultimately, you are in control of your own actions.

CAREER HANDBOOK

The Career Handbook is a practical guide to help you manage your career throughout your lifetime.

Chapter Thirteen, "Career Paths," shows you the many career areas that exist in your chosen field of study. Some of the actual jobs available in each of these career areas are outlined to show you how your chosen career may progress over the years. Chapter Fourteen, the "Glossary of Terms Used in Job Descriptions," defines some of the key words commonly found in job descriptions. This will help you use Chapter Fifteen, the "Index of Job Descriptions," which is a comprehensive list of actual job descriptions defining the job titles presented in "Career Paths." These three chapters work together to present you with a better understanding of the day-to-day job responsibilities in your chosen career and can be referred to periodically when making career decisions. Chapter Sixteen, "Career Resources," provides you with additional sources of career information that will help you guide your own job search and enhance your professional development.

Chapter Thirteen, "Career Paths," is designed to help you decide how you want to apply your degree after graduation and then provides you direction for future career moves. It is useful for self-assessment and goal setting as you conduct periodic reviews of your own career. In almost any career field, there is a wide variety of jobs that suit different interests, abilities, and personalities. The job titles listed represent that range from high people-oriented to high task-oriented jobs. They show you that you may change jobs to try many different types of work without changing the career field you have chosen. The salary ranges listed vary according to geographic location, type of industry and employer, the overall state of the economy, and your own experience level, and should always be weighed against the relative cost of living in a given area. Understanding the overview of career paths in your career field can also help you communicate to an employer that you know your long-term professional goal, that you know the series of jobs you may need to hold before getting there, and that you realize that it is necessary to start any career with an entry-level job.

In addition to helping you understand the terminology used in job descriptions, the "Glossary of Terms Used in Job Descriptions" is also a helpful tool for constructing your résumé. When used in conjunction with "Power Words for Résumés" in Chapter Four, it provides an additional resource for identifying words that best describe on your résumé what you bring to an employer. It is also good to review this chapter when preparing for a job interview so that you will be able to describe your specific skills to the interviewer.

Once you are aware of the career paths available to you and understand the main terms used in job descriptions, you should find that the "Index of Job Descriptions" will explain the responsibilities of the job(s) you are interested in.

This information is useful in clarifying whether your perception of what a job entails is accurate and should be critical to helping you decide on your career goal. Being able to articulate to an employer, during an interview, a proper understanding of the job available to you may be important to the success of your interview. This is because employers frequently find that job candidates misunderstand what many jobs entail until an explanation is provided by the employer.

Finally, you can use "Career Resources" when seeking your first job or to sharpen your career strategies from time to time as you progress in your career. Some of the resources included can help you find information on prospective employers, refine your job search skills, and improve your professional skills.

The Career Handbook is something you will find useful at many points in your career, long after your first job.

Chapter Thirteen

Career Paths

In this chapter, you will become aware of the many career choices available to you, learn how to choose a career area, and learn how to map out a plan in order to make successful career moves. If there was ever a time to do the work that you really love, to do the kind of work that you are really attracted to, it's now. Your career training enables you to choose a variety of traditional career paths. It also opens doors to many of the new and exciting career paths emerging in the workplace.

Take some time to think about any and every career direction that exists for you. When you do this, you will feel more confident about the decisions you make because you will know that you have considered all of your options. In this age of change, it will be necessary for you to consider new options periodically. Learning to be flexible now will be helpful as your world of work changes.

You have already made your first step in choosing a career area by deciding on your major or program. Unfortunately, many times students do not have access to all the information they need to decide how to best apply their professional training in the workplace. Focusing on your career means selecting an area within your field that interests you the most.

For example, if you are a Retailing major, you may choose to become involved in management, buying, distribution, visual merchandising, or sales within the retail field. As a Business Administration/Management student, you may put your professional training to work in banking, insurance, finance, personnel, retailing, advertising, production, or distribution. Your first step, then, is to look at career areas directly related to your major or program.

Don't stop there. Your talents can go to work in many other areas as well. For example, if you are pursuing professional training in Accounting, you may first look into private and public accounting firms, but you should also consider accounting work in a retail firm or a hotel as possibilities. If you are pursuing a degree in Secretarial Sciences, you may consider secretarial work in any type of business or industry that is of interest to you. You may also want to explore jobs that allow you upward mobility into management or sales.

Most important to choosing your career area is really understanding the jobs in each area. Without a clear understanding of what a job involves, you cannot really know if it's what you want, nor can you convince a potential employer that you are right for that job. Job titles don't tell us what we need to know. They are only a start. Every day, people perform in the jobs that we think we want someday. What the job really consists of or how we would spend our time every day on the job is often something we're not familiar with. Then how can we be sure this is what we really want to do? One way to find out is to

HOW TO USE "CAREER PATHS"

3

Fashion and Retail Management— Career Overview	**2** Level	Career Areas **1** Management	Buying	**4** Distribution	Sales
	Entry ($$$$)	Job titles	Job titles	Job titles	Job titles
	Mid-management/ specialists ($$$$)	Job titles	Job titles	Job titles	Job titles
	Management ($$$$)	Job titles	Job titles	Job titles	Job titles

6 ⟶ *Recommended Pre-Professional Part-Time/Summer Experience*

become familiar with job descriptions. Once employed in the workplace, you'll then be likely to say, "There's more to this job than you think there is."

The next section presents you with over 500 job titles representing 14 different career areas. The actual job descriptions for each job title can be found in Chapter Fifteen, "Index of Job Descriptions."

1. Consider the different career areas available in the field as presented in the overview.

2. Review the entry, mid-management/ specialists, and management positions and their related salary ranges.

3. Focus on the area(s) in which you have the most interest.

4. Look down that column of job titles and ask yourself what each one represents. You may wish to ask yourself, "What does a Merchandise Analyst do every day?"

5. Review the corresponding job description in Chapter Fifteen, "Index of Job Descriptions," if you are unclear about the responsibilities of a particular job title. This index also opens up a whole variety of jobs

available to you about which you may have had no previous knowledge.

6. Look at the Recommended Pre-Professional Part-Time/Summer Experience for your career area to gain insight into the kinds of part-time work employers see as valuable in order to obtain an entry-level professional position.

After each career overview, the following information is presented:

- Experience needed
- Salaries
- Qualifications
- Where the jobs are
- Trade publications
- Professional associations

"Career Paths" is your beginning to understanding your own career options. *Don't stop there!* After you have obtained your first job, you will need to refer to this information periodically to decide on your next move. By understanding the jobs in the Mid-management/ specialists and Management segment of your career, you can create a clear vision of where you are going and how long it might take to get there.

IMPORTANT POINTS TO REMEMBER ABOUT CAREER PATHS

- The salaries listed represent only an average range for the country as a whole in 1992. In general, *salaries vary according to geographic location, types of industries and employers, the overall state of the economy, and your own experience level.* You should always weigh a salary that is offered to you with how it compares to these variables.

- Under "Qualifications" you will find the most common and necessary traits you need to be successful in tomorrow's jobs! Those common qualifications often include:
  - Positive attitude
  - Enthusiasm
  - Effective written and verbal skills
  - Well-groomed appearance
  - Team worker
  - High energy level
  - Flexibility
  - Ability to learn
  - Brightness
  - Technical skills

- In "Where the Jobs Are," the most common industries where jobs exist in each career area are outlined. The industries listed are those in which entry-level jobs are most available. There may be many more types of employers depending on your level of experience and future trends in business.

- Because a successful career includes keeping up-to-date on current trends in your field and adapting to those trends, it is important to be aware of the basic "trade publications and professional associations" appropriate for your career.

- It should become obvious by studying the career paths outlined here that each career area is made up of a *planned sequence of related jobs.*

ACCOUNTING

Level	Public Accounting	Private/Mgt. Accounting	Government
1 Entry ($18,000–$23,000)	Staff Accountant Junior Accountant	Junior Accountant	Revenue Officer
2 Mid-management/ specialists ($22,000–$37,000)	Accountant Senior Accountant	Accountant Senior Accountant General Accountant Chief Internal Auditor Department Manager Tax Accountant Cost Accountant	Accountant Internal Auditor
3 Management ($30,000–$60,000+)	Manager Partner	Vice President Treasurer Controller Chief Financial Officer	Chief Internal Auditor

Recommended Pre-Professional Part-Time/Summer Work Experience
Inventory Clerk, Data Entry Clerk, Accounts Payable/Receivable Clerk, General Office Clerk, Proof-reader, Teller, Cashier, CRT Clerk, File Clerk, Salesclerk, Accounting Clerk

PUBLIC ACCOUNTING

Level	Job Title	Experience Needed	Qualifications
Entry	Staff or Junior Accountant	Professional training	**Personal:** Good communication and concentration skills. Accuracy and attention to detail. Flexibility. Objectivity. Ability to judge and make decisions. Reliability.
2	Accountant	1–3 years	
2	Senior Accountant	3–4 years	
3	Manager	5–7 years	
3	Partner	8+ years	

Salaries in Public Accounting

Level	Salary	Firm Size
Entry	$18,000 to $21,000	Medium-size firm
	$20,000 to $23,000	Large firm
2	$22,000 to $26,000	Medium-size firm
	$24,000 to $27,500	Large firm
2	$27,000 to $35,000	Medium-size firm
	$28,000 to $37,000	Large firm
3	$37,000 to $46,000	Medium-size firm
	$40,000 to $60,000	Large firm

Professional: Writing and communication skills. Exceptional mathematical ability. Commitment to professional standards. Ability to work independently.

Where the Jobs Are

CPA firms

Public accounting is divided into two tiers: the "Big Six," and other national, regional, and local practices.

Salaries vary with the size of the firm and are higher for 2- to 4-year college graduates, CPAs, and those with graduate degrees.

The "Big Six"

Arthur Andersen & Company, Chicago, IL
Coopers & Lybrand, New York, NY
DeLoitte & Touche, New York, NY
Ernst & Young, Cleveland, OH

KPMG Peat Marwick, New York, NY
Price Waterhouse & Company, New York, NY
These companies have branches throughout the country.

PRIVATE MANAGEMENT ACCOUNTING

Level	Job Title	Experience Needed
Entry	Junior Accountant	Professional training
2	Accountant	1–3 years
2	Senior Accountant	3–4 years
2	General Accountant	4–8 years
	Department Manager	4–8 years
	Chief Internal Auditor	4–8 years
3	Vice President	15+ years
	Treasurer	15+ years
	Controller	15+ years
	Chief Financial Officer	15+ years

Salaries in Private/Management Accounting

Level		
Entry	$20,000 to $22,000	Medium-size firm
	$20,000 to $23,000	Large-size firm
2	$23,000 to $29,000	Medium-size firm
	$26,000 to $31,000	Medium-large-size firm
	$28,000 to $33,000	Large-size firm
3	$30,000 to $36,000	Medium-size firm
	$36,000 to $56,000	Large-size firm

Salaries vary with the size of the firm and are higher for 2- or 4-year college graduates. CPAs, those with graduate degrees, and accountants whose jobs require extensive travel.

Qualifications

Personal: Reliability. Ability to work independently. Flexibility. Discipline.

Professional: Understanding of business and the marketplace. Willingness to increase knowledge of practical accounting techniques.

Where the Jobs Are

Private corporations
Consulting

GOVERNMENT

Level	Job Title	Experience Needed
Entry	Revenue Officer	Professional training
2	Accountant	1–3 years
2	Internal Auditor	1–3 years
3	Chief Internal Auditor	3–5 years
3	Chief Accountant	5–7 years

The goal of the accounting department of a typical government agency is to function within the budgetary constraints mandated by legislative action. The IRS is the largest employer of accountants in the United States.

Salaries in Government:

Positions are comparable to salaries in private industry, and much of the work performed is the same. Salary rates are based on varying grade levels.

Qualifications

Personal: Reliability. Ability to work independently. Flexibility. Discipline.

Professional: Knowledge of standard accounting procedures; ability to design accounting techniques; interest in publishing work in professional journals.

Where the Jobs Are

Department of Agriculture
Department of Defense Audit agencies
Department of Energy
Department of Health and Human Services
Department of the Air Force
Department of the Navy
Department of the Army
General Accounting Office
Treasury Department
(includes the Internal Revenue Service)

Special Certifications

C.M.A. *(Certificate in Management Accounting):* The C.M.A. exam is sponsored by the National Association of Accountants and tests decision-making capability and knowledge of business law, finance, and organization.

C.I.A. *(Certificate in Internal Auditing):* The C.I.A. exam is sponsored by the Institute of Internal Auditors and tests the theory and practice of internal auditing. Both exams are open to graduating seniors, but work experience is required for certification. Multiple certification is permissible and encouraged.

C.P.A. *(Certificate in Public Accounting):* The advantages of holding the C.P.A. are many, as it serves as tangible proof of your skill and your commitment to the profession. Public accounting firms, particularly the largest, often expect their accountants to receive certification as quickly as state law allows. Beyond the entry level, the C.P.A. is often a requirement for advancement. Information on how to prepare for the C.P.A. exam, as well as test dates, is available through C.P.A. review courses.

Trade Publications

CPA Journal (monthly),
New York Society of
Certified Public Accountants,
600 Third Avenue, New York, NY 10016

Government Accountant's Journal (quarterly),
Association of Government Accountants,
727 South 23rd Street, Arlington, VA 22202

Journal of Accountancy (monthly),
American Institute of
Certified Public Accountants,
1211 Avenue of the Americas,
New York, NY 10036

Management Accounting (monthly),
Warren, Gorham, and Lamont, Inc.,
210 South Street, Boston, MA 02111

The Practical Accountant (monthly),
Warren, Gorham, and Lambert, Inc.,
210 South Street, Boston, MA 02111

The Wall Street Journal (daily),
23 Cortland Street, New York, NY 10007

Professional Associations

American Institute of Certified Public Accountants
1211 Avenue of the Americas
New York, NY 10036

American Society of Women Accountants
35 East Wacker Drive
Chicago, IL 60601

Association of Government Accountants
727 South 23rd Street
Arlington, VA 22202

Institute of Internal Auditors
249 Maitland Avenue
Altamonte Springs, FL 32701

National Association of Accountants
919 Third Avenue
New York, NY 10022

BUSINESS ADMINISTRATION

Level	Banking	Insurance	Finance	Human Resources
1 Entry ($18,000–$25,000) *Management Trainee*	Bank Officer Trainee Systems Trainee	Adjuster Trainee Claims Examiner Underwriter Trainee Actuarial Trainee Beginning Agent	Registered Representative	Employment Recruiter Interviewer Personnel Assistant Job Analyst
2 Mid-management/ specialists ($20,000–$38,000)	Assistant Loan Officer Loan Officer Department Manager Supervisor Systems Analyst Systems Consultant Senior Systems Consultant Branch Manager Loan Manager	Assistant Underwriter Underwriter Specialist Senior Underwriter Assistant Actuary Actuary Senior Claims Adjuster	Investment Banker Trader Purchasing Agent Research Analyst Trust Officer Financial Analyst Portfolio Manager Credit Manager	College Recruiter Training Manager Employment Manager Corporate Recruiter Personnel Manager Wage and Salary Administrator Benefits Coordinator Labor Relations Specialist Plant Safety Specialist EEO Coordinator
3 Management ($35,000–$76,000)	Manager Division Manager Vice President President	Underwriting/ Supervisor Office Manager Chief Actuary Agent Regional Vice President Vice President	Treasurer/Controller Vice President President	Director of Human Resources Vice President of Human Resources

Level	Retailing	Advertising	Production	Distribution
1 Entry ($18,000–$25,000) *Management Trainee*	Department Manager Store Manager Trainee Buyer Trainee	Junior Copywriter Media Buyer Project Coordinator Account Executive Trainee	Expeditor Assistant Buyer Assistant Purchasing Agent Production Planner Assistant Quality Assurance Manager	*See Careers in Fashion and Retail Management*
2 Mid-management/ specialists ($20,000–$38,000)	Assistant Store Manager Sales Representative Display Coordinator Distribution Coordinator Merchandise Analyst Assistant Buyer	Copywriter Senior Copywriter Media Planner Media Department Head Project Director Research Account Director Associate Research Director Account Executive Senior Account Executive	Purchasing Agent Purchasing Manager Traffic Manager Inventory Manager Quality Assurance Manager Buyer	
3 Management ($35,000–$76,000 +)	Merchandise Manager Buyer Store Manager Operations Manager Vice President/Operations Sales Manager	Accounts Supervisor/ Manager Department Manager Copy Chief Creative Director Director of Media Advertising Research Director	Plant Manager Materials Manager Manufacturing Manager Regional Manager Operations Research Analyst Vice President/Production	

Recommended Pre-Professional Part-Time/Summer Work Experience
Salesclerk, Cashier, Messenger, Data Entry Clerk, General Office Clerk, Inventory Clerk, File Clerk, Accounting Clerk, Receptionist, Teller, Typist, CRT Clerk, Proofreader, Waitperson, Shipper/Receiver.

BANKING

Level	Job Title	Experience Needed
Entry	Bank Officer Trainee	Professional training
Entry	Systems Trainee	Professional training
2	Assistant Loan Officer	1–2 years
2	Supervisor	1–2 years
2	Systems Analyst	2 years
2	Systems Consultant	3 years
2	Department Manager	3–5 years
2	Loan Officer	3–5 years
2	Branch Manager	3–5 years
2	Senior Systems Consultant	5 years
2	Loan Manager	5–6 years
3	Division Manager	6+ years
3	Manager	6+ years
3	Vice President	8–10 years
3	President	10+ years

Salaries in Banking

Entry	$18,000 to $25,000
2	$22,000 to $31,000
2	$29,000 to $35,000
3	$35,000 to $50,000
3	$50,000+

Salaries are higher for those with 2- or 4-year college degrees.

Qualifications

Personal: Strong analytical skills. Strong negotiation skills. Strong interpersonal skills. Ability to work under pressure. Ability to work with figures.

Professional: Familiarity with business applications of software and hardware. Ability to analyze financial statements and do creative financial planning. Good business judgment.

Where the Jobs Are

Credit lending	Operations
Trusts	Systems

INSURANCE

Level	Job Title	Experience Needed
Entry	Adjuster Trainee	Professional training
Entry	Claims Examiner	Professional training
Entry	Underwriter Trainee	Professional training
Entry	Actuarial Trainee	Professional training
Entry	Sales Trainee*	Professional training
2	Assistant Underwriter	1–2 years
2	Assistant Actuary	1–2 years
2	Underwriter Specialist	2–4 years
2	Agent	2–4 years
2	Actuary	3–5 years
2	Senior Underwriter	3–5 years
2	Senior Claims Examiner	4–6 years
3	Underwriting Supervisor	6+ years
3	Office Manager	5+ years
3	Chief Actuary	6+ years
3	Regional Director	5+ years
3	Vice President	8+ years

Salaries in Insurance: (See Salaries in Banking)

New sales workers earn about $2,000 a month during the first six months of training. Most sales workers are paid on commission. The size of the commission depends on the type and amount of insurance sold. Insurance sales workers generally pay their own automobile and travel expenses. Independent sales workers must also pay office rent, clerical salaries, and other operating expenses out of their own earnings.
Salaries are higher for those with 2- and 4-year college degrees.

Qualifications

Personal: Enthusiasm. Self-motivation. Attention to detail. Good analytical skills. Excellent communication skills. Good quantitative skills. Confidence.

Professional: Accurate thinking and writing skills. Ability to write concisely. Aptitude for computers. Ability to supervise.

Where the Jobs Are

Home offices/headquarters
Branch offices
Independent agencies
Private corporations
Real estate

FINANCE

Level	Job Title	Experience Needed
Entry	Registered Representative*	Professional training
Entry	Manager Trainee	Professional training
2	Trader	1–2 years
2	Financial Analyst	2–3 years
2	Research Analyst	3–5 years
2	Investment Banker	3–5 years
2	Purchasing Agent	3–5 years
2	Portfolio Manager	5–6 years
2	Credit Manager	5–6 years
2	Trust Officer	6–8 years
3	Treasurer/Controller	6+ years
3	Vice President	8–12 years
3	President	12–15 years

Salaries in Finance: (See Salaries in Banking)

Trainees are usually paid a salary until they meet licensing and registration requirements. During training, sales workers earn $900–$1,200 a month. After licensing, earnings depend on commission from sales of stocks, bonds, life insurance, or other securities.
Salaries are higher for those with 2- or 4-year college degrees.

Qualifications

Personal: Interest in economic trends. Ability to handle frequent rejection. Ability to work independently. Good grooming. Good communication skills.

Professional: State licensing and successful completion of exams prepared by securities exchanges or NASD (National Association of Securities Dealers, Inc.)

Where the Jobs Are

Financial institutions
Banks
Private corporations
Consulting firms
Government
Securities exchanges

HUMAN RESOURCES

Level	Job Title	Experience Needed
Entry	Interviewer	Professional training
Entry	Employment Recruiter	Professional training
Entry	Personnel Assistant	Professional training
Entry	Job Analyst	Professional training
2	College Recruiter	1–3 years
2	Training Manager	2–4 years
2	Corporate Recruiter	3–5 years
2	Benefits Coordinator	1–3 years
2	Plant Safety Specialist	3–5 years
2	Equal Employment Opportunity Coordinator	1–3 years
2	Labor Relations Specialist	4–6 years
2	Wage and Salary Administrator	4–6 years
2	Employment Manager	4–6 years
2	Personnel Manager	5–7 years
3	Personnel Director	5–7 years
3	Vice President of Human Resources	7–10 years

Salaries in Personnel

Level	Salary
Entry	$18,000 to $23,000
2	$23,000 to $33,000
2	$28,000 to $38,000
3	$33,000 to $55,000
3	$55,000 to $76,000 +

Salaries are higher for those with 2- and 4-year college degrees.

Qualifications

Personal: Excellent communication skills, listening skills especially important. Ability to speak and write effectively. Ability to work under pressure.

Professional: Fair-mindedness. Good decision-making skills. Ability to enforce policies.

Where the Jobs Are

Private corporations
Education
Government agencies
Consulting firms
Independent businesses

RETAILING

(See Careers in Fashion and Retail Management)

ADVERTISING

Level	Job Title	Experience Needed
Entry	Assistant Media Planner	Professional training
Entry	Junior Copywriter	Professional training
Entry	Project Director	Professional training
Entry	Account Executive Trainee	Professional training
2	Copywriter	1–3 years
2	Account Executive	1–3 years
2	Research Account Executive	1–3 years
2	Media Planner	3–5 years
2	Associate Research Director	3–8 years
2	Senior Account Executive	5–8 years
2	Associate Media Director	5–7 years
2	Research Director	7–10 years
2	Senior Copywriter	7–10 years
2	Media Director of Planning	7–10 years
3	Accounts Supervisor/ Manager	10–13 years
3	Department Manager	10+ years
3	Copy Chief	10+ years
3	Creative Director	10+ years
3	Director of Media Advertising	10+ years
3	Research Director	10+ years

Salaries in Advertising

Level	Salary
Entry	$18,000 to $22,000
2	$20,000 to $24,000
2	$24,000 to $26,000
2	$26,000 to $30,000
2	$30,000 to $33,000
2	$33,000 to $38,000
3	$38,000 to $41,000
3	$41,000 to $47,000
3	$47,000 to $62,000
3	$62,000 to $75,000 +

Salaries are higher for those with 2- or 4-year college degrees.

Qualifications

Personal: Strong interpersonal skills. Ability to work with a team. Problem-solving mentality.

Professional: Good writing skills, knowledge of the media. Sales ability. Negotiation skills.

Where the Jobs Are

Advertising agencies
Media
Private corporations
Consulting
Freelancing

PRODUCTION

Level	Job Title	Experience Needed
Entry	Expeditor	Professional training
Entry	Assistant Buyer	Professional training
Entry	Assistant Purchasing Agent	Professional training
Entry	Production Planner	Professional training
Entry	Assistant Quality Assurance Manager	Professional training
2	Purchasing Agent	1–3 years
2	Purchasing Manager	3–5 years
2	Traffic Manager	2–4 years
2	Inventory Manager	2–4 years
2	Quality Assurance Manager	3–5 years
2	Buyer	4–6 years
3	Plant Manager	5–6 years
3	Materials Manager	5–6 years
3	Manufacturing Manager	5–6 years
3	Regional Manager	6–8 years
3	Operations Research Analyst	6–8 years
3	Vice President/ Production	7–10 years

Salaries in Production:

(See Salaries in Banking)

Qualifications

Personal: Good organizational skills. Aptitude for figures. Ability to plan and make quick decisions. Flexibility.

Professional: Ability to interpret computer data. Ability to supervise and think ahead.

Where the Jobs Are

Manufacturing
Distribution
Private corporations

DISTRIBUTION

(See Careers in Fashion and Retail Management)

Trade Publications

Advertising Age (weekly),
Crain Communications, Inc.,
740 North Rush Street, Chicago, IL 60611

Adweek (weekly),
Adweek Publications,
820 Second Avenue, New York, NY 10017
(regional editions for East, Southeast, West, Southwest, and Midwest)

ABA Banking Journal (monthly),
345 Hudson Street, New York, NY 10014

American Banker (daily),
One State Street Plaza, New York, NY 10014

The Banker's Magazine (bimonthly),
Warren, Gorham, and Lamont, Inc.,
210 South Street, Boston, MA 02111

Bank News (monthly),
912 Baltimore Avenue, Kansas City, MO 64105

Professional Associations

The Advertising Council
825 Third Avenue
New York, NY 10022

Advertising Research Foundation Information Center
3 East 54th Street
New York, NY 10022

American Advertising Federation
1400 K Street, N.W.
Suite 1000
Washington, DC 20005

American Association of Advertising Agencies
200 Park Avenue
New York, NY 10017

Association of National Advertisers
155 East 44th Street
New York, NY 10017

American Bankers Association
1120 Connecticut Avenue, N.W.
Washington, DC 20036

Consumer Bankers Association
1725 K Street, N.W.
Washington, DC 20006

National Association of Bank Women
111 East Wacker Drive
Chicago, IL 60601

United States League of Savings Association
111 East Wacker Drive
Chicago, IL 60601

American Management Association
135 West 50th Street
New York, NY 10020

COMPUTER SYSTEMS

Level	Programming	Operations	Marketing/Sales	Support Services
1 Entry *($18,000–$25,000)*	Programmer Trainee Programmer Analyst	Tape Librarian Data Entry Supervisor Computer Operator	Sales Representative	Instructor Product Support Representative Service Representative

2
Mid-management/
   specialists
($21,000–$34,000)
	Senior Programmer
	Senior Analyst
		Supervisor/Systems
		   Operators
		Peripheral Systems
		   Operator
		MIS Supervisor
		Systems Analyst
			Account
			   Representative
				Training Manager
				Documentation
				   Specialist
				District Manager

3
Management
($30,000–$75,000 +)
   MIS Director
	Lead Programmer
	Lead Analyst
	Manager of
	   Programming
		Operations Manager
		EDP Auditor
		Manager/Systems
		   Analysis
			Account Supervisor
			Vice President/
			   Account Services
				Consultant
				Regional Manager
				Vice President
				President

Recommended Pre-Professional Part-Time/Summer Work Experience
CRT Clerk, Typist, Data Entry Clerk, Coder, Salesclerk, File Clerk, Cashier, General Office Clerk

PROGRAMMING

Level	Job Title	Experience Needed	Qualifications
Entry	Programmer Trainee	Professional training	**Personal:** Patience. Persistence. Ability to work with extreme accuracy. Ability to work under pressure and with deadlines. Good written and verbal communication skills.
Entry	Programmer Analyst	Professional training	
2	Senior Programmer	1–3 years	**Professional:** Ability to think logically. Capable of doing highly analytical work. Problem-solving ability. Decision-making skills. Team worker.
2	Senior Analyst	1–3 years	
3	Lead Programmer	3–5 years	
3	Lead Analyst	3–5 years	
3	Manager of Programming	3–5 years	
3	MIS Director	6–8 years	

Where the Jobs Are

Salaries in Programming

Level	Salary
Entry	$18,000 to $22,000
Entry	$20,000 to $24,000
2	$22,000 to $28,000
2	$28,000 to $34,000
3	$34,000 to $40,000

Salaries are higher for those with 2- or 4-year college degrees.

Where the Jobs Are

   Manufacturing firms
   Data processing service organizations
   Government
   Banks
   Insurance
   Education

OPERATIONS

Level	Job Title	Experience Needed	Qualifications
Entry	Tape Librarian	Professional training	
Entry	Data Entry Supervisor	Professional training	
Entry	Computer Operator	Professional training	
2	Systems Operators Supervisor	1–2 years	
2	Peripheral Equipment Operator	1–2 years	
2	Systems Analyst	2–4 years	
2	MIS Supervisor	2–4 years	
3	Operations Manager	3–6 years	
3	EDP Auditor	3–6 years	
3	Manager of Systems Analysis	6–8 years	
3	MIS Director	6–10 years	

Personal: Patience. Persistence. Ability to work under pressure. Flexibility. Good communication skills. Detail oriented. Manual dexterity. Interest in learning new procedures.

Professional: Ability to make quick decisions and supervise others. Analytical skills essential. Team worker.

Where the Jobs Are

Manufacturing
Data processing service organizations
Government
Banks
Insurance
Education

Salaries in Operations:

(See Salaries in Programming)

MARKETING/SALES

Level	Job Title	Experience Needed	Qualifications
Entry	Sales Representative	Professional training	
2	Account Representative	1–3 years	
3	Account Supervisor	3–6 years	
3	Vice President/ Account Services	6–10 years	

Personal: Excellent verbal communication skills. Confidence. Enthusiasm. Well-groomed. Ability to work independently. Self-motivated. Flexibility.

Professional: Product knowledge. Perception of customer needs. Willingness to learn.

Salaries in Marketing/Sales

Level	Salary
Entry	$19,000 to $24,000
2	$24,000 to $26,000
3	$26,000 to $34,000
3	$34,000 to $54,000
3	$54,000 to $75,000+

Salaries are higher for those with 2- or 4-year college degrees.

Where the Jobs Are

Computer service organizations
Consulting
Computer manufacturers
Government

SUPPORT SERVICES

Level	Job Title	Experience Needed
Entry	Product Support Representative	Professional training
Entry	Service Representative	Professional training
2	Training Manager	2–4 years
2	Documentation Specialist	1–2 years
2	District Manager	3–5 years
2	Academic Department Head	3–5 years
3	Consultant	5+ years
3	Regional Manager	5–8 years
3	Vice President	8–10 years
3	President	8–10+ years

Qualifications

Personal: Excellent communication skills. Self-motivated. Well-groomed. Patience. Ability to work independently. Confidence.

Professional: Product knowledge. Perception of customer needs. Team worker. Ability to make decisions.

Where the Jobs Are

Computer service organizations
Computer manufacturers
Consulting
Education
Banks
Insurance
Manufacturing

Salaries in Support Services

Entry	$19,000 to $25,000
2	$21,000 to $26,000
2	$24,000 to $30,000
3	$30,000 to $35,000
3	$35,000 to $55,000+

Salaries are higher for those with 2- or 4-year college degrees.

Trade Publications

Byte (monthly),
70 Main Street, Peterborough, NH 03458

Computer Decisions (monthly),
50 Essex Street, Rochelle Park, NJ 07662

Computer Design (monthly),
11 Goldsmith Street, Littleton, MA 01460

Computer Times,
P.O. Box 13918, Philadelphia, PA 19101

Computer and Electrical Engineering (quarterly),
Pergamon Press, Maxwell House, Fairview Park, Elmsford, NY 10523

Computer and People (bimonthly),
Berkley Enterprises, Inc.,
815 Washington Street, Newtonville, MA 02160

Computerworld (weekly),
CW Communications, Inc.,
Box 880, 375 Cochituate Road,
Framingham, MA 01701

Datamation (monthly),
Technical Publishing Company,
666 Fifth Avenue, New York, NY 10103

Data Processor,
IBM Corporation,
1133 Westchester Avenue, White Plains, NY 10604

Information Systems News (bimonthly),
333 East Shore Road, Manhasset, NY 11030

Software News (monthly),
5 Kane Industrial Drive, Hudson, MA 01749

Professional Associations

American Foundation of Information Processing Societies
1815 North Lynn Street
Suite 800
Arlington, VA 22209

American Society for Information Science
1010 Sixteenth Street, N.W.
Washington, DC 20036

Association for Computational Linguistics
c/o Dr. D. E. Walker
SRI International
Menlo Park, CA 94025

Association for Computer Programmers and Analysts
294 Main Street
East Greenwich, RI 02818

Association for Systems Management
24587 Bagley Road
Cleveland, OH 44138

Microcomputer Software Association
1300 North 17th Street, No. 300
Arlington, VA 22209

Women in Data Processing
P. O. Box 8117
San Diego, CA 92102

COURT REPORTING AND RELATED CAREERS

Level	Court Reporting	Hearing Reporting	Legislative Reporting	Conference Reporting	Freelance Reporting
1 Entry *($16,000–$23,000)*	Court Reporter	Hearing Reporter	Legislative Reporter	Conference Reporter	Freelance Reporter
2 Mid-management/ specialists *($23,000–$42,000)*	*See Paralegal Careers*				
3 Management *($42,0J0–$60,000)*					

Recommended Pre-Professional Part-Time/Summer Work Experience
Typist, CRT Clerk, General Office Clerk, Messenger, File Clerk, Court Clerk, Coder, Research Assistant, Law Clerk

COURT REPORTING AND RELATED CAREERS

Level	Job Title	Experience Needed
Entry	Court Reporter	Professional training
Entry	Hearing Reporter	Professional training
Entry	Legislative Reporter	Professional training
Entry	Conference Reporter	Professional training
Entry	Freelance Reporter	Professional training
2	Paralegal	2–4 years *(with further education)*
2	Legal Assistant	2–4 years
2	Legal Technician	2–4 years
2	Paralegal Instructor	2–4 years
2	Proofreader	2–4 years
2	Marketing Representative	2–4 years
2	Sales Representative	2–4 years
2	Paralegal Supervisor	4–6 years
2	Senior Legal Assistant	4–6 years
2	Research Assistant	5–8 years
2	Information Specialist	5–8 years
2	Litigation Paralegal	5–8 years
2	Placement Director	5–8 years
2	Editor	5–8 years
2	Systems Programmer	5–8 years
3	Law Office Administrator	8–10 years
3	Lawyer	8–10 years *(with further education)*
3	Law Office Administrator	8–10 years
3	Law Library Manager	8–10 years
3	Program Director	8–10 years
3	Consultant/Adviser	8–10 years
3	Marketing Analyst	8–10 years

Salaries in Court Reporting and Related Careers

Entry	$16,000 to $20,000
Entry	$18,000 to $23,000
2	$23,000 to $28,000
2	$28,000 to $34,000
2	$34,000 to $42,000
3	$42,000 to $60,000 +

Qualifications

Personal: Strong concentration. Physical stamina. Manual dexterity. Detail-oriented. Professional appearance. Ability to work under pressure.

Professional: Accurate thinking and spelling. Transcription skills. Familiarity with legal terminology. Excellent written and verbal communication skills. Positive attitude. High energy level.

Where the Jobs Are

Courts
Legal firms/departments
Freelancing
Business and industry *(meetings and conferences)*
Conventions
Sales
Stockholders' meetings

Trade Publications

American Bar Association Journal,
750 N. Lake Shore Drive, Chicago, IL 60611

National Shorthand Reporters Association,
118 Park Street, Southeast, Vienna, VA 22180

Professional Association

National Shorthand Reporters Association
118 Park Street, Southeast
Vienna, VA 22180

DATA ENTRY

Level	Operations
1 Entry ($14,000–$17,000)	Data Entry Operator Keypunch Operator Tape Librarian

2
Mid-management/
  specialists
  ($17,000–$22,000)
	Computer Operator
	Peripheral Equipment Operator
	Supervisor of Data Entry Services

3	

(*See Careers in Computer Systems: Programming, Operations, Marketing/Sales, and Support Services.*)

Recommended Pre-Professional Part-Time/Summer Work Experience
Keypunch Operator, CRT Clerk, Typist, General Office Clerk, Word Processing Operator

OPERATIONS

Level	Job Title	Experience Needed
Entry	Data Entry Operator	Professional training
Entry	Tape Librarian	Professional training
2	Computer Operator	2–4 years
2	Peripheral Equipment Operator	2–4 years
2	Supervisor of Data Entry Services	4–6 years

Salaries in Data Entry

Entry	$14,000 to $17,000
2	$17,000 to $22,000
3	(*See Salaries in Computer Systems*)

Qualifications

Personal: Attention to detail. Good attention span. Ability to do repetitive work. Ability to work under close supervision. Patience. Manual dexterity.

Professional: Positive attitude. Enthusiasm. Team worker. Ability to make decisions. Problem-solving skills. Excellent communications skills.

Where the Jobs Are

Insurance companies
Research organizations
Education
Hospitals
Government
Computer service organizations
Banks

Trade Publications

(*See Careers in Computer Systems*)

Professional Associations

(*See Careers in Computer Systems*)

DENTAL ASSISTANT

Level	Private Practices, Hospitals, Health Maintenance Organizations	Education	Marketing/Sales
1 Entry ($14,000–$19,000)	Dental Assistant	Instructor	Sales Representative
2 Mid-management/ specialists ($19,000–$23,000)	Clinical Dental Assistant Administrative Dental Assistant Dental Hygienist *(with further education)* Claims Examiner Claims Representative Research Assistant	Academic Department Head	Sales Manager
3 Management ($23,000–$32,000+)	Office Manager Research Analyst Dentist *(with further education)*	School Director Administrator/Education	Director of Marketing and Sales

Recommended Pre-Professional Part-Time/Summer Work Experience
Receptionist, File Clerk, Typist, CRT Clerk, Sales, Accounting Clerk

PRIVATE PRACTICES, HOSPITALS, HEALTH MAINTENANCE ORGANIZATIONS

Level	Job Title	Experience Needed	
Entry	Dental Assistant	Professional training	
2	Clinical Dental Assistant	1–2 years	
2	Administrative Dental Assistant	1–2 years	
2	Dental Hygienist	*Further education*	
2	Medical Claims Examiner	1–2 years	
2	Medical Claims Representative	1–2 years	
2	Research Assistant	2–4 years	
3	Office Manager	4–6 years	
3	Research Analyst	4–6 years	
3	Dentist	*Further education*	

Qualifications

Personal: Patience. Concentration. Good grooming and hygiene. Manual dexterity. Congenial personality. Ability to work with people who may be under stress.

Professional: Knowledge of medical terminology. Ability to learn on the job. Familiarity with billing procedures and health plans.

Where the Jobs Are

Private practices
Hospitals
Health maintenance organizations
State and local public health departments
Government *(hospitals and dental clinics of the U.S. Public Health Service and the Veterans Administration)*

Salaries in Private Practices, Hospitals, Health Maintenance Organizations

Entry	$14,000 to $19,000
2	$17,000 to $21,000
2	$21,000 to $23,000
3	$23,000 to $26,000
3	$26,000 to $32,000 +

Salaries are higher for those with 2- or 4-year college degrees.

EDUCATION

Level	Job Title	Experience Needed
Entry	Instructor	Professional training and/or college degree
2	Academic Department Head	4–5 years
3	Administrator/ Education	6–8 years
3	School Director	8–10+ years

Qualifications

Personal: Patience. Good communication skills. Ability to manage.

Professional: Awareness of policies and laws in the health care field. Planning and organizational skills. Ability to work with budgets.

Where the Jobs Are

Dental schools
Hospital dental departments

Salaries in Education:

(See Salaries in Teacher Education)

SALES/MARKETING

Level	Job Title	Experience Needed	Qualifications
Entry	Sales Representative	Professional training	*Personal:* Positive attitude. Good communication
2	Sales Manager	3–5 years	skills. Ability to work independently.
3	Director of	5 + years	Self-motivated. Tolerance for rejection.
	Marketing/Sales		Confidence.

Salaries in Sales/Marketing:

(See Salaries in Careers in Marketing)

Professional: Product knowledge. Perception of customer needs. Familiarity with medical terminology.

Where the Jobs Are

Medical suppliers
Dental suppliers

Trade Publications

The Dental Assistant,
American Dental Assistants Association,
Suite 1130, 666 N. Lake Shore Drive,
Chicago, IL 60611

Dental Assisting,
P.O. Box 7573, Waco, TX 76714

Dental Products,
Readers Service Center,
P.O. Box 2610, Clinton, IA 52735

Dental Management,
7500 Old Oak Blvd., Cleveland, OH 44130

Dental Economics,
P.O. Box 3408, Tulsa, OK 74101

The Journal of Dental Education,
American Association of Dental Schools,
1625 Massachusetts Ave., NW,
Washington, DC 20036

Dental Abstracts,
American Dental Association,
211 East Chicago Avenue, Chicago, IL 60611

Professional Associations

American Dental Assistants Association
Suite 1130
666 N. Lake Shore Dr.
Chicago, IL 60611

National Association of Dental Assistants
3837 Plaza Drive
Fairfax, VA 22030

Commission on Dental Accreditation
American Dental Association
211 E. Chicago Ave.
Suite 1814
Chicago, IL 60611

Dental Assisting National Board, Inc.
666 North Lake Shore Dr.
Suite 1136
Chicago, IL 60611

DRAFTING

Level	Operations	Support Services	Education
1 Entry ($19,000–$24,000)	Junior Drafter	Junior Drafter	Instructor
2 Mid-management/ specialists ($24,000–$29,000)	Senior Drafter	Junior Consultant	Academic Department Head
3 Management *with further* *education* ($29,000–$50,000+)	Engineer Designer Architect	Senior Consultant	Program Director School Director

Recommended Pre-Professional Part-Time/Summer Work Experience
CRT Clerk, Data Entry Operator, Runner for Architectural, Engineering, or Construction Firm

OPERATIONS

Level	Job Title	Experience Needed
Entry	Junior Drafter	Professional training
2	Senior Drafter	4–6 years
3	Engineer	*With further education*
3	Designer	*With further education*
3	Architect	*With further education*

Salaries in Operations

Entry	$19,000 to $24,000
2	$24,000 to $29,000
3	$29,000 to $50,000+

Salaries are higher for those with 2- or 4-year college degrees.

Qualifications

Personal: Good eyesight. Manual dexterity. Attention to detail. Patience. Ability to work independently. Accuracy. Neatness. Excellent communication skills. Ability to work under pressure.

Professional: Ability to do free-hand drawings of three-dimensional objects. Artistic ability. Ability to conceptualize. Ability to meet deadlines. Team worker.

Where the Jobs Are

Engineering and architectural firms

Durable goods and manufacturing industries
  (machinery, electrical equipment, and fabricated metals)

Construction

Transportation

Communications

Utilities industries

SUPPORT SERVICES

Level	Job Title	Experience Needed	Qualifications
Entry	Junior Drafter	Professional training	
2	Senior Drafter	4–6 years	
2	Junior Consultant	6–8 years	
3	Senior Consultant	8–10 years	

Qualifications

Personal: Positive attitude. Enthusiasm. High energy level. Excellent communication skills. Professional appearance.

Professional: Technical knowledge. Perception of customers' needs. Team worker. Ability to work independently. Strong marketing and sales skills.

Salaries in Support Services:

(See Salaries in Operations)

Where the Jobs Are:

(See "Where the Jobs Are" in Operations)

EDUCATION

Level	Job Title	Experience Needed
Entry	Instructor	Professional training and/or college degree
2	Academic Department Head	4–6 years
3	Program Director	6–8 years
3	School Director	8–10 years

Qualifications

Personal: Positive attitude. Enthusiasm. High energy level. Excellent communication skills. Listening skills. Flexibility. Ability to work under pressure.

Professional: Ability to organize and plan. Technical knowledge. Managerial skills. Ability to work with budgets. Team worker.

Salaries in Education:

(See Salaries in Teacher Education)

Where the Jobs Are

Technical schools
Vocational schools
Drafting departments

Trade Publication

Design and Drafting News,
American Institute for Design and Drafting,

966 Hungerford Drive, Suite 10-B,
Rockville, MD 20854

Professional Associations

American Institute for Design and Drafting
966 Hungerford Drive
Suite 10-B
Rockville, MD 20854

American Institute of Technical Illustrators Association
2513 Forest Leaf Parkway
Suite 906
Ballwin, MO 63011

Coordinating Council for Computers in Construction
1221 Avenue of the Americas
New York, NY 10020

National Association of Trade and Technical Schools
2021 K Street, N.W.
Washington, DC 20006

ELECTRONICS

Level	Repair	Research	Support Services	Production	Education
1 Entry ($19,000–$24,000)	Electronics Technician	Electronics Technician	Sales/Field Representative Customer Service Representative	Electronics Technician	Instructor
2 Mid-management/ specialists ($22,000–$28,000)	Robotics Technician Broadcast Technician Engineering Technician Communications/ Equipment Technician Computer Technician Digital Technician Office Machine Repairer Commercial/Industrial Technician Medical Technician Health Technician Service Technician	Design Technician Research Technician	Production Technician Instructor Sales/Service Manager Training Supervisor	Production Technician	Academic Department Head
3 Management ($28,000–$40,000+)	Electronics Engineer *(with further education)*	Director of Research and Development	Consultant Administrator Director of Marketing and Sales	Production Manager	Program Director School Director

Recommended Pre-Professional Part-Time/Summer Work Experience
Assistant Technician, Repair Person, CRT Clerk, Computer Operator, Data Entry Operator

REPAIR

Level	Job Title	Experience Needed	*Qualifications*
Entry	Electronics Technician	Professional training	**Personal:** Ability to do detailed work. Ability to
2	Robotics Technician	1–3 years	work independently. Accuracy. Manual dexterity.
2	Broadcast Technician	1–3 years	Good communication skills.
2	Engineering Technician	1–3 years	
2	Communications Equipment Technician	1–3 years	**Professional:** Aptitude for mathematics and science. Aptitude for technical work. Creative
2	Medical Technician	1–3 years	talent. Perception of customers' needs.
2	Health Technician	1–3 years	Problem-solving ability. Team worker.
3	Service Technician	1–3 years	
3	Electronics Engineer	*With further education*	*Where the Jobs Are*

Salaries in Repair

Entry	$19,000 to $22,000	
2	$22,000 to $25,000	
2	$25,000 to $28,000	
3	$28,000 to $35,000	
3	$35,000 to $40,000+	

Salaries are higher for those with 2- or 4-year college degrees.

Where the Jobs Are

Defense contractors
Private corporations
Government
Education
Broadcasting
Computer service organizations
Research organizations
Radio and TV stations

RESEARCH

Level	Job Title	Experience Needed
Entry	Electronics Technician	Professional training
2	Design Technician	3–5 years
2	Research Technician	3–5 years
3	Director of Research and Development	6–10 years *With further education*

Salaries in Research

Level	Salary
Entry	$19,000 to $24,000
2	$22,000 to $25,000
2	$25,000 to $28,000
3	$28,000 to $35,000
3	$35,000 to $40,000+

Salaries are higher for those with 2- or 4-year college degrees.

Qualifications

Personal: Ability to do detailed work. Ability to work independently. Accuracy. Good communication skills. Resourcefulness. Flexibility. Analytical skills.

Professional: Aptitude for mathematics and science. Aptitude for technical work. Ability to interpret and predict. Familiarity with computer. Problem-solving ability. Team worker. Ability to conceptualize.

Where the Jobs Are

Defense contracts
Private corporations
Government
Education

SUPPORT SERVICES

Level	Job Title	Experience Needed
Entry	Sales/Field Representative	Professional training
Entry	Customer Service Representative	Professional training
2	Instructor	1–3 years
2	Sales/Service Manager	2–5 years
2	Training Supervisor	2–5 years
3	Consultant	5–7 years
3	Administrator/Educator	6–8 years
3	Director of Marketing and Sales	7–10 years *With further education*

Salaries in Support Services:

(See Salaries in Careers in Marketing and Teacher Education)

Qualifications

Personal: Positive attitude. Enthusiasm. Good communication skills. Well-groomed appearance. Self-motivated. Ability to work independently. Confidence. Tolerance for rejection.

Professional: Product knowledge. Perception of customers' needs. Effective marketing and sales skills.

Where the Jobs Are

Defense contractors
Private corporations
Government
Education
Manufacturers of electronic equipment

PRODUCTION

Level	Job Title	Experience Needed
Entry	Electronics Technician	Professional training
2	Production Technician	2–4 years
3	Production Manager	5–7 years

Salaries in Production:

(See Salaries in Electronics Repair)

Qualifications

Personal: Accuracy. Good communication skills. Manual dexterity. Ability to do detailed work.

Positive attitude. Enthusiasm. Ability to work under pressure.

Professional: Ability to plan, organize, coordinate, and supervise. Concern for quality. Team worker. Knowledge of safety procedures. Aptitude for figures, finances, inventories, and quotas.

Where the Jobs Are

Manufacturing

EDUCATION

Level	Job Title	Experience Needed
Entry	Instructor	Professional training and/or college degree
2	Academic Department Head	4–6 years
3	Program Director	6–8 years
3	School Director	8–10 years

Salaries in Education:

(See Salaries in Teacher Education)

Qualifications

Personal: Positive attitude. Enthusiasm. High energy level. Excellent communication skills. Listening skills. Flexibility. Ability to work under pressure.

Professional: Ability to organize and plan. Technical knowledge. Managerial skills. Ability to work with budgets. Team worker.

Where the Jobs Are

Technical schools
Vocational schools
Electronic departments

Trade Publications

EDN,
Cahners Publishing Company,
Cahner Building, 275 Washington Street,
Newton, MA 02158

Electrionics,
Lake Publishing Corp.,

Box 159, 17730 West Peterson Road,
Libertyville, IL 60048

Electronics,
McGraw-Hill Publications,
1221 Avenue of the Americas,
New York, NY 10020

Professional Associations

International Society of Certified Electronic Technicians
2708 W. Berry
Suite 3
Fort Worth, TX 76109

Jets Inc.
345 East 47th Street
New York, NY 10017

FASHION AND RETAIL MANAGEMENT

Level	Management	Buying	Distribution	Visual Merchandising and Design	Sales
1 Entry ($15,000–$24,000)	Manager Trainee Department Manager Assistant Store Manager Customer Service Representative	Buyer Trainee	Merchandise Planner	Window Trimmer Display Coordinator	Sales Representative
2 Mid-management/ specialists ($19,000–$30,000)	Assistant Store Manager Area Manager Group Manager Divisional Manager Personnel Assistant Training Specialist Credit Manager	Junior Buyer Merchandise Analyst Fashion Coordinator	Administrative/ Analyst Planner MIS Specialist Coordinator of Scheduling Traffic Manager Production Coordinator Inventory Coordinator Transportation Specialist	Display Director Freelancer Fashion Writer Design Assistant *(with further education)* Fashion Display Specialist	Sales Manager District Sales Manager
3 Management ($25,000–$70,000 +)	Store Manager Personnel Manager Operations Manager Director of Training Director of Human Resources Vice President/Human Resources Vice President/ Operations	Buyer Merchandise Manager Vice President/ Merchandising	MIS Director Transportation Manager Administrative Manager Inventory Control Manager Distribution Manager Warehousing/Operations Manager Vice President/ Operations	Consultant Fashion Designer *(with further education)*	Regional Sales Manager Vice President/ Sales Vice President/ Manufacturing

Recommended Pre-Professional Part-Time/Summer Work Experience
Sales, Shipping/Receiving, Cashier, Waitperson, Inventory Clerk, Posting Clerk, Data Entry Clerk, CRT Clerk, Telephone Sales, Demonstrators, General Office Clerk

MANAGEMENT

Level	Job Title	Experience Needed
Entry	Manager Trainee	Professional training
Entry	Department Manager	Professional training
Entry	Assistant Store Manager	Professional training
Entry	Customer Service Representative	Professional training
2	Assistant Store Manager*	1–3 years
2	Area Manager	1–3 years
2	Group Manager	2–4 years
2	Divisional Manager	3–5 years
2	Personnel Assistant	3–5 years
2	Training Specialist	3–5 years
2	Credit Manager	5–6 years
3	Personnel Manager	6–8 years
3	Operations Manager	1–10 years
3	Store Manager*	3–8 years
3	Director of Training	5–7 years
3	Director of Human Resources	7–9 years
3	Vice President/ Operations	9+ years
3	Vice President/Human Resources	9+ years

*Varies greatly depending on size and type of retail operation.

Salaries in Management

Entry	$16,000 to $24,000
2	$19,000 to $30,000
3	$30,000 to $45,000+

Salaries are higher for those with 2- and 4-year college degrees and vary greatly with the size and type of retail operation.

Qualifications

Personal: Enthusiasm. Positive attitude. Ability to learn quickly. Flexibility. Willingness to work weekends, nights, and holidays. Willingness to relocate helpful. Diplomacy.

Professional: Demonstrated leadership ability. Aptitude for dealing with figures, finances, inventories, and quotas. Team worker.

Where the Jobs Are

Department stores
Specialty stores
Bookstores
Grocery/supermarkets
Boutiques
Computer sales centers
Government surplus organizations

BUYING

Level	Job Title	Experience Needed
Entry	Buyer Trainee	Professional training
2	Junior Buyer	1–3 years
2	Merchandise Analyst	3–5 years
2	Fashion Coordinator	1–3 years
3	Buyer	5–7 years
3	Merchandise Manager	5–7 years
3	Vice President of Merchandising	7–10 years

Salaries in Buying

Entry	$16,000 to $22,000
2	$20,000 to $25,000
2	$22,000 to $29,000
3	$25,000 to $60,000
3	$35,000 to $70,000+

Salaries are higher for those with 2- or 4-year college degrees and vary greatly depending on the size and type of retail operation.

Qualifications

Personal: Ability to make quick decisions. Ability to work at a fast pace. Ability to conceptualize. Good written and verbal communication. Creativity. Risk taker. Negotiation skills. Willingness to travel extensively.

Professional: Product knowledge. Aptitude for dealing with figures, finances, inventories, and quotas. Marketing and sales skills.

Where the Jobs Are

Department stores
Specialty stores buying offices
Resident buying offices

DISTRIBUTION

Level	Job Title	Experience Needed	Qualifications
Entry	Merchandise Planner	Professional training	*Personal:* Ability to write and speak effectively. Patience. Listening skills. Ability to get along with people. Attention to detail. Organizational skills. Initiative. Good decision-making skills.
2	Inventory Coordinator	1–2 years	
2	Production Coordinator	1–2 years	
2	Traffic Manager	2–4 years	
2	Transportation Specialist	2–4 years	*Professional:* Familiarity with computers. Ability to plan and supervise. Aptitude for figures, finances, inventories, and quotas.
2	Administrative/Analyst Planner	3–5 years	
2	Coordinator of Scheduling	3–5 years	
2	MIS Specialist	3–5 years	*Where the Jobs Are*
3	Distribution Manager	4–6 years	Distribution centers
3	Transportation Manager	4–6 years	Manufacturing firms
3	Administrative Manager	4–6 years	Carriers
3	Inventory Control Manager	4–6 years	Public warehouses
3	Warehousing/Operations Manager	4–6 years	Material handling equipment manufacturers and dealers
3	MIS Director	6–10 years	Consulting firms
3	Vice President/ Operations	6–10 years	Education

Salaries in Distribution

Print media

		Communications
Entry	$17,000 to $22,000	Government
2	$20,000 to $25,000	Computer service organizations
2	$25,000 to $30,000	
2	$28,000 to $32,000	
3	$32,000 to $36,000	
3	$36,000 to $40,000	
3	$40,000 to $50,000+	

Salaries are higher for those with 2- or 4-year college degrees.

VISUAL MERCHANDISING AND DESIGN

Level	Job Title	Experience Needed	Salaries in Visual Merchandising	
Entry	Window Trimmer	Professional training	**Entry**	$15,000 to $19,000
Entry	Display Coordinator	Professional training	**Entry**	$19,000 to $23,000
2	Fashion Display Specialist	1–3 years	2	$20,000 to $25,000
2	Display Director	3–5 years	2	$25,000 to $30,000
2	Freelancer	2–5 years	3	$30,000 to $35,000
2	Fashion Writer	2–5 years	3	$35,000 to $50,000
2	Design Assistant	*With further education*	3	$50,000 to $65,000+
3	Consultant	5–7 years		
3	Fashion Designer	*With further education*		

Salaries are higher for those with 2- or 4-year college degrees.

Qualifications

Personal: Ability to conceptualize. High energy level. Ability to make quick decisions. Ability to work under pressure.

Professional: Ability to work with budget restrictions. Willingness to travel. Willingness to work long hours including nights, weekends, and holidays. Familiarity with current trends and events.

Where the Jobs Are

Manufacturers' showrooms
Design houses
Retail stores
Advertising agencies
Magazines
Consulting
Apparel manufacturers

SALES

Level	Job Title	Experience Needed
Entry	Sales Representative	Professional training
2	Sales Manager	2–5 years
2	District Sales Manager	4–6 years
3	Regional Sales Manager	5–8 years
3	Vice President of Sales	7–10 years

Salaries in Sales:

(See Salaries in Marketing Careers)

Qualifications

Personal: Positive attitude. Enthusiasm. High energy level. Ability to take rejection. Ability to work independently. Self-motivated. Negotiation skills. Confidence. Excellent communication skills. Tolerance for rejection.

Professional: Product knowledge. Perception of customer needs. Willingness to learn. Diplomacy. Good grooming.

Where the Jobs Are

Clothing manufacturers
Design houses
Apparel manufacturers
Resident buying offices
Computer manufacturers

Trade Publications

Advertising Age (weekly),
Crain Communications,
740 North Rush Street, Chicago, IL 60611

Journal of Retailing (quarterly),
New York University,
202 Tisch Building,
New York, NY 10003

Stores Magazine (monthly),
National Retail Merchants Association,
100 West 31st Street, New York, NY 10001

Women's Wear Daily (daily),
Fairchild Publications, Inc.,
7 East 12th Street, New York, NY 10003

Professional Associations

American Marketing Association
250 South Wacker Drive
Chicago, IL 60606

American Retail Federation
1616 H. Street, N.W.
Washington, DC 20006

Association of General Merchandise Chains
1625 I Street, N.W.
Washington, DC 20006

National Retail Merchants Association
100 West 31st Street
New York, NY 10001

FOOD SERVICE

Level	Production	Support	Control	Service
1 Entry *($19,000–$24,000)*	Sauce Cook Roasting Cook Soup Cook Vegetable Cook Seafood Cook Pastry Cook Baker Garde Manger Rounds Cook/ Swing Cook Butcher Commis Line Cook Prep Cook Sous Chef Pantry Person	Food Service Salesperson Sanitation Supervisor	Purchasing Assistant Manager Trainee	Bartender Assistant Steward Waiter
2 Mid-management/ specialists *($24,000–$38,000)*	Chef Pastry Chef Assistant Chef Assistant Pastry Chef Kitchen Manager Catering Manager Cafeteria Manager Food Production Manager Banquet Manager	Product Development Technologist Menu Planner Chef Instructor Director of Recipe Development Nutritionist Administrative Dietitian Quality Assurance Specialist Research and Development Specialist Sales and Marketing Specialist Packaging Specialist Home Economics Teacher Food Service Engineer Account Executive Training Manager Personnel Director Sales Manager Director of Marketing and Advertising Marketing and Promotion Manager Facilities Designer Real Estate Manager	Assistant Manager Merchandising Supervisor Storeroom Supervisor Purchasing Agent Accountant Computer Specialist Assistant Food and Beverage Manager Production Manager Food Service Manager Unit Manager Vending Manager Purchasing Manager Quality Control Manager Restaurant Manager	Wine Steward Head Bartender Dining Room Manager Hostperson Head Waiter Dining Room Captain Banquet Captain
3 Management *($38,000–$60,000 +)*	Executive Chef Chef de Cuisine	Educator/Administrator Food Service Consultant	Food and Beverage Manager Controller Regional Vice President District Manager Owner/Operator General Manager	Beverage Manager Food Service Director Maitre d'Hotel

Recommended Pre-Professional Part-Time/Summer Experience
Cook, Grill Person, Prep Cook, Baker, Dishwasher, Checker and Cashier, Receiver, Storeroom Clerk, Barback, Waitperson, Counterworker,
Hostperson, Busperson, Dining Room Attendant.

PRODUCTION

Level	Job Title	Experience Needed
Entry	Sauce Cook	Professional training
Entry	Roasting Cook	Professional training
Entry	Soup Cook	Professional training
Entry	Vegetable Cook	Professional training
Entry	Seafood Cook	Professional training
Entry	Pastry Cook	Professional training
Entry	Baker	Professional training
Entry	Garde Manger	Professional training
Entry	Rounds Cook/ Swing Cook	Professional training
Entry	Butcher	Professional training
Entry	Commis	Professional training
Entry	Line Cook	Professional training
Entry	Prep Cook	Professional training
Entry	Sous Chef	Professional training
Entry	Pantry Person	Professional training
2	Assistant Chef	2–4 years
2	Assistant Pastry Chef	2–4 years
2	Chef	4–6 years
2	Pastry Chef	4–6 years
2	Kitchen Manager	5–7 years
2	Catering Manager	5–7 years
2	Cafeteria Manager	5–7 years
2	Banquet Manager	5–7 years
2	Food Production Manager	6–8 years
3	Chef de Cuisine	8+ years
3	Executive Chef	8+ years

In all career areas in the food service industry it is important to note that the experience needed to progress to different positions varies widely according to the size, type, and volume of the operation.

Salaries in Production*

Entry	$19,000 to $22,000
2	$22,000 to $27,000
2	$27,000 to $38,000
3	$38,000 to $45,000
3	$45,000 to $60,000+

*Some positions, including Kitchen Managers, Banquet Chefs, Banquet Managers, and Sales Personnel, earn bonuses and/or commissions based on sales volume. Chefs' salaries are frequently based on food cost percentages and labor cost percentages.

Salaries vary widely according to the size, type, and location of the food service operation. In many large or fine-dining estab-lishments and luxury hotels, top management positions are salaried over $100,000.

Special combinations of bonus, housing, meals, clothing allowance, company car, etc., are often in addition to salary.

Qualifications

Personal: Positive attitude. Enthusiasm. High energy level. Confidence. Diplomacy. Accuracy and attention to detail. Reliability. Excellent communication skills. Ability to work under pressure. Ability to handle stress. Good grooming and hygiene habits. Professional appearance.

Professional: Knowledge of and commitment to professional standards. Team worker. Perception of customer needs. Creative talent. Ability to conceptualize. Aptitude for finances, figures, inventories, and budgets.

Where the Jobs Are

Restaurants

Hotels

Motels

Resorts

Private businesses

Institutional food service operations (*schools, universities, in-plant, hospitals, health care facilities, etc.*)

Clubs

Transportation

Education

Catering firms

Fast-food operations

Franchises*

Contract food operations

Government

*Franchising is a form of licensing by which the owner (the franchisor) obtains distribution through affiliated dealers (the franchisee). Franchise agreements call for the parent company to give an independent businessperson rights to a successful restaurant concept and trademark, plus assistance in organizing, training, merchandising, and management.

SUPPORT SERVICES

Level	Job Title	Experience Needed
Entry	Food Service Salesperson	Professional training
Entry	Sanitation Supervisor	Professional training
2	Menu Planner	1–3 years
2	Chef Instructor	1–3 years
2	Nutritionist	1–3 years
2	Home Economics Teacher	1–3 years
2	Administrative Dietitian	1–3 years
2	Quality Assurance Specialist	3–5 years
2	Product Development Technologist	3–5 years
2	Research and Development Specialist	3–5 years
2	Sales and Marketing Specialist	3–5 years
2	Packaging Specialist	3–5 years
2	Food Service Engineer	3–5 years
2	Quality Assurance Specialist	3–5 years
2	Account Executive	3–5 years
2	Facilities Designer	3–5 years
2	Training Manager	5–7 years
2	Sales Manager	5–7 years
2	Marketing Manager	5–7 years
2	Marketing and Promotion Manager	5–7 years
2	Real Estate Manager	5–7 years
2	Director of Recipe Development	6–8 years
2	Personnel Director	6–8 years
2	Director of Marketing and Advertising	6–8 years
3	Educator/Administrator	8–10+ years
3	Food Service Consultant	8–10+ years

Salaries in Support Services

Entry	$19,000 to $24,000
2	$24,000 to $28,000
2	$28,000 to $35,000
2	$35,000 to $40,000
3	$40,000 to $50,000
3	$50,000 to $60,000+

Qualifications

Personal: Positive attitude. Enthusiasm. Excellent verbal and written communication skills. Ability to judge and make decisions. Accuracy and attention to detail. Well groomed. Ability to work independently.

Professional: Knowledge of and commitment to professional standards. Technical knowledge. Product knowledge. Strong marketing and sales skills. Perception of customer needs. Creative talent. Ability to conceptualize. Team worker.

Where the Jobs Are

Restaurants
Hotels
Motels
Resorts
Private businesses
Institutional food service operations *(schools, universities, in-plant, hospitals, health care facilities, etc.)*
Clubs
Transportation
Education
Catering firms
Fast-food operations
Franchises*
Contract food operations
Consulting
Wholesalers
Restaurant equipment suppliers
Manufacturers of food products
Government

(See note regarding franchises under Production heading.)

CONTROL

Level	Job Title	Experience Needed	Qualifications

Level *Job Title* *Experience Needed*

Level	Job Title	Experience Needed
Entry	Purchasing Assistant	Professional training
Entry	Manager Trainee	Professional training
2	Assistant Manager	2–4 years
2	Accountant	2–4 years
2	Purchasing Agent	2–4 years
2	Computer Specialist	2–4 years
2	Merchandising Supervisor	3–5 years
2	Storeroom Supervisor	3–5 years
2	Assistant Food and Beverage Manager	3–5 years
2	Production Manager	4–6 years
2	Food Service Manager	4–6 years
2	Unit Manager	4–6 years
2	Vending Manager	4–6 years
2	Purchasing Manager	5–7 years
2	Quality Control Manager	5–7 years
2	Restaurant Manager	5–7 years
3	Food and Beverage Manager	6–8 years
3	Controller	8–10 years
3	District Manager	8–10 years
3	Regional Vice President	8–10 years
3	Owner/Operator	8–10 years
3	General Manager	8–10 years

Salaries in Control

Entry	$19,000 to $23,000
2	$23,000 to $26,000
2	$26,000 to $32,000
2	$32,000 to $38,000
3	$38,000 to $45,000
3	$45,000 to $60,000 +

Qualifications

Personal: Positive attitude. Enthusiasm. Ability to make quick and accurate decisions. Attention to detail. Excellent written and verbal communication skills. Confidence. Ability to handle pressure.

Professional: Demonstrated leadership ability. Aptitude for dealing with figures, finances, inventories, and quotas. Team worker. Product knowledge. Perception of customers' needs. Planning and organizational skills. Ability to work with budgets.

Where the Jobs Are

Restaurants

Hotels

Motels

Resorts

Institutional food service operations *(schools, universities, in-plant, hospitals, health care facilities, etc.)*

Clubs

Catering firms

Fast-food operations

Franchises

Contract food operations

Lounges

Drinking establishments

Government

SERVICE

Level	Job Title	Experience Needed	Qualifications
Entry	Bartender	Professional training	
Entry	Assistant Steward	Professional training	
Entry	Professional Waiter	Professional training	
2	Hostperson	1–3 years	
2	Wine Steward	1–3 years	
2	Head Bartender	1–3 years	
2	Dining Room Manager	2–5 years	
2	Head Waiter	2–5 years	
2	Dining Room Captain	2–5 years	
2	Banquet Captain	2–5 years	
3	Beverage Manager	4–6 years	
3	Food Service Director	5–7 years	
3	Maitre d'Hotel	7–10 years	

Personal: Positive attitude. Enthusiasm. High energy level. Good communication skills. Ability to work under pressure. Well groomed. Professional appearance. Flexibility.

Professional: Product knowledge. Perception of customer needs. Team worker. Demonstrated leadership ability. Commitment to professional standards. Ability to supervise others. Good organizational and planning skills.

Salaries in Service*

Entry	$19,000 to $22,000
2	$20,000 to $25,000
2	$25,000 to $30,000
3	$30,000 to $35,000
3	$35,000 to $45,000 +

In many service positions, especially at the entry level, tips and gratuities constitute a portion of the salary. Salaries involving tips and gratuities vary according to the volume and type of operation.

Where the Jobs Are

Restaurants
Hotels
Motels
Resorts
Lounges
Drinking establishments
Transportation
Clubs
Franchises
Institutional food service operations (*in-plant*)
Contract food operations
Government

Trade Publications

Nations Restaurant News,
Lebhar-Friedman,
425 Park Avenue, New York, NY 10022

Restaurants and Institutions,
Cahners Publishing Co.,
Cahners Plaza, 1350 East Touhy Avenue,
P.O. Box 5080, Des Plaines, IL 60018

Restaurant Business,
633 Third Avenue, New York, NY 10017

Restaurant Management,
Harcourt, Brace, Jovanovich,
7500 Old Oak Blvd., Cleveland, OH 44130

Professional Associations

American Culinary Federation (*ACF*)
Box 3466
St. Augustine, FL 32084

National Restaurant Association (*NRA*)
311 First Street, N.W.
Washington, DC 20001

Council on Hotel, Restaurant and Institutional Education (*CHRIE*)
Henderson Blvd., S-208
University Park, PA 16802

International Food Service Executives Association
111 East Wacker Dr.
Chicago, IL 60601

HOSPITALITY

Level	Rooms Division	Food and Beverage Services	Support
1 Entry *($19,000–$25,000)*	Guest Services Agent Reservationist Information Specialist Head Cashier Concierge Front Desk Supervisor Inspector Assistant Manager *(Front Office)* Assistant Housekeeper Housekeeper Team Leader *(Floor Supervisor)*	*See Food Service Careers— Production, Control, and Service*	*See Food Service Careers— Support* Accountant Night Auditor Sales Trainee Sales Representative
2 Mid-management/ specialists *($25,000–$42,000)*	Front Office Manager Rooms Attendant Executive Housekeeper Superintendent of Service Rooms Division Supervisor	*See Food Service Careers— Production, Control, and Service*	*See Food Service Careers— Support* *See Travel/Tourism Careers— Hotels, Motels, Resorts* Sales Director Group Sales Manager Area Sales Manager Auditor Corporate Account Executive Association Account Executive International Account Executive Tour and Travel Account Executive
3 Management *($38,000–$65,000 +)*	Resident Manager Assistant Hotel Manager Vice President/Operations General Manager	*See Food Service Careers— Production, Control, and Service*	*See Food Service Careers— Support* *See Travel/Tourism Careers— Hotels, Motels, Resorts* Chief Accountant Vice President/Finance Vice President/Marketing

Recommended Pre-Professional Part-Time/Summer Work Experience
Room Clerk, Starter, Telephone Operator, Messenger, Bellhop, Lobby Porter, Maid, Linen Room Attendant, Cashier, Seamstress, Doorperson, Cook, Waitperson, Busperson, Pantry Worker

ROOMS DIVISION

Level	Job Title	Experience Needed
Entry	Guest Services Agent	Professional training
Entry	Reservationist	Professional training
Entry	Information Specialist	Professional training
Entry	Head Cashier	Professional training
Entry	Concierge	Professional training
Entry	Front Desk Supervisor	Professional training
Entry	Inspector/ress	Professional training
Entry	Assistant Manager (Front Office)	Professional training
Entry	Assistant Housekeeper	Professional training
Entry	Housekeeper	Professional training
Entry	Team Leader (Floor Supervisor)	Professional training
2	Front Office Manager	1–2 years
2	Rooms Attendant	1–2 years
2	Executive Housekeeper	2–4 years
2	Superintendent of Service	4–6 years
2	Rooms Division Supervisor	4–6 years
3	Resident Manager	6–8 years
3	Assistant Hotel Manager	6–8 years
3	Vice President/ Operations	8–10 years
3	General Manager	8–10 years

*Salaries in Rooms Division**

Level	Salary
Entry	$19,000 to $24,000
2	$24,000 to $28,000
3	$28,000 to $38,000
3	$38,000 to $43,000
3	$43,000 to $46,000
3	$46,000 to $65,000+

Salaries in Rooms Divisions vary widely according to the type of hotel. In many large or luxury hotels, top management positions are salaried over $100,000. Special combinations of bonus, housing, meals, clothing allowance, company car, etc., are often in addition to salary. For details on salaries in the Hospitality Industry, consult the Roth Young Hospitality Industry Wage and Salary Review.

Qualifications

Personal: Positive attitude. Enthusiasm. High energy level. Diplomacy. Courtesy. Confidence. Ability to make quick decisions and work independently. Good grooming and professional appearance. Ability to handle pressure. Excellent communication skills.

Professional: Computer knowledge helpful. Aptitude for figures, finances, inventories, and quotas. Knowledge of and commitment to professional standards. Team worker. Ability to plan, organize, and forecast.

Where the Jobs Are

Hotels

Motels

Resorts

Inns

Bed and breakfast operations

FOOD AND BEVERAGE SERVICE

Level	Job Title	Experience Needed	Qualifications:
Entry	See Food Service Careers— Control and Services	Professional training	(See Qualifications in Food Service Careers—Production, Control, and Service)
2	See Food Service Careers— Control and Services	Professional training	
3	See Food Service Careers— Control and Services	Professional training	Where the Jobs Are

Salaries in Food and Beverage Services:

(See Salaries in Food Service Careers—Production, Control, and Service)

Where the Jobs Are

Hotels
Motels
Resorts
Inns
Bed and breakfast operations

SUPPORT

Level	Job Title	Experience Needed
Entry	See Food Service Careers—Support	Professional training
Entry	Accountant	Professional training
Entry	Night Auditor	Professional training
Entry	Sales Trainee	Professional training
Entry	Sales Representative	Professional training
2	See Food Service Careers—Support See Travel/Tourism Careers—Hotels, Motels, and Resorts	
2	Auditor	2–4 years
2	Group Sales Manager	2–4 years
2	Area Sales Manager	3–5 years
2	Corporate Account Executive	2–4 years
2	International Account Executive	3–5 years
2	Tour and Travel Account Executive	3–5 years
3	See Food Service Careers—Support See Travel/Tourism Careers—Hotels, Motels, and Resorts	
3	Chief Accountant	
3	Vice President/ Finance	
3	Vice President/ Marketing	

Salaries in Support:

(See Salaries in Food Service Careers—Support and Salaries in Travel/Tourism Careers—Hotels, Motels, and Resorts)

Qualifications:

(See Qualifications in Food Service Careers—Support and Qualifications in Travel/Tourism Careers—Hotels, Motels, and Resorts)

Where the Jobs Are

Hotels
Motels
Resorts
Inns
Bed and breakfast operations

Trade Publications

Hotel & Motel Management,
545 Fifth Ave., New York, NY 10017

Lodging Hospitality,
1100 Superior Ave., Cleveland, OH 44114

Hotel & Motel Red Book,
American Hotel Association Directory
Corporation,
888 Seventh Ave., New York, NY 10019

*Cornell Hotel and Restaurant Administration
Quarterly,*
School of Hotel Administration,
Cornell University, Ithaca, NY 14853

Nations Restaurant News,
Lebhar-Friedman, Inc.,
425 Park Ave., New York, NY 10022

Restaurant and Institutions,
Cahners Publishing Co.,
Cahners Plaza, 1350 East Touhy Ave.,
P.O. Box 5080, Des Plaines, IL 60018

Professional Associations

American Hotel and Motel Association
888 Seventh Avenue
New York, NY 10019

**Council on Hotel, Restaurant, and Institutional
Education** *(CHRIE)*
Henderson Bldg., S-208
University Park, PA 16802

**Hotel Sales and Marketing Association
International**
1400 K St., NW, Suite 810
Washington, DC 20005

National Executive Housekeepers Association
1001 Eastwind Dr., Suite 301
Westerville, OH 43081

Foodservice and Lodging Institute
1919 Pennsylvania Ave., NW
Washington, DC 20006

American Bed and Breakfast Association
6811 Kingwood Drive
Falls Church, VA 20042

Club Managers Association of America
7615 Winterberry Place
Bethesda, MD 20817

National Restaurant Association
311 First St., NW
Washington, DC 20001

International Food Service Executives' Association
111 East Wacker Drive
Chicago, IL 60601

MARKETING

Level	Sales/Management	Market Research	Telemarketing	Retailing
1 Entry ($17,000–$23,000)	Sales Representative Customer Service Representative	Coder-Editor Junior Analyst Associate Analyst	Telemarketing Representative Junior Account Executive	Buyer Trainee Sales Representative
2 Mid-management/ specialists ($21,000–$50,000)	Sales Supervisor Branch Sales Manager District Sales Manager Regional Sales Manager Central Region Sales Manager Advertising Manager	Analyst Senior Analyst Research Manager Product Manager	Telemarketing Trainer Account Executive Telemarketing Communicator Script Writer Supervisor Telemarketing Center Manager	Assistant Buyer Sales Manager Buyer Merchandise Manager
3 Management ($35,000–$65,000 +)	National Sales Manager Vice President/Marketing and Sales President	Market Research Director Vice President President	Executive Administrator	Executive

Recommended Pre-Professional Part-Time/Summer Work Experience
Sales, Telemarketing, General Office, Demonstrator, Messenger, Research Clerk, Coder, Data Entry Clerk, CRT Clerk, Waitperson

SALES/MANAGEMENT

Level	Job Title	Experience Needed	Qualifications
Entry	Sales Representative	Professional training	**Personal:** Positive attitude. Enthusiasm. Flexibility. High energy level. Good listening skills. Ability to speak and write effectively. Tolerance for rejection. Initiative. Self-motivation. Resourcefulness. Goal orientation.
Entry	Customer Service Representative	Professional training	
2	Sales Supervisor	1–2 years	
2	Branch Sales Manager	2–4 years	
2	District Sales Manager	3–5 years	**Professional:** Logic. Product knowledge. Perception of customer needs. Time management skills. Commitment. Good grooming. Professional social skills.
2	Regional Sales Manager	5 + years	
2	Central Region Sales Manager	6–8 years	
2	Advertising Manager	6–8 years	
3	National Sales Manager	7–9 years	
3	Vice President/Marketing and Sales	7–9 years	
3	President	8–10 years	

Where the Jobs Are

Salaries in Sales/Management

Entry	$17,000 to $23,000
2	$23,000 to $35,000
2	$35,000 to $50,000
3	$50,000 to $65,000
3	$65,000 +

Salaries are higher for those with 2- or 4-year college degrees.

Private industry
Advertising
Insurance
Financial services
Retailing
Computer services
Publishing houses
Equipment suppliers
Product manufacturers

MARKET RESEARCH

Level	Job Title	Experience Needed	Qualifications
Entry	Coder-Editor	Professional training	**Personal:** Detail-oriented. Good communication skills. Good organizational skills. Initiative. Patience. Resourcefulness. Ability to handle confidential information.
Entry	Junior Analyst	Professional training	
Entry	Associate Analyst	Professional training	
2	Analyst	2–4 years	
2	Senior Analyst	4–6 years	
2	Research Manager	4–6 years	**Professional:** Familiarity with computers. Aptitude for figures. Analytical thinking. Problem solving. Ability to conceptualize. Ability to evaluate and predict.
2	Product Manager	6–8 years	
3	Market Research Director	7–9 years	
3	Vice President	7–9 years	
3	President	10 years +	

Salaries in Market Research

Entry	$17,000 to $23,000
2	$21,000 to $25,000
2	$23,000 to $27,000
2	$26,000 to $32,000
2	$32,000 to $40,000 +
3	$35,000 to $40,000
3	$40,000 to $50,000 +

Salaries are higher for those with 2- or 4-year college degrees.

Where the Jobs Are

Private industry
Government

TELEMARKETING

Level	Job Title	Experience Needed	Qualifications
Entry	Telemarketing Representative	Professional training	**Personal:** Positive attitude. Good listening skills. Enthusiasm. Goal orientation. Self-motivation. Tolerance for rejection.
Entry	Junior Account Executive	Professional training	
2	Telemarketing Trainer	2–4 years	**Professional:** Product knowledge. Perception of customers' needs.
2	Account Executive	2–4 years	
2	Telemarketing Communicator	2–4 years	
2	Script Writer	2–4 years	
2	Supervisor	5–7 years	
2	Telemarketing Center Manager	5–7 years	
3	Executive/Administrator	7–10 years	

Salaries in Telemarketing

Entry	$17,000 to $22,000
2	$22,000 to $35,000
2	$35,000 to $50,000
3	$50,000 +

Salaries are higher for those with 2- or 4-year college degrees.

Where the Jobs Are

Private industry
Education
Government
Telemarketing
Consulting
Advertising agencies
Computer service organizations
Publishing houses

RETAILING

(See Careers in Fashion and Retail Management)

Trade Publications

Telemarketing Magazine,
17 Park Street, Norwalk, CT 06854

Teleprofessional Magazine,
Box 123, Del Mar, CA 92014

Telemarketing Insiders Report,
470 Main Street, Suite 108, Keyport, NJ 07735

Professional Associations

Telemarketing Recruiters, Inc.
114 East 32nd Street
New York, NY 10016

Telemarketing Council
Direct Marketing Association
6 East 43rd Street
New York, NY 10017

American Telemarketing Association
104 Wilmot Street
Deerfield, IL 60615

MEDICAL ASSISTANT

Level	Private Practices, Hospitals, Health Maintenance Organizations	Education	Medical Suppliers
1 Entry ($16,000–$23,000)	Medical Assistant	Instructor	Sales Representative
2 Mid-management/ specialists ($23,000–$28,000)	Claims Examiner Claims Representative Research Assistant Clinical Medical Assistant Administrative Medical Office Assistant	Department Head Medical Librarian	Sales Manager
3 Management ($28,000–$35,000 +)	Medical Records Administrator Office Manager Nurse (With further education) Research Analyst Doctor (With further education)	School Director Administrator/ Education	Director of Marketing and Sales

Recommended Pre-Professional Part-Time/Summer Work Experience
Office Clerk, Receptionist, General Office Clerk, Lab Assistant, Nurse's Aide, Volunteer

PRIVATE PRACTICES, HOSPITALS, HEALTH MAINTENANCE ORGANIZATIONS

Level	Job Title	Experience Needed
Entry	Medical Assistant	Professional training
2	Claims Examiner	1–3 years
2	Claims Representative	2–5 years
2	Claims Medical Assistant	1–3 years
2	Administrative Medical Office Assistant	3–5 years
3	Medical Records Administrator	5–7 years
3	Nurse	With further education
3	Research Analyst	7–10 years
3	Doctor	With further education

Qualifications

Personal: Listening skills. Courtesy. Neat, well-groomed appearance. Patience.

Professional: Ability to train on the job. Confidentiality. Computer and word processing skills. Good organizational and management skills.

Where the Jobs Are

Physicians' group practice
Physician's independent practice
Clinics
Free-standing emergency centers
Hospitals
Nursing homes
Health care centers
Rehabilitation centers
Health maintenance organizations

Salaries in Private Practices, Hospitals, Health Maintenance Organizations

Level	Salary
Entry	$16,000 to $23,000
2	$23,000 to $25,000
2	$25,000 to $28,000
3	$28,000 to $31,000
3	$31,000 to $35,000 +

Salaries are higher for those with 2- or 4-year college degrees.

EDUCATION

Level	Job Title	Experience Needed	
Entry	Instructor	Professional training and/or college degree	
2	Academic Department Head	4–5 years	
2	Medical Librarian	4–5 years	
3	Administrator/ Education	6–8 years	
3	School Director	8–10+ years	

Qualifications

Personal: Patience. Good communication skills. Ability to manage.

Professional: Awareness of policies and laws in the health care field. Planning and organizational skills. Ability to work with budgets.

Salaries in Education:

(See Salaries in Teacher Education)

Where the Jobs Are

> Career schools
> Hospitals
> Medical assistant departments

MEDICAL SUPPLIERS

Level	Job Title	Experience Needed
Entry	Sales Representative	Professional training
2	Sales Manager	3–6 years
3	Director of Marketing and Sales	7–10 years *(May need further education)*

Qualifications

Personal: Positive attitude. Good communication skills. Ability to work independently. Self-motivated. Tolerance for rejection. Confidence.

Professional: Product knowledge. Perception of customer needs. Familiarity with medical terminology.

Salaries with Medical Suppliers:

(See Salaries in Careers in Marketing)

Where the Jobs Are

> Medical supply companies
> Pharmaceutical houses

Trade Publication

Professional Medical Assistant,
American Association of Medical Assistants,
20 North Wacker Drive, Chicago, IL 60606

Professional Associations

The American Association of Medical Assistants
20 North Wacker Drive
Suite 1575
Chicago, IL 60606

American Medical Technologists
Registered Medical Assistants
710 Higgins Rd.
Park Ridge, IL 60068

PARALEGAL

Level	Private Practices, Community Legal Services, Government Agencies	Corporations	Law Libraries	Education	Legal Publishing Houses	Computer Firms
1 Entry ($19,000–$24,000)	Paralegal Legal Assistant	Paralegal	Legal Technician	Paralegal Instructor	Paralegal	Sales Representative
2 Mid-management/ specialists ($24,000–$40,000)	Paralegal Supervisor	Senior Legal Assistant	Research Assistant Information Specialist Litigation Paralegal	Placement Director	Editor	Systems Programmer
3 Management ($40,000–$55,000 +)	Law Office Administrator Lawyer (With further education)	Law Office Administrator	Law Library Manager	Program Director	Consultant/ Adviser	Marketing Analyst

Recommended Pre-Professional Part-Time/Summer Work Experience
General Office Clerk, Messenger, Library Clerk, Research Assistant, Coder, Legal Secretary, Court Reporter, Sales, Telemarketing

PRIVATE PRACTICES, COMMUNITY LEGAL SERVICES, GOVERNMENT AGENCIES

Level	Job Title	Experience Needed
Entry	Paralegal	Professional training
Entry	Legal Assistant	Professional training
2	Paralegal Supervisor	2–5 years
3	Law Office Administrator	5–7 years
3	Lawyer	With further education

Salaries in Private Practices, Community Legal Services, Government Agencies*

Entry	$19,000 to $24,000 (10–25% for overtime)
2	$24,000 to $34,000
2	$34,000 to $40,000
3	$40,000 to $55,000 +

*After two years on the job, Paralegal salaries often increase by more than 20%.

Qualifications

Personal: Courtesy. Proven written and verbal communication skills. Interest in current events and history. Detail-oriented. Patience.

Professional: Familiarity with legal terminology. Research and investigative skills. Ethics. Confidentiality. Logic. Team worker.

Where the Jobs Are

Community legal service projects
Government agencies
Private practices

CORPORATIONS

Level	Job Title	Experience Needed	Qualifications
Entry	Paralegal	Professional training	*Personal:* Positive attitude. Professional appearance. Enthusiasm. Detail-oriented. Proven written and verbal communication skills. Patience.
2	Senior Legal Assistant	2–5 years	
3	Law Office Administrator	5–8 years	

Salaries in Corporations:

(See Salaries in Private Practices, Community Legal Services, and Government Agencies)

Professional: Familiarity with legal terminology. Research and investigative skills. Ethics. Confidentiality. Logic. Team worker.

Where the Jobs Are

> Private corporations
> Public businesses

LAW LIBRARIES

Level	Job Title	Experience Needed	Qualifications
Entry	Legal Technician	Professional training	*Personal:* Positive attitude. Detail-oriented. Patience. Interest in current events and history.
2	Research Assistant	3–6 years	
2	Information Specialist	4–7 years	
2	Litigation Paralegal	5–7 years	
3	Law Library Manager	7–10 years	

Salaries in Law Libraries:

(See Salaries in Private Practices, Community Legal Services, Government Agencies)

Professional: Familiarity with legal terminology. Research and investigative skills. Ethical. Confidentiality.

Where the Jobs Are

> Law libraries

EDUCATION

Level	Job Title	Experience Needed	Qualifications
Entry	Paralegal Instructor	Professional training	*Personal:* Leadership qualities. Excellent communication skills. High energy level. Positive attitude. Enthusiasm. Patience.
2	Placement Director	3–5 years	
3	Program Director	6–10 years	

Salaries in Education:

(See Salaries in Teacher Education)

Professional: Ethics. Knowledge of subject matter. Team worker. Well organized. Willingness to retrain.

Where the Jobs Are

> Education
> Private corporations
> Consulting

LEGAL PUBLISHING HOUSES

Level	Job Title	Experience Needed	Qualifications
Entry	Paralegal	Professional training	**Personal:** Positive attitude. Enthusiasm.
Entry	Proofreader	Professional training	Detail-oriented. Proven written and verbal
Entry	Marketing Representative	Professional training	communication skills. Initiative. Professional appearance.
2	Junior Editor	3–5 years	
3	Senior Editor	6–8 years	**Professional:** Problem-solving ability. Analytical
3	Consultant/Adviser	8–10 years	thinking. Ability to conceptualize.

Decision-making skills. Familiarity with legal terminology.

Salaries in Legal Publishing Houses

Entry	$19,000 to $24,000
Entry	$24,000 to $26,000
2	$26,000 to $30,000
3	$30,000 to $37,000
3	$37,000 to $50,000 +

Where the Jobs Are

Legal publishing houses

COMPUTER FIRMS

Level	Job Title	Experience Needed	Qualifications
Entry	Sales Representative	Professional training	**Personal:** Excellent verbal communication skills.
2	Systems Programmer	3–5 years	Confidence. Enthusiasm. Professional appearance.
3	Marketing Analyst	5–8 years	Ability to work independently. Self-motivated. Flexibility.

Salaries in Computer Firms:

Professional: Product knowledge. Perception of customer needs. Willingness to learn. Problem-solving skills. Decision-making skills.

Where the Jobs Are

Computer manufacturers
Computer sales firms
Research organizations
Consulting
Computer service organizations

Trade Publications

National Paralegal Reporter,
National Federation of Paralegal Associations,
P.O. Box 40158, Overland Park, KS 66204

American Association for Paralegal Education Newsletter,
American Association for Paralegal Education,
P.O. Box 40244, Overland Park, KS 66204

Bulletin of the American Association for Paralegal Education,
American Association
for Paralegal Education,
P.O. Box 40244, Overland Park, KS 66204

International Legal Practitioner,
International Bar Association,
Two Harewood Place, Hanover Square,
London WIR 2HB, England, United Kingdom

Professional Associations

National Association of Paralegal Personnel
Box 8202
Northfield, IL 60093

National Association of Legal Assistants
1420 S. Utica
Tulsa, OK 74104

National Paralegal Association
10 South Pine Street
Doylestown, PA 18901

National Federation of Paralegal Associations
Box 40158
Overland Park, KS 66204

American Bar Association
750 N. Lake Shore Drive
Chicago, IL 60611

Standing Committee on Legal Assistants
American Bar Association
750 North Lake Shore Drive
Chicago, IL 60611

SECRETARIAL SCIENCES

Level	Administration	Information Processing	Specialization

1
Entry
($17,000–$24,000)
	Receptionist
	Secretary
	Administrative Secretary
	Executive Secretary
		Word Processor
		Page Creator
		Editor
		Coder
		Proofreader
			Legal Secretary
			Medical Secretary
			Technical Secretary
			School Secretary
			Membership Secretary
			Sales Secretary
			Travel Secretary
			Social Secretary
			International Group
			    Secretary
			Statistical Typist
			City Mortgage and
			    Real Estate Secretary

2
Mid-management/
    specialists
($24,000–$29,000)
	Administrative Assistant
	Conference and Meeting
	    Coordinator
	Department Manager
		Information Packager
		Systems Administrator
		Information Broker
		Information Manager
		Coding Clerk Supervisor
			Paralegal
			Legal Assistant
			Personnel Clerk
			Medical Records Technician
			Customer Service
			    Representative

3 Management ($29,000–$40,000+)	Executive Assistant Private Secretary Office Manager	Production Planner Financial Analyst Marketing Director Research Analyst (See Careers in Word Processing)	Personnel Assistant Sales Assistant Manager Trainee Office Manager (See Paralegal Careers)

Recommended Pre-Professional Part-Time/Summer Work Experience
Sales, File Clerk, CRT Clerk, Typist, Receptionist, Word Processor, Data Entry Operator, Inventory Clerk, Computer Operator, Library Assistant, General Office Clerk, Messenger

ADMINISTRATION

Level	Job Title	Experience Needed	Qualifications
Entry	Receptionist	Professional training	
Entry	Secretary	Professional training	
Entry	Administrative Secretary	Professional training	
Entry	Executive Secretary	Professional training	
2	Administrative Assistant	1–3 years	
2	Conference and Meeting Coordinator	2–4 years	
2	Department Manager	3–5 years	
3	Executive Assistant	4–6 years	
3	Private Secretary	5–7 years	
3	Office Manager	5–7 years	

Qualifications

Personal: Positive attitude. Enthusiasm. Detail-oriented. Excellent communication skills. Flexibility. Ability to work well under pressure. Self-starter. Dependable.

Professional: Good typing, spelling, and grammar skills. Decision-making skills. Professional appearance. Responsible. Team worker. Resourcefulness. Ability to work independently.

Salaries in Administration

Entry	$17,000 to $24,000
2	$24,000 to $29,000
3	$29,000 to $40,000+

Where the Jobs Are

Insurance	Medical offices
Banking	State and local government
Hotels	Federal government
Travel corporations	Manufacturing
Education	Private corporations
Law offices	

INFORMATION PROCESSING

Level	Job Title	Experience Needed
Entry	Word Processor*	Professional training
Entry	Page Creator	Professional training
Entry	Editor	Professional training
Entry	Coder	Professional training
Entry	Proofreader	Professional training
2	Information Packager	2–4 years
2	Systems Administrator	2–4 years
2	Information Broker	2–4 years
2	Information Manager	3–5 years
2	Coding Clerk Supervisor	3–5 years
3	Production Planner	4–6 years
3	Financial Analyst	5–7 years
3	Marketing Director	7–10 years
3	Research Analyst	7–10 years

*See Careers in Word Processing.

Salaries in Information Processing

Entry	$17,000 to $22,000
2	$23,000 to $27,000
3	$27,000 to $33,000+

Qualifications

Personal: Positive attitude. Enthusiasm. Detail-oriented. Excellent written communication skills. Ability to work well under pressure. Ability to meet deadlines.

Professional: Proofreading skills, ability to edit texts effectively. Good typing, spelling, and grammar. Ability to work independently. Team worker. Professional appearance.

Where the Jobs Are

Insurance

Banking

Education

Publishing houses

Advertising agencies

Media

Law offices

State and local government

Federal government

Private corporations

SPECIALIZATION

Level	Job Title	Experience Needed
Entry	Legal Secretary	Professional training
Entry	Medical Secretary	Professional training
Entry	Technical Secretary	Professional training
Entry	School Secretary	Professional training
Entry	Membership Secretary	Professional training
Entry	Sales Secretary	Professional training
Entry	Travel Secretary	Professional training
Entry	Social Secretary	Professional training
Entry	International Group Secretary	Professional training
Entry	Statistical Typist	Professional training
Entry	City Mortgage and Real Estate Secretary	Professional training
2	Paralegal*	3–5 years
2	Legal Assistant	3–5 years
2	Personnel Clerk	3–5 years
2	Medical Records Technician	3–5 years
2	Customer Service Representative	3–5 years
3	Personnel Assistant	5–7 years
3	Sales Assistant	5–7 years
3	Management Trainee	5–7 years
3	Office Manager	6–8 years

*See Paralegal Careers.

Salaries in Specialization

Entry	$17,000 to $22,000
2	$22,000 to $27,000
3	$27,000 to $35,000 +

Qualifications

Personal: Positive attitude. Enthusiasm. Excellent verbal and written communication skills. Flexibility. Ability to work well under pressure. Dependable.

Professional: Good typing, spelling, and grammar skills. Decision-making skills. Professional appearance. Team worker. Resourcefulness. Ability to work independently. Knowledge of specialized terminology.

Where the Jobs Are

Law offices
Hospitals
Medical offices
Travel corporations
Hotels
Real estate companies
Insurance
Banking
Education
State and local government
Federal government

TRAVEL/TOURISM

Level	Travel Agencies	Corporate Travel	Tourist Bureaus/Offices	Convention and Visitors' Bureaus
1 Entry ($13,000–$19,000)	Travel Counselor Reservationist Travel Agent Receptionist	Reservationist Travel Agent Receptionist Travel Counselor	Information Coordinator	Coordinator/Travel Information Center Coordinator of Membership Sales
2 Mid-management/ specialists ($19,000–$24,000)	Incentive Travel Specialist Outside Sales Agent Employment Interviewer	Travel Specialist	Attractions Specialist Research Analyst Surveyor Assistant Marketing Director Interpreter	Destinations Promoter Public Relations Specialist Convention Sales Manager Convention Center Manager Finance Manager Director of Transportation
3 Management ($24,000–$45,000 +)	Travel Director Travel Agency Manager Personnel Manager Owner/Operator	Travel Director Corporate Travel Manager	Director of Marketing and Sales State Travel Director Chief Tourism Officer Deputy Commissioner of Tourism Development Commissioner of Tourism	Executive Director Vice President/Sales and Marketing

Level	Chambers of Commerce	Department of Economic Development	Education	Tour Operations
1 Entry ($13,000–$19,000)	Membership Coordinator	Information Coordinator	Instructor	Tour Guide Tour Escort Tourist Information Assistant
2 Mid-management/ specialists ($19,000–$24,000)	Sales Manager Research Analyst Program Coordinator	Economic Development Coordinator Demographer Urban Planner Director of Public Safety	Academic Department Head	Tour Operator Director of Escort Services Director of Tour Guides Tour Director
3 Management ($24,000–$45,000 +)	Executive Director Vice President/ Marketing and Sales	Executive Director	Education Consultant	Manager of Tour Operations

Recommended Pre-Professional Part-Time/Summer Work Experience
Sales, Receptionist, General Office Clerk, Volunteer, Coder, Telephone Salesperson, Waitperson, Travel Assistant

Level	Associations	Conference and Meeting Planning	Hotels, Motels, and Resorts	Public Relations
1 Entry ($13,000–$19,000)	Sales Representative Coordinator of Membership Sales	See Careers in Hotels, Motels, and Resorts	Reservationist Reservations Manager Reception Manager Front Desk Clerk Concierge	Account Representative
2 Mid-management/ specialists ($19,000–$24,000)	Public Relations Specialist Research Analyst Meeting Planner Special Events Coordinator Sales Manager		Meeting Planner Conference Planner Convention Planner Front Office Manager Mail and Information Coordinator Special Events Coordinator Conference Service Coordinator	Account Manager Speaker Informer Research and Evaluator Special Events Coordinator Press Coordinator Communications Technician
3 Management ($24,000–$45,000 +)	Director of Marketing and Sales Executive Director Vice President/Marketing and Sales		Group Sales Manager Convention Sales Manager	Account Executive Director of Public Relations Vice President/ Communications

Level	Travel Writing	Airlines/Airports	Car Rental Agencies	Cruiselines
1 Entry ($13,000–$19,000)	Travel Writer	Reservationist Customer Service Representative Flight Attendant Ticket Agent Sales Representative	Customer Service Agent Rental Sales Representative	Sales Representative Reservationist
2 Mid-management/ specialists ($19,000–$24,000)	Proofreader Coder Freelancer	Airport Operations Agent Passenger Service Agent Ramp Agent Customs Inspector	Station Manager Lead Agent	Activities Coordinator Health Club Director Recreation Director
3 Management ($24,000–$45,000 +)	Travel Editor	Supervisor of Gate Services Airline Schedule Analyst Airport Manager Airport Security Officer Schedule Planning Manager	City Manager	Cruise Director Director of Sales and Marketing

Recommended Pre-Professional Part-Time/Summer Work Experience
Sales, Receptionist, General Office Clerk, Volunteer, Coder, Telephone Salesperson, Waitperson, Travel Assistant

TRAVEL AGENCIES

Level	Job Title	Experience Needed	Qualifications
Entry	Travel Counselor	Professional training	*Personal:* Positive attitude. High energy level.
Entry	Reservationist	Professional training	Enthusiasm. Ability to work with budgets.
Entry	Travel Agent	Professional training	Negotiation skills. Good communication skills.
Entry	Receptionist	Professional training	Effective interpersonal skills. Flexibility. Patience.
2	Incentive Travel Specialist	1–2 years	
2	Outside Sales Agent	1–2 years	*Professional:* Familiarity with computers. Familiarity with geographic areas and
2	Employment Interviewer	2–4 years	destinations. Strong marketing and sales skills.
3	Travel Director	4–6 years	
3	Travel Agency Manager	4–6 years	*Where the Jobs Are*
3	Personnel Manager	4–6 years	Travel Agencies
3	Owner/Operator	Varies	Department Stores

Salaries in Travel Agencies

Entry	$13,000 to $16,000
Entry	$16,000 to $19,000
2	$19,000 to $22,000
3	$22,000 to $26,000 +

CORPORATE TRAVEL

Level	Job Title	Experience Needed	Qualifications
Entry	Reservationist	Professional training	*Personal:* Good communication skills. Effective
Entry	Travel Agent	Professional training	interpersonal skills. Professional appearance.
Entry	Receptionist	Professional training	Positive attitude. Enthusiasm. Articulate.
Entry	Travel Counselor	Professional training	Initiative. Flexible.
2	Travel Specialist	1–3 years	
3	Travel Director	3–5 years	*Professional:* Awareness of product knowledge.
3	Corporate Travel Manager	3–5 years	Strong sales and marketing skills.

Salaries in Corporate Travel

Where the Jobs Are

Entry	$17,000 to $20,000
Entry	$20,000 to $22,000
2	$22,000 to $25,000
2	$25,000 to $28,000
3	$28,000 to $31,000
3	$31,000 to $35,000 +

Corporate travel firms
Private industry
Government

TOURIST BUREAUS/OFFICES

Level	Job Title	Experience Needed	Qualifications
Entry	Information Coordinator	Professional training	**Personal:** Positive attitude. Enthusiasm. Resourcefulness. Ability to communicate well. Effective interpersonal skills. Flexibility. Detail-oriented. Well groomed.
2	Attractions Specialist	Professional training	
2	Research Analyst	1–3 years	
2	Surveyor	1–3 years	**Professional:** Ability to interpret, predict, and organize. Knowledge of area lodging, restaurants, attractions. Strong marketing and sales skills. Familiarity with computers. Attention to national trends. Successful completion of civil service exam.
2	Assistant Marketing Director	3–5 years	
2	Interpreter	3–5 years	
3	Director of Marketing and Sales	5–8 years	
3	State Travel Director	5–8 years	
3	Chief Tourism Officer	8–10 years	*Where the Jobs Are*
3	Deputy Commissioner of Tourism Development	8–10 years	Research division
3	Commissioner of Tourism	8–10 years	Promotion division

Salaries in Tourist Bureaus/Offices

Information division

News division

Public affairs division

Entry	$13,000 to $16,000
2	$16,000 to $19,000
2	$19,000 to $21,000
2	$21,000 to $24,000
3	$24,000 to $27,000
3	$27,000 to $34,000
3	$34,000 to $50,000 +

CONVENTION AND VISITORS' BUREAUS

Level	Job Title	Experience Needed	Qualifications
Entry	Coordinator/Travel Information Center	Professional training	**Personal:** Positive attitude. Enthusiasm. Accurate writing skills. Detail-oriented. Flexibility. Good communication skills. Effective interpersonal skills. Well groomed. Resourcefulness.
Entry	Coordinator of Membership Sales	Professional training	
2	Destination Promoter	1–3 years	
2	Public Relations Specialist	1–3 years	**Professional:** Ability to conceptualize. Strong marketing and sales skills. Good organizational skills. Knowledge of area attractions, services, lodging, and restaurants.
2	Convention Sales Manager	3–5 years	
2	Convention Center Manager	3–5 years	
2	Finance Manager	3–5 years	
2	Director of Transportation	3–5 years	
3	Executive Director	5–7 years	*Where the Jobs Are*
3	Vice President of Sales and Marketing	7–10 years	Convention and Visitors' Bureaus

Salaries in Convention and Visitors' Bureaus:

See Salaries in Travel/Tourism—Tourist Bureaus/Offices)

CHAMBERS OF COMMERCE

Level	Job Title	Experience Needed	Qualifications
Entry	Membership Coordinator	Professional training	*Personal:* Positive attitude. Enthusiasm. Resourcefulness. Ability to communicate well.
2	Sales Manager	3–5 years	Flexibility. Detail-oriented. Well groomed.
2	Research Analyst	1–3 years	
2	Program Coordinator	1–3 years	*Professional:* Awareness of area businesses.
3	Executive Director	5–7 years	Ability to coordinate and plan. Strong marketing
3	Vice President/ Marketing and Sales	7–10 years	and sales skills.

Salaries with Chambers of Commerce:

(See Careers in Travel/Tourism—Tourist Bureau Offices)

Where the Jobs Are

Sales
Research
Promotion

DEPARTMENTS OF ECONOMIC DEVELOPMENT

Level	Job Title	Experience Needed	Qualifications
Entry	Information Coordinator	Professional training	*Personal:* Detail-oriented. Ability to work independently. Accurate writing skills.
2	Economic Development Coordinator	1–3 years	Resourcefulness.
2	Demographer	2–4 years	*Professional:* Familiarity with computers. Ability
2	Urban Planner	2–4 years	to evaluate, plan, coordinate, and interpret data.
2	Director of Public Safety	3–5 years	Awareness of local and national economic trends.
3	Executive Director	5–7 years	

Salaries with Departments of Economic Development

(See Salaries in Travel/Tourism—Tourist Bureau/ Offices)

Where the Jobs Are

Promotion
Research

EDUCATION

Level	Job Title	Experience Needed	Qualifications
Entry	Instructor	Professional training and/or college degree	**Personal:** Listening skills. Patience. Enthusiasm. Positive attitude. Detail-oriented. Flexibility. High energy level. Good communication skills.
2	Academic Department Head	4–5 years	
3	School Director/ Administrator	6–8 years	**Professional:** Familiarity with computers. Broad knowledge of Travel/Tourism industry. Good organizational skills.
3	Education Consultant	8–10 years	

Salaries in Education:

(See Salaries in Careers in Teacher Education)

Where the Jobs Are

    Schools
    Consulting firms
    Travel companies

TOUR OPERATIONS

Level	Job Title	Experience Needed	Qualifications
Entry	Tour Guide	Professional training	**Personal:** High energy level. Enthusiasm. Positive attitude. Effective interpersonal skills.
Entry	Tour Escort	Professional training	
Entry	Tourist Information Assistant	Professional training	**Professional:** Problem-solving ability. Leadership skills. Ability to settle complaints and give advice. Background in geography.
2	Tour Operator	1–2 years	
2	Director of Escort Services	3–5 years	
2	Director of Tour Guides	3–5 years	*Where the Jobs Are*
2	Tour Director	3–5 years	Tour operators
3	Manager of Tour Operations	5+ years	Attractions

    Government
    Private industry

Salaries in Tour Operations:

(See Salaries in Travel/Tourism—Travel Agencies)

ASSOCIATIONS

Level	Job Title	Experience Needed	Qualifications
Entry	Sales Representative	Professional training	*Personal:* Good communication skills. Enthusiasm. Positive attitude. Initiative. Detail-oriented. Accurate writing skills.
Entry	Coordinator of Membership Sales	Professional training	
2	Public Relations Specialist	1–3 years	*Professional:* Strong marketing and sales skills. Familiarity with computers. Awareness of local and national business interests. Ability to supervise.
2	Research Analyst	1–3 years	
2	Meeting Planner	1–3 years	
2	Special Events Coordinator	1–3 years	
2	Sales Manager	3–5 years	
3	Director of Sales and Marketing	5–7 years	*Where the Jobs Are*
3	Executive Director	5–7 years	Professional associations
3	Vice President/Marketing and Sales	7–10 years	Chambers of commerce

Salaries with Associations:

(See Salaries in Travel/Tourism—Tourist Bureaus/Offices)

CONFERENCE AND MEETING PLANNING

(See Careers in Travel/Tourism—Hotels, Motels, and Resorts)

Where the Jobs Are

Company or corporate meeting planners

Associations *(or similar and usually not-for-profit organizations)*

Independent meeting planners

HOTELS, MOTELS, AND RESORTS

Level	Job Title	Experience Needed
Entry	Reservationist	Professional training
Entry	Reservations Manager	Professional training
Entry	Reception Manager	Professional training
Entry	Front Desk Clerk	Professional training
Entry	Concierge	Professional training
2	Meeting Planner	1–2 years
2	Conference Planner	1–2 years
2	Convention Planner	1–2 years
2	Front Office Manager	1–2 years
2	Mail and Information Coordinator	1–2 years
2	Special Events Coordinator	3–5 years
2	Conference Service Coordinator	3–5 years
3	Group Sales Manager	5+ years
3	Convention Sales Manager	5+ years

Salaries in Hotels, Motels, and Resorts

Entry	$16,000 to $22,000
2	$22,000 to $25,000
2	$25,000 to $29,000+
3	$29,000 to $33,000
3	$33,000 to $35,000+

Qualifications

Personal: Positive attitude. High energy level. Patience. Confidence. Good grooming. Professional appearance. Flexibility. Excellent interpersonal skills.

Professional: Negotiation skills. Sales and marketing skills. Ability to supervise.

Where the Jobs Are

Hotels
Motels
Resorts

PUBLIC RELATIONS

Level	Job Title	Experience Needed
Entry	Account Representative	Professional training
2	Account Manager	1–3 years
2	Speaker	2–4 years
2	Informer	2–4 years
2	Researcher and Evaluator	2–4 years
2	Special Events Coordinator	2–4 years
2	Press Coordinator	3–6 years
2	Communications Technician	3–6 years
3	Account Executive	6–8 years
3	Director of Public Relations	6–8 years
3	Vice President of Communications	8–10 years

Salaries in Public Relations:

(See Salaries in Careers in Marketing—Advertising/Public Relations)

Qualifications

Personal: Excellent written and verbal communication skills. Effective interpersonal skills. Detail-oriented. Positive attitude. Enthusiasm. High energy level. Flexibility. Ability to work under pressure.

Professional: Ability to meet deadlines. Strong sales and marketing skills. Ability to supervise.

Where the Jobs Are

Convention and visitors' bureaus
Hotels, motels, and resorts
Civic centers
Tourist bureaus/offices
Chambers of commerce
Conference and meeting planning
Departments of economic development

TRAVEL WRITING

Level	Job Title	Experience Needed
Entry	Travel Writer	Professional training
2	Proofreader	1–2 years
2	Coder	1–2 years
2	Freelancer	2–4 years
3	Travel Editor	5–8 years

Salaries in Travel Writing:

Salaries can pay well but will vary. Many publications feel that travel is a perk and pay less—even one third—for travel stories than for other features.

Qualifications

Personal: Excellent writing skills. Detail-oriented. High energy level.

Professional: Ability to conceptualize. Knowledge of subject matter. Ability to meet deadlines.

Where the Jobs Are

Travel journals
Publishing houses
Magazines
Public relations departments
Advertising agencies
Research organizations

AIRLINES/AIRPORTS

Level	Job Title	Experience Needed
Entry	Reservationist	Professional training
Entry	Custom Service Representative	Professional training
Entry	Flight Attendant	Professional training
Entry	Ticket Agent	Professional training
Entry	Sales Representative	Professional training
2	Airport Operations Agent	1–3 years
2	Passenger Service Agent	1–2 years
2	Ramp Agent	1–2 years
2	Customs Inspector	1–3 years
3	Supervisor of Gate Services	3–5 years
3	Airline Schedule Analyst	3–5 years
3	Airport Manager	5–8 years
3	Airport Security Officer	3–5 years
3	Schedule Planning Manager	5–7 years

Salaries in Airlines/Airports

Entry	$16,000 to $20,000
2	$20,000 to $23,000
2	$23,000 to $25,000
3	$25,000 to $28,000
3	$28,000 to $32,000
3	$32,000 to $39,000+

Qualifications

Personal: Positive attitude. Enthusiasm. Good communication skills. Effective interpersonal skills. Well groomed. Willingness to work nights, holidays, and weekends. Flexibility.

Professional: Awareness of airline/airport policies and procedures. Familiarity with computers. Supervisory skills. Planning skills.

Where the Jobs Are

Airlines
Airports

CAR RENTAL AGENCIES

Level	Job Title	Experience Needed
Entry	Customer Service Agent	Professional training
Entry	Rental Sales Representative	Professional training
2	Station Manager	1–3 years
2	Lead Agent	1–3 years
3	City Manager	3–5 years

Qualifications

Personal: Positive attitude. Enthusiasm. High energy level. Good communication skills. Effective interpersonal skills.

Professional: Ability to work with figures. Negotiation skills. Knowledge of geographic areas helpful. Resourcefulness.

Salaries with Car Rental Agencies

Level	Salary
Entry	$13,000 to $19,000
2	$19,000 to $24,000
3	$24,000 to $35,000
3	$35,000 to $50,000+

Where the Jobs Are

> Car rental agencies
> Airports
> Hotels
> Major shopping malls

CRUISELINES

Level	Job Title	Experience Needed
Entry	Sales Representative	Professional training
Entry	Reservationist	Professional training
2	Activities Coordinator	1–3 years
2	Health Club Director	2–4 years
2	Recreation Director	2–4 years
3	Cruise Director	5–8 years
3	Director of Sales and Marketing	7–9 years

Qualifications

Personal: Positive attitude. High energy level. Enthusiasm. Good communication skills. Effective interpersonal skills. Flexibility.

Professional: Knowledge of safety policies and procedures. Strong marketing and sales skills.

Where the Jobs Are

> Cruiselines (on board)
> Cruiselines (on land)

Salaries with Cruiselines*

Level	Salary
Entry	$13,000 to $19,000
Entry	$19,000 to $21,000
2	$21,000 to $23,000
2	$23,000 to $26,000
3	$26,000 to $37,000+

*Most sales positions pay 25% in incentive pay and bonuses.

Trade Publications

Meeting News,
1515 Broadway, New York, NY 10036

Travel Weekly,
One Park Avenue, New York, NY 10016

International Travel News,
2120-28th Street,
Sacramento, CA 95818

Travelhost,
8080 N. Central Exp., 14th Floor, Dallas, TX 75206

Courier,
National Tour Association,
546 East Main Street, Lexington, KY 40058

Professional Associations

National Tour Association
546 East Main Street
Lexington, KY 40058

Travel Industry Association of America
Suite 600
1899 L. St., NW
Washington, DC 20036

Association of Travel Marketing Executives
804 D. St., NE
Washington, DC 20002

Travel and Tourism Research Association
Box 8066
Foothill Station
Salt Lake City, UT 84108

International Association of Convention & Visitor Bureaus
Box 758
Champaign, IL 61820

American Society of Travel Agents
4400 MacArthur Blvd., NW
Washington, DC 20007

WORD PROCESSING

Level	Corporations	Education	Vendor Companies	Consulting	Employment Agencies
1 Entry ($17,000–$20,000)	Word Processor Lead Word Processing Operator	Instructor	Sales Representative	Training Specialist	Instructor
2 Mid-management/ specialists ($20,000–$24,000)	Coordinator/Scheduler Records Manager Proofreader Trainer	Academic Department Head	Marketing Support Representative Sales Manager	Consultant	Employment Counselor
3 Management ($24,000–$28,000+)	Administrative Support Manager Night Shift Supervisor Word Processing Center Manager	Program Director Consultant	Director of Marketing and Sales Vice President/Marketing and Sales	President/Owner	Owner/ Manager

Recommended Pre-Professional Part-Time/Summer Work Experience
Data Entry Operator, Clerk Typist, Messenger, Word Processing Operator Trainee, File Clerk, CRT Clerk

CORPORATIONS

Level	Job Title	Experience Needed
Entry	Word Processor	Professional training
Entry	Lead Word Processing Operator	Professional training
2	Coordinator/Scheduler	1–3 years
2	Records Manager	3–5 years
2	Proofreader	1–3 years
2	Trainer	3–5 years
3	Administrative Support Manager	5–7 years
3	Night Shift Supervisor	4–6 years
3	Word Processing Center Manager	5–7 years

Salaries in Corporations

Level	Salary
Entry	$17,000 to $20,000
2	$20,000 to $22,000
2	$22,000 to $24,000
3	$24,000 to $26,000
3	$26,000 to $28,000+

Qualifications

Personal: Positive attitude. Detail-oriented. Ability to work independently. Ability to make accurate decisions. Confidence. Enthusiasm.

Professional: Ability to type. Good spelling, punctuation, and grammar. Ability to handle advanced electronic equipment. Team worker.

Where the Jobs Are

Law departments
Personnel
Claims area
Records department
Communications
Medical department
Word processing center

EDUCATION

Level	Job Title	Experience Needed	Qualifications
Entry	Instructor	Professional training and/or college degree	*Personal:* Patience. Good communication skills. Ability to manage. Detail-oriented.
2	Academic Department Head	4–5 years	*Professional:* Knowledge of various types of word processing equipment. Willingness to retrain as needed.
3	Program Director	6–8 years	
3	Consultant	8–10 years	

Salaries in Education:

(See Salaries in Teacher Education)

Where the Jobs Are

Schools
Consulting firms

VENDOR COMPANIES

Level	Job Title	Experience Needed	Qualifications
Entry	Sales Representative	Professional training	*Personal:* Positive attitude. High energy level. Initiative. Self-motivated. Enthusiasm. Ability to work independently.
2	Marketing Support Representative	1–3 years	
2	Sales Manager	3–5 years	*Professional:* Product knowledge. Perception of customer needs. Strong sales and marketing skills.
3	Director of Sales and Marketing	5–7 years	
3	Vice President of Marketing and Sales	7–10 years	

Salaries with Vendor Companies:

(See Careers in Marketing—Sales/Management)

Where the Jobs Are

Word processing manufacturing firms
Office equipment suppliers

CONSULTING

Level	Job Title	Experience Needed	Qualifications
Entry	Training Specialist	Professional training and/or college degree	*Personal:* Positive attitude. Enthusiasm. Ability to work independently. Effective written and verbal communication skills. Flexibility.
2	Consultant	1–5 years	
3	President/Owner	6+ years	

Salaries in Consulting:

(See Salaries in Computer Systems—Support Services)

Professional: Product knowledge. Perception of customer needs. Strong marketing and sales skills.

Where the Jobs Are

Freelancing
Education
Equipment manufacturers
Private corporations

EMPLOYMENT AGENCIES

Level	Job Title	Experience Needed
Entry	Instructor	Professional training
2	Employment Counselor	1–3 years
3	Owner/Manager	3–6 years

Salaries in Employment Agencies:

Vary but are usually based on a base salary plus commissions on the number of candidates successfully placed in jobs. Percentages of commission progress with salary amounts; however, compensation in employment agencies also can include bonuses and travel reimbursement. As an owner, compensation is earned after all of the overhead costs for running the business (rent, salaries, equipment, etc.) are paid.

Qualifications

Personal: Assertiveness. Ability to work under pressure. Good communication skills. Effective interpersonal skills. Positive attitude. Enthusiasm. Persistence. Patience. Risk taker. High energy level.

Professional: Ability to assess clients' needs. Strong business ethics. Good business judgment. Ability to manage. Strong marketing and sales skills.

Where the Jobs Are

> Temporary employment agencies
> Permanent placement agencies

Trade Publications

Logos,
Information Management and
Processing Association,
P.O. Box 16267, Lansing, MI 48901

The Word,
Office Technology Management Association,
9401 West Beloit Road, Suite 101,
Milwaukee, WI 53227

Professional Associations

Information Management and Processing Association
P.O. Box 16267
Lansing, MI 48901

National Association of Professional Word Processing Technicians
110 W. Byberry Road
Philadelphia, PA 19116

Office Technology Management Association
9401 W. Beloit Road
Suite 101
Milwaukee, WI 53227

Word Processing Society, Inc.
P.O. Box 92553
Milwaukee, WI 53202

Chapter Fourteen

Glossary of Terms Used in Job Descriptions

accept To receive with consent; to take without protest.

accountability The state of being subject to judgment for an action or result which a person has been given authority and responsibility to perform.

act To exert one's power so as to bring about a result; to carry out a plan or purpose. (See *execute*, *implement*, and *perform*.)

add To affix or attach; to find the sum of figures.

administer To direct the application, execution, use, or general conduct of.

adopt To take and apply or put into action.

advise To give recommendations to. (See *propose* and *recommend*.) To offer an informed opinion based on specialized knowledge.

affirm To confirm or ratify.

align To arrange or form in a line.

amend To change or modify.

analyze To study the factors of a situation or problem in order to determine the outcome or solution; to separate or distinguish the parts of a process or situation so as to discover their true relationships.

This glossary was developed in 1981 by Richard B. Shore and Patricia Alcibar for American Management Associations. Used by permission.

From: JoAnn Sperling, *Job Descriptions in Human Resources* (New York: Amacom [A Division of American Management Association], 1985).

anticipate To foresee events, trends, consequences, or problems in order to deal with them in advance.

apply To adjust or direct; to put in use.

appraise To evaluate as to quality, status, or effectiveness of.

approve To sanction officially; to accept as satisfactory; to ratify thereby assuming responsibility for. (*Used only in the situation where the individual has final authority.*)

arrange To place in proper or desired order; to prepare for an event. (See *prepare*.)

ascertain To find out or learn with certainty.

assemble To collect or gather together in a predetermined order or pattern. (See *collect*, *compile*, and *coordinate*.)

assign To give specific duties to others to perform. (See *delegate*.)

assist To lend aid or support in some undertaking or effort. (*No authority over the activity is implied.*)

assume To take upon oneself; to undertake; to take for granted.

assure To confirm; to make certain of. (See *ensure*.)

attach To bind, fasten, tie, or connect.

attend To be present for the purpose of listening or contributing.

audit To examine and review a situation, condition, or practice, and conclude with a detailed report on the findings.

authority The power to influence or command thought, opinion, or behavior.

authorize To empower; to permit; to establish by authority.

balance To arrange or prove so that the sum of one group equals the sum of another.

batch To group into a quantity for one operation.

calculate To ascertain by mathematical processes; to reckon by exercise of practical judgment.

cancel To strike or cross out.

carry To convey through the use of the hands.

center To place or fix at or around the center; to collect to a point.

chart To draw or exhibit in a graph.

check To examine for a condition; to compare for verification. (See *control, examine, inspect, monitor,* and *verify.*)

circulate To distribute in accordance with a plan. (See *disseminate.*)

classify To separate into groups having systematic relations.

clear To get the agreement or disagreement of others.

close To terminate or shut down.

code To transpose words or figures into symbols or characters. (Also *encode.*)

collaborate To work or act jointly with others.

collate To bring together in a predetermined order.

collect To gather facts or data; to assemble; to accumulate. (See *assemble* and *compile.*)

compile To collect into a volume; to compose out of materials from other documents.

compose To make up, fashion, or arrange.

concur To agree with a position, statement, act, or opinion.

conduct To lead, guide, or command the efforts of others toward producing a chosen result.

confer To converse with others to compare views. (See *consult, discuss,* and *negotiate.*)

consolidate To combine separate items into a single whole.

construct To set in order mentally; to arrange.

consult To seek advice of others; to confer.

control To exert power over in order to guide or restrain; to measure, interpret, and evaluate for conformance with plans or expected results.

cooperate To work jointly with others. (See *collaborate.*)

coordinate To bring into common action or condition so as to harmonize by regulating, changing, adjusting, or combining. (See *assemble.*)

copy To transfer or reproduce information.

correct To rectify; to make right.

correlate To establish a mutual or reciprocal relationship; to put in relation to each other.

cross foot To add across, horizontally.

cross off To line out, strike out.

cross out To eliminate by lining out.

date stamp To affix or note a date by stamping.

decide To choose from among alternatives or possibilities so as to end debate or uncertainty.

delegate To entrust to the care or management of another; to authorize or empower another to act in one's place. (*See assign, authorize,* and *represent.*)

delegation Assigning to a subordinate the responsibility and commensurate authority to accomplish an objective or specific result.

delete To erase; to remove.

design To conceive and plan in the mind for a specific use; to create, fashion, execute, or construct according to a plan. (See *develop, devise, formulate,* and *plan.*)

determine To make a decision; to bring about; to cause; to decide and set limits to, thereby fixing definitely and unalterably. To find out something not before known as a result of an intent to find defined and precise truth.

develop To conceive and create; to make active, available, or usable; to set forth or make clear, evident, or apparent.

development The result of developing.

devise To come up with something new, especially by combining known ideas or principles. (See *design, develop, formulate,* and *plan.*)

direct To lead, guide, or command the efforts of others toward producing a chosen result. (See *conduct, manage,* and *supervise.*)

direction Guidance or supervision of others.

disassemble To take apart. (Also *dissemble.*)

discover To find out something not known before as a result of chance, exploration, or investigation. (See *ascertain* and *determine.*)

discuss To exchange views for the purpose of convincing or reaching a conclusion.

dissemble To take apart. (Also *disassemble.*)

disseminate To spread information or ideas. (See *circulate, distribute, issue,* and *release.*)

distribute To divide or separate into classes; to pass around; to allot; to deliver to named places or persons. (See *circulate, disseminate, issue,* and *release.*)

divide To separate into classes or parts subject to mathematical division.

draft To compose or write papers and documents in preliminary or final form, often for the approval or clearance of others.

duty Assigned task.

edit To revise and prepare for publication.

endorse To express approval of; to countersign.

ensure To make safe or certain. (See *assure.*)

establish To set up or bring into existence on a firm basis.

evaluate To ascertain or determine the value of.

examine To investigate; to scrutinize; to subject to inquiry by inspection or test.

execute To put into effect; to follow through to the end.

exercise To employ actively, as in authority or influence.

expedite To accelerate the movement or progress of; to remove obstacles.

facilitate To make easy or less difficult.

feed To supply material to a machine.

figure To compute.

file To lay away papers, etc., arranged in some methodical manner.

fill in To enter information on a form.

find To locate by search.

flag To mark distinctively.

follow up To check the progress of; to see if results are satisfactory.

formulate To develop or devise a plan, policy, or procedure; to put into a systemized statement.

furnish To give or supply. (See *provide.*)

goal An objective.

guidance Conducting or directing along a course of action.

implement To carry out; to perform acts essential to the execution of a plan or program; to give effect to.

inform To instruct; to communicate knowledge.

initiate To originate; to introduce for the first time.

insert To put or thrust in.

inspect To examine carefully for suitability or conformance with standards. (See *check, control, examine, monitor,* and *verify.*)

instruct To impart knowledge to; to give information or direction to; to show how to do.

instructions To furnish with directions; to inform.
Specific: Precise and detailed directions that closely limit what can be done or how it can be done.
General: Directions that are merely outlined, hence do not closely limit what can be done or how it can be done.

intensive Exhaustive or concentrated.

interpret To explain or clarify; to translate.

interview To question in order to obtain facts or opinions.

inventory A list of items; stock on hand.

investigate To study closely and methodically.

issue To distribute formally.

itemize To set or note down in detail; to set by particulars.

line To cover the inside surface of; to draw lines on.

list To itemize.

locate To search for and find; to position.

maintain To keep up-to-date or current; to keep at a given level or in working condition.

manage To control and direct; to guide; to command the efforts of others toward producing a chosen result. (See *supervise.*)

measure To find the quality or amount of; to ascertain dimension, count, intensity, etc.

merge To combine.

mix To unite or blend into one group or mass.

monitor To observe or check periodically for a specific purpose.

multiply To perform the operation of multiplication.

negotiate To exchange views and proposals with an eye to reaching agreement by sifting possibilities, proposals, and pros and cons.

nonroutine Irregular or infrequent situations that arise relating to business or official duties. Characteristic of higher-level jobs.

note To observe, notice.

notify To give notice to; to inform.

objective A desired result. (See *goal.*)

observe To perceive, notice, watch.

obtain To gain possession of; to acquire.

open To enter upon; to spread out; to make accessible.

operate To conduct or perform activity.

organization Individuals working together in related ways within a specific structure toward a common end.

organize To arrange in interdependent parts; to systematize.

originate To produce as new; to invent.

outline To make a summary of the significant features of a subject.

participate To take part in.

perform To carry out; to accomplish; to execute.

place To locate an employee in a job.

plan To devise or project a method or course of action.

policy A definite course or method of action selected from among alternatives and in light of given conditions, to guide and determine present and future decisions.

position description A document that describes the purpose, scope, duties, responsibilities, authorities, and working relationships associated with a position or entity to be occupied and performed by one person.

position specification A document that describes the physical characteristics, knowledge, skill, experience, and education requirements of a person who would be ideally suited to perform a specific job.

post To announce by public, written notice; to transfer or carry information from one record to another.

practice To work repeatedly to gain skill.

prepare To make ready for a special purpose.

principle A governing law of conduct; a fundamental belief serving as a responsible guide to action; a basis for policy.

procedure A particular way of accomplishing something or of acting; a series of steps followed in a regular, definite order; a standardized practice.

proceed To begin or carry out.

process To subject to some special treatment; to handle in accordance with prescribed procedures.

program A series of planned steps toward an objective.

promote To act so as to increase sales or patronage; to advance someone to a higher level or job.

propose To offer for consideration or adoption; to declare an intention.

provide To supply for use; to make available; to furnish.

purchase To buy or procure.

purpose Something set up as an objective or end to be attained; a reason.

rate To appraise or assess; to give one's opinion of the rank or quality of.

receive To take something that is offered or sent.

recommend To advise or counsel a course of action or to suggest for adoption a course of action.

reconstruct To restore; to construct again.

record To register; to make a record of.

refer To direct attention to.

register To enter in a record or list.

release To authorize the publication of, dissemination of.

remit To transmit or send money as payment.

render To furnish, contribute.

report To supply or furnish organized information.

represent To act for or in place of; to serve as a counterpart of; to substitute in some capacity for.

request To ask for something.

require To demand as necessary or essential.

requisition A document making a request.

research Inquiry into a specific subject from several sources.

responsibility The quality or state of being accountable for.

responsible for Having caused; accountable for.

review To examine, usually with intent to approve or dissent; to analyze results in order to give an opinion.

revise To change in order to make new, to correct, to improve, or bring up-to-date.

route To prearrange the sending of an item to the location to which it is to be sent.

routine Regular procedure, or normal course of business or official duties.

scan To examine point by point; to scrutinize.

schedule To plan a timetable; to set specific times for.

screen To examine so as to separate into two or more groups or classes, usually rejecting one or more.

search To look over and through for the purpose of finding something.

secure To get possession of; to obtain; to make safe.

select Chosen from a number of others of a similar kind.

separate To set apart from others for special use; to keep apart.

serve To hold an office; to act in a capacity; to discharge a duty or function.

sign To authorize by affixing one's signature.

sort   To put in a definite place or rank according to kind, class, etc.

stack   To pile up.

standard of performance   A statement of the conditions that will exist when a job is acceptably done. Whenever possible, the elements of the statement include specific reference to quantity, quality, cost, and time.

stimulate   To excite, rouse, or spur on.

study   To consider attentively; to ponder or fix the mind closely upon a subject.

submit   To present information for another's judgment or decision.

subtotal   An interim total.

subtract   To deduct one number from another.

summarize   To give only the main points.

supervise   To oversee a work group—leading, guiding, or commanding its efforts to produce a chosen result.

support   To provide service, assistance, or supplies to another person or department.

survey   To ascertain facts regarding conditions or the condition of a situation usually in connection with the gathering of information.

tabulate   To form into a table by listing; to make a listing.

trace   To record the transfer of an application or document; to copy as a drawing.

train   To increase skill or knowledge by capable instruction.

transcribe   To make a typed copy from shorthand notes or dictated record; to write a copy of.

transpose   To transfer; to change the usual place or order.

underline   To emphasize or identify by drawing a line under the characters or subject.

verify   To prove to be true or accurate; to confirm or substantiate; to test or check the accuracy of.

Chapter Fifteen

Index of Job Descriptions

Academic Department Head
Administers affairs of an academic department. May administer department's budget and recruit academic personnel. Conducts meetings to discuss current teaching strategies and obtains recommendations for changes within the department.

Account Executive
Responsible for the development of and service of a customer account. Brings business to the firm. Consults with the client and collaborates with associates to find best strategies for servicing clients.

Account Executive (Advertising)
Meets with clients. Participates in meetings with other departments on the ideas for a campaign. Plans overall strategy for clients. Keeps up-to-date on media rate changes and new media outlets. Serves as a link between the agency and the clients.

Account Executive (Food Service)
Initiates and signs new customers, which includes scouting new business, helping survey clients' needs, writing formal request letters, and making formal presentations, usually accompanied by management representative(s). Representative of the food service contractor who deals directly with the liaison designate of the client.

Account Executive (Public Relations)
Meets with clients to determine needs for public relations program. May review company strategies and goals, current customer base, and reputation with the public. Recommends public relations program. Keeps up-to-date on new and existing programs and policies. Serves as a link between the public relations firm and the clients.

Account Executive (Telemarketing)
Organizes and manages a program internally once it has been brought in by a telemarketing representative. Coordinates script writing, script testing, list preparation, forms design (to record sales and customer data), and client reports. Monitors the project and provides regular reports for the client.

Account Executive Trainee (Advertising)
Fields material from other departments. Takes calls from clients. Keeps in touch with traffic department on schedules for ads and spots.

Account Manager
Develops an efficient coverage pattern for the territory. Decides on the call frequency for major accounts. Develops a sales plan for the territory. Promotes, sells, and services product line. Reviews customer-call reports. Coordinates activities at individual key customer locations.

Account Representative
(See *Account Executive*)

Account Supervisor
(See *Account Manager*)

Accounts Supervisor/Manager
(See *Account Manager*)

Accountant
Helps businesses and individuals set up financial recordkeeping. Examines, analyzes, and interprets accounting records for the purpose of giving advice or preparing statements. Estimates future revenues and expenditures to prepare budget.

Accountant (Food Service)
Prepares and analyzes financial reports that furnish up-to-date financial information.

Accountants employed by large restaurant firms may travel extensively to audit or work for clients or branches of the firm.

Accountant (Hospitality)
Sets up the financial recordkeeping for the hotel or other lodging facility. Estimates future revenues and expenditures to prepare the operation's budget for each year.

Activities Coordinator (Cruiselines)
Plans and implements activities for passengers on cruiselines.

Actuarial Trainee
Works for insurance companies analyzing statistics to determine probabilities of accident, death, injury, earthquake, flood, fire, etc., so that the rates charged for insurance policies will bring in profits for the company while still being competitive with those of other insurance carriers.

Actuary
Uses mathematical skills to predict probabilities of events that will be used for insurance plans and pension programs.

Adjuster
Investigates and settles claims of losses suffered by policyholders of all kinds of insurance.

Adjuster Trainee
Assists with investigations and settling claims of losses suffered by policyholders of all kinds of insurance.

Administrative Analyst/Planner
Responsibilities include developing any new systems and setting up any long-range planning systems; responsible for the planning group, which actually plans each day's shipment to distribution centers. Works on product allocation and inventory control. Responsible for anything that might affect the distribution area.

Administrative Assistant
An administrative support job performed with little or no supervision, and one that is a step higher than an executive secretary. Handles dissemination of contract information or works with a chief officer of a company in preparing corporate reports. Often involves supervision of others.

Administrative Dental Assistant
Checks office and laboratory supplies; maintains waiting, reception, and examination rooms in a

neat and orderly condition; answers telephones; greets patients and other callers; records and files patient data and medical records; fills out medical reports and insurance forms; handles correspondence, schedules appointments, and arranges for hospital admission and laboratory services. May transcribe dictation and handle the bookkeeping and billing.

Administrative Dietitian
Responsible for training and supervision of food service supervisor and assistants in food preparation and formulating policies, enforcing sanitary and safety regulations. Buys food, equipment, and other supplies, so must understand purchasing and budgeting.

Administrative Manager
Provides maximum support to all divisions through the regional or district distribution centers and ensures that timely, cost-effective service is provided to those units and their customers. Supervises personnel, equipment, materials, facilities, product handling, inventory control, building services, customer relations, order processing, office services, and district operations.

Administrative Medical Office Assistant
(See *Administrative Dental Assistant*)

Administrative Secretary
Handles everything except dictation and typing. Duties range from filing and setting up filing systems, routing mail, and answering telephones to more complex work such as answering letters, doing research, and preparing statistical reports.

Administrative Support Manager
(Word Processing)
Responsible for the operation of the entire word processing center.

Administrator (Education)
Directs the administration of an educational institution, or a division of it, within the authority of the governing board. Develops or expands programs or services. Administers fiscal operations such as budget planning, accounting, and establishing costs for the institution. Directs hiring and training of personnel. Develops policies and procedures for activities within area of responsibility.

Administrator (Education)
Involved with curriculum and program development and directing teaching personnel of the school system. Confers with teaching and

administrative staff to plan and develop curriculum designed to meet needs of the students. Visits classrooms to observe effectiveness of instructional methods and materials. Evaluates teaching techniques and recommends changes for improving them. Conducts workshops and conferences for teachers to study new classroom procedures, new instructional materials, and other aids to teaching.

Advertising Manager
Plans and executes advertising policies of an organization. Confers with department heads to discuss possible new accounts and to outline new policies or sales promotion campaigns. Confers with officials of newspapers, radio, and television stations and then arranges billboard advertising contracts. Allocates advertising space to department. May authorize information for publication.

Agent (Insurance)
Sells traditional life insurance to clients. May also sell mutual funds and other equity-based products. Many agents also qualify as financial planners after obtaining certification. Explains financial products in detail to prospective clients. Processes necessary paperwork when closing a sale.

Airline Schedule Analyst
Reviews schedules for all incoming and outgoing flights. Makes recommendations for changes in schedules to ensure maximum service while still maintaining strict procedures.

Airport Manager
Responsible for operating a safe facility and fund raising. Keeps the public informed on safety decisions affecting the area surrounding the airport.

Airport Operations Agent
Customer service agent responsible for assigning boarding times, lifting tickets; coordinates baggage service; announces flight arrivals to main desk.

Airport Security Officer
Notes suspicious persons and reports to superior officer. Reports hazards. Inspects baggage of passengers. Assists passengers with lost luggage claims. Directs passengers to appropriate boarding areas. Warns or arrests persons violating ordinances. Issues tickets to traffic violators. Maintains overall security of the airport.

Analyst (Marketing)
(See *Market Research Analyst*)

Architect
Involved with all aspects of the planning, design, and construction of buildings. Prepares proposals which include illustrations and scaled drawings. Draws the structural system as well as the other elements that go into the project. Provides advice about choosing contractors.

Area Manager (Retail)
Manages a selling center within a store. This would include a small group of departments carrying related merchandise.

Area Sales Manager (Hospitality)
Responsible for sales promotion for a group of hotel properties in a specified geographic area.

Assistant Actuary
(See *Actuary*)

Assistant Buyer (Production)
(See *Buyer-Production*)

Assistant Chef
(See *Chef*)

Assistant Club Manager
(See *Club Manager*)

Assistant Food and Beverage Manager
(See *Food and Beverage Manager*)

Assistant Hotel Manager
Assists with supervising the operations of the different departments of a hotel: food service, housekeeping, front office, and maintenance. Ensures the smooth functioning and profitability of the hotel by maintaining the property and quality guest service.

Assistant Housekeeper
(See *Housekeeper*)

Assistant Loan Officer
(See *Loan Officer*)

Assistant Manager (Food Service)
Performs supervisory duties under the manager's direction. Must be capable of filling in when the manager is absent, thus needs good management skills and knowledge of the operation.

Assistant Manager (Front Office)
(See *Front Office Manager*)

Assistant Manager Trainee (Recreation)
(See *Assistant Club Manager*)

Assistant Marketing Director (Travel)
Assists with the development of competitive strategies for clients. Reviews services and products being offered and evaluates client's market position. Assists companies with monitoring themselves to make sure they are delivering what is promised.

Assistant Media Planner
Learns to interpret rate cards of various media. Analyzes audience ratings. Writes letters and memos. Compares media alternatives. Prepares and delivers presentations to clients. Talks with sales representatives from various media. Evaluates media buying.

Assistant Pastry Chef
(See *Pastry Chef*)

Assistant Professor
A designation of faculty rank used to refer to faculty members with some, but not extensive, teaching experience in their area of expertise. (See *Professor*)

Assistant Purchasing Agent
(See *Purchasing Agent*)

Assistant Quality Assurance Manager
(See *Quality Assurance Manager*)

Assistant Store Manager
(See *Store Manager*)

Assistant Travel Editor
(See *Travel Editor*)

Assistant Underwriter
(See *Underwriter*)

Assistant Wine Steward
(See *Wine Steward*)

Associate Analyst (Marketing)
(See *Market Research Analyst*)

Associate Media Director
Makes decisions on media buying. Reviews alternative selections and results of ratings to determine decision.

Associate Professor
A higher designation of faculty rank used to refer to faculty members with more extensive teaching experience in their area of expertise. Often, this ranking is also marked by research work, publications, or industry experience. (See *Professor*)

Associate Research Director (Advertising)
Evaluates information published by the government, trade, or other groups as relates to individual ad campaigns. Evaluates suggestions and findings of the research account executive to determine best approach to each ad campaign. Keeps campaigns operating within specified guidelines.

Association Account Executive (Hospitality)
Responsible for the development of and service of professional or trade association business coming into the hotel or other related facility.

Attractions Specialist
Has specific knowledge of local attractions and how to promote them. Provides input on target population for promotional effort.

Auditor (Hospitality)
Examines and analyzes accounting records of hotel or food service operation and prepares reports concerning its financial status and operating procedures. Analyzes data to check for duplication of effort, extravagance, fraud, or lack of compliance with management's established policies.

Baker
Prepares all the baked items that are not desserts, such as breads, rolls, muffins, danish, and croissants for use in dining rooms of hotels and restaurants and related facilities. Depending on the size of the staff and the operation, may also make pies, cakes, and some pastry items.

Bank Manager
Manages, directs, and coordinates activities of workers engaged in accounting and recording of financial transactions, setting up trust or escrow accounts, probating estates, and administering trust or mortgage accounts. Develops relationships with customers, business, community, and civic organizations to promote goodwill and generate new business.

Bank Officer Trainee
Gains experience in the main functions of the banking business. These include the trust department, where money is invested for families, institutions, or other businesses; the credit department, where decisions are made on loaning

money to customers and operations, where all of the normal business functions (data processing, personnel, public relations, and accounting) are monitored.

Banquet Captain
May greet the host, hostess, and guests. Ensures that everything is as ordered. Ensures that all party rooms are in order at all times and checks before and after a function to make sure that the patrons are satisfied. Presents the bill for signature or payment when the function is over. Pays employees at the end of the function.

Banquet Manager
Arranges banquet and food service functions. Arranges banquet details after they have been agreed upon by the catering manager and the customer. Prepares and updates banquet menus. Reports inventory needs to purchasing agent and storeroom, and may supervise the scheduling of staff to work the functions.

Bartender
Mixes and serves alcoholic and nonalcoholic drinks for patrons of a bar following standard recipes. Mixes ingredients, such as liquor, soda, water, sugar, and bitters to prepare cocktails and other drinks. Serves wine and draught or bottled beer. Collects money for drinks served. Orders or requisitions liquors and supplies. Places bottled goods and glasses to make an attractive display. May slice and pit fruit for the garnishing of drinks. May prepare appetizers, such as pickles, cheese, and cold meat.

Benefits Coordinator
Administers various employee benefit programs such as group insurance—life, medical, and dental; accident and disability insurance; pensions; investment savings; and health maintenance organizations. Initiates medical and option forms and/or affidavits; arranges for their completion and submission within time limits. Implements new benefit programs; arranges and conducts employee information presentations and enrollments. Ensures program compliance with governmental regulations.

Beverage Manager
Responsible for compiling statistics of liquor costs, sales, profits, and losses. Inventories the bar as needed, sometimes daily, and prepares the daily consumption report that is forwarded to the auditing office. Issues merchandise to all bar areas, but usually does not buy liquor. Instead, forwards purchase orders to a central purchasing agent, who may order for several hotels in a chain.

Branch Manager
Plans, coordinates, controls the work flow, updates systems, strives for administrative efficiency, and is responsible for all functions of a branch office.

Branch Sales Manager
Makes a direct sales effort to the customers in the area to sell a product line. Provides management with sales and booking forecasts on a monthly, quarterly, and annual basis. Keeps abreast of prices and performance of competitors' products in his or her territory. Handles service and related problems as they arise. Trains and supervises sales staff.

Broadcast Technician
Performs the work of an electronics technician, specifically on various types of broadcast equipment. (See *Electronics Technician*)

Butcher
Responsible for cutting, boning, and otherwise caring for and preparing meats for cooking.

Buyer (Production)
Responsible for placing orders, expediting back orders, and processing paperwork for stock and nonstock supplies. This includes processing requisitions, researching products, clarifying specifications, typing purchase orders, following up on back orders, selecting vendors, maintaining up-to-date product information files, and utilizing computer terminals and hand-held order entry devices to place order.

Buyer (Retail)
Selects the goods to be sold by retail stores or wholesale outlets. Buyers also help to plan the selling programs for the goods they have purchased. They normally specialize in one type of goods such as men's clothing, housewares, or accessories.

Buyer Trainee (Retail)
Assists supervising buyer. Places orders and speaks with manufacturers by telephone. Supervises the inspection and unpacking of new merchandise and overseeing its distribution.

Cafeteria Manager
In charge of a unit with as few as 1 employee to as many as 70 or more. Oversees all employees, sometimes giving limited on-the-job training. Hiring and firing responsibilities. Purchases what is needed for unit, usually from a central purchasing office, and keeps records of the same.

Camp Manager
Directs and coordinates activities of workers concerned with preparation and maintenance of buildings and facilities in residential camp; coordinates through staff or personally directs staff in preparing and maintaining such camp facilities as dining halls, etc., used by resident employees. Schedules purchase and delivery of food supplies. Enforces safety and sanitation regulations.

Catering Manager
Works with the Executive Chef on menus, food quality, or service problems. Responsible for arranging any catered functions held at the establishment, from weddings to conventions, from banquets to dances. Draws up necessary contracts. Helps customers select menu, decorations, and room arrangement and transmits these requirements to various departments for execution.

Central Region Sales Manager
Responsible for sales function in the central region. (See *Regional Sales Manager*).

Chef
Supervises, coordinates, and participates in activities of cooks and other kitchen personnel engaged in preparing foods for a hotel, restaurant, cafeteria, or other establishment. Estimates food consumption, and requisitions or purchases foodstuffs. Receives and checks recipes. Supervises personnel engaged in preparing, cooking, and serving meats, sauces, vegetables, soups, and other foods. May employ, train, and discharge workers. In small establishments, may maintain time and payroll records.

Chef de Cuisine (Maitre de Cuisine)
In complete charge of food services. Reporting to the Food and Beverage Director in large operations or to the owner or manager in smaller operations; may assume duties of the Food and Beverage Director as well when needed.

Chef Instructor
Brings a chef's perspective to the "lab" classroom and teaches hands-on cooking techniques. (See *Instructor*)

Chief Accountant
Responsible for the supervision and control of the general accounting functions. This includes general ledger, payables, payroll, property, budget reporting, and statistical accumulation. Responsible for financial statement and report preparation and budget reviews. Supervises and trains employees in accounting, payroll, and accounts payable.

Chief Accountant (Hospitality)
Responsible for the supervision and control of the general accounting functions of the hotel. This includes night audit functions, general ledger, payables, payroll, property, budget reporting, and statistical accumulation. Responsible for financial statement and report preparation and budget reviews. Supervises and trains hotel employees in accounting, payroll, and accounts payable.

Chief Actuary
Oversees the calculation of probabilities of death, sickness disability, injury, property loss, fire, and other hazards. Evaluates and analyzes relevant statistics. Determines the rate of expected losses due to the issuance of various types of policies. Determines the various provisions contained in insurance policies.

Chief Financial Officer
Develops corporate financial objectives. Establishes policies and procedures for the effective recording, analyzing, and reporting of all financial matters. Directs the controller, treasury, and corporate financial services activities to ensure that each of these functions meets established goals and provides effective service to the corporation as a whole.

Chief Internal Auditor
(See *Internal Auditor*)

Chief Tourism Officer
Oversees the staff engaged in tourism development for a particular area. Works within established budgets. Approves promotional campaigns.

City Manager
Responsible for managing inbound business for a car rental company.

City Mortgage and Real Estate Secretary
Works with real estate investment officers and provides secretarial support for an investment team. Prepares commitment letters and various reports, maintains files, and handles telephone communications.

Claims Examiner
Analyzes insurance claims to determine extent of insurance carrier's liability and settles claims with claimants in accordance with policy provisions. Investigates questionable inquiries.

Claims Representative
Reviews insurance claim forms for completeness; secures and adds missing data; and transmits claims for payment or for further investigation.

Clinical Dental Assistant
Reviews patients' records and presents them to the dentist; obtains information needed to update medical histories; takes patient X rays; assists the dentist in examining patients; instructs about medications.

Clinical Medical Assistant
Receives patients' height, weight, temperature, and blood pressure; obtains medical histories; performs basic laboratory tests; prepares patients for examination or treatment; assists the physician in examining patients. Instructs patients about medication and self-treatment, draws blood, prepares patients for X rays, takes EKGs, and applies dressings.

Club Manager
Estimates and orders food products and coordinates activity of workers engaged in selling alcoholic and nonalcoholic beverages for consumption on the premises. May manage staff involved in operating club with recreational facilities for private groups or the general public. Responsible for grounds and buildings, payroll, and promotion.

Coder
Converts routine items of information obtained from records and reports into codes for processing by data typing using predetermined coding systems.

Coder-Editor
Synthesizes the results of questionnaires or mail or telephone surveys. The results are then reviewed by the research analyst.

Coding Clerk Supervisor
Supervises and coordinates activities of workers engaged in converting routine items of information from source documents into codes to prepare records for data processing. Modifies, revises, or designs forms and initiates procedures to develop more efficient methods of data input.

Cold Cook (Garde Manger)
Responsible for cold hors d'oeuvres, cold plates, salads, buffets, ice and vegetable carvings, tallow and butter sculpturing, etc.

College Recruiter
Interviews college graduates on campus. Works in conjunction with the policies and standards approved by the Employment Manager.

Commis
A professional assistant in the kitchen or dining room.

Commissioner of Tourism
Promotes overall tourism efforts. Generates new sources for funding. Interfaces with businesses in the community to gain support for tourism development.

Communications Equipment Technician
Performs the work of an electronics technician specifically on various types of communications equipment. (See *Electronics Technician*)

Communications Technician
May direct activities of production, circulation, or promotional personnel. May prepare news or public relations releases, special brochures, and similar materials. Assigns staff member, or personally interviews individuals and attends gatherings to obtain items for publication, verify facts, and clarify information.

Computer Operator
Operates computer equipment to ensure that tasks are processed in accordance with a schedule of operations. Maintains and completes daily logs. Maintains an accurate report of equipment and/or software malfunctions.

Concierge

Handles guests' problems in a hotel, makes reservation requests with restaurants and transportation facilities, arranges tours, procures theater tickets, and handles a host of other activities.

Conference and Meeting Coordinator

Coordinates the planning and execution of conferences and meetings on and off site. Notifies attendees of details. Makes necessary facilities arrangements. Makes travel arrangements if required. Oversees the function and conducts postmeeting evaluation.

Conference Planner

Compiles list of individuals or groups requesting space for activities and schedules needed facilities. Notifies program participants of locations assigned. Maintains schedules and records of available space, space used, and cancellations. Requisitions needed equipment. Arranges for services during the conference. Follows up with client after the conference for evaluation of services provided.

Conference Reporter

Attends conferences at the request of the conference coordinator. Records minutes of the meetings and activities that occur during the conference. Types up summaries and distributes to requesting parties.

Conference Service Coordinator

Books the meetings, services them, and follows up with a postmeeting evaluation.

Consultant

Consults with client to determine need or problem, conducts studies and surveys to obtain data, and analyzes data to advise on or recommend a solution. Advises client on alternate methods of solving problem or recommends a specific solution. May negotiate contract for consulting service.

Consultant/Adviser (Paralegal)

Assists the legal publisher in planning new kinds of books to be written either about the paralegal profession or the procedures utilized by paralegals in law offices.

Controller

Directs financial affairs of an organization. Prepares financial analyses of operations for guidance of management. Establishes major economic objectives and policies for the company. Prepares reports that outline company's financial position in areas of income, expenses, and earnings based on past, present, and future operations. Directs preparation of budgets and financial forecasts.

Convention Center Manager

Manages the building, does marketing and public relations for events at the center. Responsible for entire budget for the center and supervises personnel.

Convention Planner

Arranges space and facilities for convention. Keeps exhibitors and attendees informed of procedures and policies for participation. Assigns troubleshooters to be available to provide needed services during the convention and minimizes situations that may result in a safety, legal, or logistical problem.

Convention Sales Manager

Responsible for generating convention business at hotel, civic center, or other appropriate facility. Oversees sales staff. Approves advertising and rate packages. Handles projections on business and expected income. Works within established budgets.

Cook

Prepares, seasons, and cooks soups, meats, vegetables, desserts, and other foodstuffs for consumption in hotels and restaurants. Reads menu to estimate food requirements and orders food from supplier or procures it from storage. Adjusts thermostat controls to regulate temperature of ovens, broilers, grills, and roasters. Measures and mixes ingredients according to recipe, using a variety of kitchen utensils and equipment, such as blenders, mixers, grinders, slicers, and tenderizers to prepare soups, salads, gravies, desserts, sauces, and casseroles. Bakes, roasts, broils, and steams meat, fish, vegetables, and other foods. Observes and tests foods being cooked by tasting, smelling, and piercing with fork to determine that it is cooked. Carves meats, portions food on serving plates, adds gravies, sauces, and garnishes servings to fill orders.

Coordinator of Membership Sales

Maintains prospect lists for membership in travel clubs or travel associations. Coordinates marketing programs to solicit new membership.

Explains membership policies and benefits and receives payment of membership dues. Makes decisions on appropriateness of membership.

Coordinator/Scheduler (Word Processing)
Sees that there is an even flow of work to the word processor.

Coordinator of Scheduling (Retail)
Prepares production schedules. Determines type and quantity of material needed to process orders. Issues work orders. Calculates costs for manufacturing.

Coordinator/Travel Information Center
Supervises and coordinates activities of workers engaged in greeting and welcoming motorists at state highway information center. Provides information, such as directions, road conditions, and vehicular travel regulations. Provides maps, brochures, and pamphlets to assist motorists in locating points of interest or in reaching destination. May direct tourists to rest areas, camps, resorts, historical points, or other tourist attractions.

Copy Chief
Supervises one or more copywriters in an advertising agency, department, or service, whose function it is to assign the work of preparing the textual matter for advertisements; supervises the actual writing and transmits the completed work in accordance with the existing traffic arrangement in the firm. Coordinates copywriting activities with the layout, art, and production departments of the organization.

Copywriter
Writes original advertising material about products or services for newspapers, magazines, radio and television, posters, or other media.

Corporate Account Executive (Hospitality)
Responsible for the development of and service of corporate (business and industry) business coming into the hotel.

Corporate Recruiter
Recruits corporate-level staff for the organization. Works in conjunction with the policies and standards approved by the Employment Manager.

Corporate Travel Manager
Sets up travel budget, establishing policies for employees to follow; acts as a liaison with an outside travel agency that actually handles the arrangements; also involves personnel relocation as well as meetings and convention planning. May administer corporate aircraft, transportation to training programs, the car pool, and possibly group recreational trips or vacations for employees; may also negotiate discounts with travel suppliers.

Court Reporter
Makes accurate records of what is said during proceedings of all types. Memorizes and then reproduces the appropriate symbols that are involved in shorthand and machine reporting. All types of recordings, manual, machine, and tape, are transcribed accurately and typed in the required format.

Creative Director
Develops basic presentation approaches and directs layout design and copywriting for promotional material. Reviews materials and information presented by client and discusses various production factors to determine most desirable presentation concept. Confers with heads of art, copywriting, and production departments to discuss client requirements and scheduling, outlines basic presentation concepts, and coordinates creative activities.

Credit Manager
Responsible for the collection of accounts deemed to be delinquent and for determining when the accounts should be referred to an outside agency for further collection efforts. Generates reports on a daily and monthly basis. Posts cash on a daily basis.

Cruise Director
Supervises all activity on board the cruiseline. Responsible for overall safety and service of passengers. Oversees staff on board.

Customer Service Agent (Travel)
Arranges for car rental on-site at rental company by phone with travel agent or in person with individual customer. Processes contracts and arranges billing upon return of the rental vehicle.

Customer Service Manager (Retail)
Responsibilities include making certain that shipments take place as scheduled. Acts as a liaison between customers and the sales force. Spends most of the time on administrative duties, including reviewing performance standards. Also trains personnel.

Customer Service Representative
Responds to customer inquiries and performs a variety of duties related to customer service. Works with customers to offer alternatives to unresolvable problems. Receives, researches, and answers customer inquiries and requests regarding accounts, products, rates, and services. Develops and maintains company's image and corporate philosophy in the community.

Customer Service Representative (Airlines)
Duties include booking onward flight reservations, securing hotel and car rental reservations, and ticketing passengers in flight.

Customer Service Representative (Retail)
Resolves customer complaints and requests for refunds, exchanges, and adjustments. Provides customers with catalogs and information concerning prices, shipping time, and costs. Approves customers' checks and provides check-cashing service according to exchange policy. Issues temporary charges. Keeps records of items in layaway, receives and posts customer payments, and prepares and forwards delinquent notices.

Customs Inspector
Inspects baggage, articles worn or carried by persons, and vessels, vehicles, or aircraft entering or leaving the United States to enforce customs and related laws.

Data Entry Operator
Operates keyboard machine to transcribe data onto magnetic tape for computer input. Examines codes on forms and source documents to determine work procedures.

Data Entry Supervisor
Accountable for quality, productivity, cost effectiveness, and timeliness of work to ensure efficient and effective conversion and verification of data into computer readable forms. Directs distribution of work; prioritizes allocation of resources to meet schedules. Sets performance standards and reviews policies for data entry personnel.

Dean
Develops academic policies and programs for college or university. Directs and coordinates activities of academic department heads within the college. Participates in activities of faculty committees and in the development of academic

budgets. Serves as a liaison with accrediting agencies that evaluate academic programs.

Demographer
Plans and conducts demographic research and surveys to study the population of a given area and affecting trends.

Dental Assistant
Helps dentist during the examination and treatment of patients. Sets up and maintains instruments, arranges appointments, and keeps records of patients.

Dental Hygienist
Licensed to clean teeth under the supervision of a dentist. Instructs patients in dental care, diet, and nutrition for proper mouth care.

Dentist
Helps patients take care of their teeth and gums, either to correct dental problems or to advise patients on ways to prevent future cavities and gum problems.

Department Manager (Office)
Directs and coordinates departmental activities and functions utilizing knowledge of department functions and company policies, standards, and practices. Gives work directions, resolves problems, prepares work schedules, and sets deadlines to ensure completion of operational functions. Evaluates procedures and makes recommendations for improvements. Assigns or delegates responsibility for specific work.

Department Manager (Retail)
Supervises and coordinates activities of personnel in one department of a retail store. Assigns duties to workers and schedules lunch, breaks, work hours, and vacations. Trains staff in store policies, department procedures, and job duties. Evaluates staff. Handles customer complaints. Ensures that merchandise is correctly priced and displayed. Prepares sales and inventory reports. Plans department layout. Approves checks for payment and issues credit and cash refunds.

Deputy Commissioner of Tourism Development
Establishes goals, policies, and procedures of tourism development for a given area.

Design Assistant
Researches colors by contacting color forecasting services. Visits color forecasters to see

presentations. Finds new garments on the market and in stores. Contacts fabric salespeople by phone for fabric samples. Keeps records, does patterns, and keeps design room organized.

Design Technician
Tests and assists in the design of all kinds of electronics equipment developed by Electronics-Design Engineers. Performs the work of an electronics technician. (See *Electronics Technician*)

Designer (Drafting)
Makes design drawings to assist in developing experimental ideas evolved by research engineers, using specifications and sketches, and employing knowledge of engineering theory and its applications to solve mechanical and fabrication problems.

Destination Promoter
Sells meeting and convention planners, tour operators, and wholesalers on the idea of choosing a destination for their program. Services individual travelers with information and products that will make their business or pleasure trips more satisfying.

Dining Room Captain
Under the general supervision of the dining room manager, dining room captains are in charge of one section of the dining room. They instruct, supervise, and give help to the staff working their area when needed. Dining room captains watch all the tables under their jurisdiction to detect any dissatisfaction and may make adjustments in response to complaints.

Dining Room Manager
Supervises all dining room staff and activities, including staff training, scheduling of staff working hours, keeping time records, and assigning workstations. Should be capable of working in a formal public atmosphere.

Director of Escort Services
Responsible for the hiring, training, and assignment of tour escorts. Trains the escorts in the areas for which they will be responsible.

Director of Human Resources
Oversees the day-to-day activities of the human resources staff. Ensures that staff complies with policies set and approved by the Vice President of Human Resources and senior management. (See *Vice President of Human Resources*)

Director of Marketing and Sales
Supervises sales department. Coordinates sales and marketing departments to develop and implement an effective marketing effort. Responsible for increasing sales volume through direct sales efforts and by assisting sales reps in the field. Coordinates future market growth plans with regard to products, services, and markets. May plan and implement advertising and promotion activities.

Director of Marketing/Sales (Cruiselines)
Develops pricing strategies for packages sold to groups and individuals. Establishes advertising and promotion programs. Reviews competition's strategies for attracting clients and implements competitive strategies.

Director of Marketing and Advertising (Food Service)
Plans and carries out advertising and promotional programs. Works with company's top-level management to prepare an overall marketing plan. Arranges with various suppliers regarding schedule and cost of brochures, menus, advertisements, etc., being promoted. Responsible for the advertising budget.

Director of Media Advertising
Defines corporate media objectives. Provides media information and advice to the company. Measures media costs against industry standards. Searches for new, creative ways to use media. Recommends controls, quality, and cost of media purchases.

Director of Public Relations
Plans, directs, and conducts public relations program designed to create and maintain a public informed of employer's programs, accomplishments, and point of view.

Director of Public Safety
Responsible for the safety of the people and equipment in a city, town, or state.

Director of Recipe Development
Creates new recipes for the menus of larger restaurants or restaurant chains. Requires thorough knowledge of food preparation and the ability to apply this knowledge creatively.

Director of Research and Development
Directs and coordinates activities concerned with research and development of new concepts, ideas,

basic data on, and applications for organization's products, services, or ideologies. Reviews and analyzes proposals submitted to determine if benefits derived and possible applications justify expenditures. Develops and implements methods and procedures for monitoring projects. May negotiate contracts with consulting firms to perform research studies.

Director of Sales and Marketing
(See *Director of Marketing and Sales*)

Director of Tour Guides
Responsible for the hiring, training, and assignment of tour guides.

Director of Training
Oversees training function for an entire company at all locations. Responsible for approval of recommended programs and proposed budgets. (See *Training Manager*)

Director of Transportation
Responsible for getting convention goers from their hotels to and from the center; trafficking trucks in and out of the building; working with the city to make sure street lights are working; dealing with city's Taxi and Limousine Commission to ensure there are adequate services for the center.

Display Coordinator
Designs and implements the window decorations and interior displays that are so important in promoting sales. Must work well within limitations of time, space, and money.

Display Director
Supervises the display of merchandise in windows, in showcases, and on the sales floor of retail stores. Schedules plans for displays and ensures staff follows store plan. Often responsible for several stores within a designated division.

Distribution Manager (Retail)
Oversees the routing of merchandise from one branch store to another on the basis of sales. Analyzes reports of stock on hand and kind and amount sold.

District Manager
Manages personnel for an assigned district, ensuring the development and accomplishment of established objectives. Trains, develops, and motivates staff. Recruits new hires. Maintains good business relationships with customers through periodic contacts and proper handling of administrative functions.

District Manager (Food Service)
Supervises smaller facilities in certain areas. Purchasing, negotiation, and supervision of area personnel are main responsibilities.

District Sales Manager
Actually carries out "cold calls," maintains reporting forms and proper business files, holds periodic meetings with sales staff.

District Sales Manager (Travel)
Administers city ticket and reservations offices and promotes and develops airline passenger and cargo traffic in the district.

Divisional Manager (Banking)
Responsible for the activities of a related group of departments in a bank, such as all departments involved with customer service versus operations or systems.

Divisional Manager (Retail)
Retail executive responsible for the activities of a related group of selling departments or divisions.

Doctor (Medical)
Examines patients, orders or executes various tests and X rays to provide information on patient's condition. Analyzes reports and findings of tests and of examinations and diagnoses condition. Recommends treatment.

Documentation Specialist
Makes computer technology accessible to people who have no computer background. Translates the technology into plain, comprehensive English. Writes promotional brochures and advertising copy.

Drafter
Develops detailed design drawings and related specifications of mechanical equipment according to engineering sketches and design-proposal specifications. Often calculates the strength, quality, quantity, and cost of materials. Usually specializes in a particular field of work such as mechanical, electrical, electronic, aeronautical, structural, or architectural drafting.

Drafter (Computer Assisted—CADD)
Drafts layouts, drawings, and designs for applications in such fields as aeronautics,

architecture, or electronics, according to engineering specifications, using the computer. Locates file relating to projection database library and loads program into computer. Retrieves information from file and displays information on cathode ray tube (CRT) screen using required computer languages. Displays final drawing on screen to verify completeness, after typing in commands to rotate or zoom in on display to redesign, modify, or otherwise edit existing design. Types command to transfer drawing dimensions from computer onto hard copy.

Economic Development Coordinator
Directs economic development planning activities for city, state, or region. Negotiates with industry representatives to encourage location in an area. Directs activities, such as research, analysis, and evaluation of technical information to determine feasibility and economic impact of proposed expansions and developments.

Editor
Reads the manuscripts and rough drafts of authors and other writers that are to be published in a magazine, book, or newspaper. Corrects grammatical errors and makes suggestions for improving readability and consistency of style.

Editor (Word Processing)
Helps design the overall package and rough out the information to be contained on each page of a videotex display. Once the information is set up, the page creator takes over.

EDP Auditor
Monitors computer functions of the entire company and operational procedures and reports findings back to top management with recommendations for improvements. EDP Auditors make specific recommendations for improved accuracy, procedures, and security.

Education Consultant
Develops programs for in-service education of teaching personnel. Reviews and evaluates curricula used in schools and assists in adaptation to local needs. Prepares or approves manuals, guidelines, and reports on educational policies. Conducts research into areas such as teaching methods and strategies.

Educator/Administrator (Food Service)
Designs and teaches courses tailored to students of food service, such as sanitation, food service

management, and nutrition. Develops curriculum and hires staff. Works with designated budget to purchase equipment and materials needed to operate the school. Seeks support from industry with instruction and funding.

Electronics Engineer
Works on research and development, production, and quality control problems. The electronics engineer is highly specialized and may work in a specific area such as the design and implementation of solid-state circuitry in radar, computers, or calculators.

Electronics Technician
Repairs and maintains machines and equipment used in processing and assembly of electronic components. Starts equipment or machine. Reads blueprints and schematic drawings to determine repair procedures. Dismantles machine. Removes and sets aside defective units for repair or replacement. Starts repaired or newly installed machines and verifies readiness for operation.

Employment Agency Owner
Manages employment services and business operations of private employment agency. Directs hiring, training, and evaluation of employees. Analyzes placement reports to determine effectiveness of employment interviewers. Investigates and resolves customer complaints.

Employment Counselor (Word Processing)
Screens and places word processing professionals in available jobs.

Employment Interviewer
(See *Interviewer*)

Employment Manager
Oversees the recruiting function. This includes soliciting qualified applicants through various sources including advertising and college recruiting. Oversees screening, interviewing, and selection procedures. Responsible for overseeing the hiring of all personnel.

Employment Recruiter
Matches job seekers with job openings that employers have listed with placement firms, employment agencies, or governmental employment offices.

Engineer
Applies the theories and principles of science and mathematics to practical technical problems.

Designs and develops consumer products. Determines the general way the device will work, designs and tests all components, and fits them together in an integrated plan. Evaluates overall effectiveness of the new device, as well as its cost and reliability.

Engineering Technician
Develops and tests machinery and equipment, applying knowledge of mechanical engineering technology, under direction of engineering and scientific staff.

Equal Employment Opportunity Coordinator
Monitors and enforces governmental regulations concerning equal employment practices in all levels of the organization. Maintains required records to verify adherence to approved affirmative action plan.

Executive Administrator (Education)
Makes projections for future needs; oversees curriculum and policy decisions. Hires and supervises personnel; prepares school budget. Works with local groups to ensure the best interest of the community is being met.

Executive Chef
Coordinates activities of and directs indoctrination and training of chefs, cooks, and other kitchen personnel engaged in preparing and cooking food. Plans menus and utilization of food surpluses and leftovers, taking into account probable number of guests, marketing conditions, population, and purchases or requisitions foodstuffs and kitchen supplies. Reviews menus, analyzes recipes, determines food, labor, and overhead costs, and assigns prices to the menu items. Observes methods of food preparation and cooking, sizes of portions, and garnishing of foods to ensure food is prepared in prescribed manner. Develops exclusive recipes and varied menus.

Executive Director
Develops and coordinates an administrative organization plan and staff to carry out the plan. Delegates authority and responsibility for the execution of the organization's many departments and functions. Establishes operating policies and procedures; standards of service and performance. Involved with fund raising. Serves on various civic committees.

Executive/Administrator (Telemarketing)
Directs the planning and operations of telemarketing function. Sets goals and objectives for telemarketing programs and establishes budgets as well as sales goals. Guides development of telemarketing programs and evaluates available systems applications.

Executive Assistant
Member of the management team that is responsible for overseeing the overall administrative functions of an office. Ensures productivity of office staff. Makes recommendations for improved systems. Supervises staff. Handles special projects and confidential materials. Assists executive. Represents the company at professional and community events on a regular basis. Often acts as a spokesperson for the executive.

Executive Director, Associations
Directs and coordinates activities of professional or trade associations in accordance with established policies to further achievement of goals, objectives, and standards of the profession or association. Directs or participates in the preparation of educational and informative materials for presentation to membership or public in newsletters, magazines, news releases, or on radio or television.

Executive Director, Chamber of Commerce
Directs activities to promote business, industrial, and job development, and civic improvements in the community. Administers programs of departments and committees which perform such functions as providing members with economic and marketing information, promoting economic growth and stability in the community, and counseling business organizations and industry on problems affecting local economy. Coordinates work with that of other community agencies to provide public services. Prepares and submits annual budgets to elected officials for approval. Studies governmental legislation, taxation, and other fiscal matters to determine effect on community interests, and makes recommendations based on organizational policy.

Executive Director, Convention Bureau
Directs activities of convention bureau to promote convention business in the area. Administers

promotional programs. Coordinates efforts with local hotels, restaurants, transportation companies, exhibit centers, and other related facilities. Works within specified budgets. Serves on various civic and community boards to enhance the position of the bureau.

Executive Director, Department of Economic Development
Directs activities of the department. Ensures that demographic and economic information is maintained. Decides on research projects to be conducted. Directs publications prepared for public information. Works in conjunction with local and national agencies.

Executive Housekeeper
Supervises housekeeping staff. May hire and train new employees. Orders supplies, takes inventories and keeps records, prepares budgets, sees to needed repairs, draws up work schedules, inspects rooms. May be in charge of interior decoration.

Executive Secretary
Schedules meetings, takes minutes at meetings, and then transcribes and types them; composes letters; evaluates priority of incoming mail and telephone calls. Organizes and executes special projects and reports. May prepare budget reports. Works with a minimum of supervision; initiates much of own work according to office priorities.

Expeditor
Ensures that merchandise and supplies that have been ordered are received when and where needed.

Facilities Designer
Plans and designs utilization of space and facilities for hotels, food service operations, and other related properties. Draws design layout, showing location of equipment, furniture, work spaces, doorways, electrical outlets, and other related facilities. May review real estate contracts for compliance with regulations and suitability for occupancy. Suggests decor that is both practical and attractive to suit the purpose of the facility as well as maximize client business.

Fashion Coordinator
Offers advice to the buying staff in large department stores on changing tastes, trends, and styles. Works with buying staff to be sure that the store's merchandise is completely up-to-date.

Fashion Designer
Creative specialist responsible for designing coats, suits, dresses, as well as other lines of apparel. Adapts higher-priced merchandise to meet the price range of the customers.

Fashion Display Specialist
Responsible for designing display windows and display units within department or clothing stores. May have supervisory responsibilities as a coordinator for chain of stores.

Fashion Writer
Writes articles on the subject of fashion. Writes press releases and complete public relations projects. Writes about projected fashion trends, designers, new store openings. Writes newsletters for stores and buying offices. Covers fashion shows and does research.

Finance Manager
Directs activities of workers engaged in performing such financial functions as accounting and recording financial transactions. Establishes procedures for control of assets, records, loan collateral, and securities.

Financial Analyst
Performs the quantitative analysis required for strategic planning and investments. Evaluates the financing and refinancing of certain projects and lines of credit. Prepares various reports for management. Collects data for financial comparisons with similar companies and securities.

Flight Attendant
Directly responsible for making passengers' flight comfortable, enjoyable, and safe. Ensures cabin is in order and that supplies and equipment are on board. Greets passengers as they board the plane. Helps passengers with carry-on luggage and with finding their seats. Instructs passengers before take-off in the location and proper usage of oxygen masks and other emergency equipment and exits. Serves meals and beverages.

Food and Beverage Manager
Responsible for compiling statistics of food and liquor costs, sales, and profits and losses. May

also develop the procedures of portion control and item usage. May inventory bars as needed and prepare daily consumption reports that are forwarded to the auditing office. Takes inventory of foodstuffs with the chef, and works closely with the chef on matters of buying and producing.

Food Director (Recreation)
Responsible for all food service areas at a particular theme park, amusement park, arcade, or other type of recreational facility. Supervises the procurement and preparation of food and drinks for concession stands, snack bars and dining halls, and rooms. Hires and trains staff. Maintains control of food costs and inventories. Deals directly with suppliers in ordering and paying for all food products. Enforces sanitation policies and health department codes throughout all food service facilities.

Food Production Manager
Responsible for all food preparation and supervision of kitchen staff. Workers must possess leadership skills and have knowledge of food preparation techniques, quality, and sanitation standards and cost control methods.

Food Service Consultant
Advises clients on site selection for food service operation, menu design and selection, interior decor, equipment, and overall design and layout of dining facility. Advises owner/operator of expected food and beverage costs, and helps to develop effective pricing strategy for all menu items.

Food Service Director
Exercises general supervision over all production areas in one or more kitchens. Also responsible for all the service that may be needed on counters and in the dining rooms. Responsible for the buying of food, its storage, its preparation, and the service necessary to handle large groups.

Food Service Engineer
Analyzes and creates efficient and cost-effective production processes, designs manufacturing equipment, or operates a plant's physical systems.

Food Service Manager
Responsible for the operation's accounts and records and compliance with all laws and regulations, especially those concerning licensing, health, and sanitation.

Food Service Salesperson
Tells customers how a given item performs against the competition, how it will benefit the buyer, and ultimately, how it can increase profits and encourage repeat business. Demonstrates new products, gives customers actual product samplings, advises on menu ideas and serving suggestions, and even helps work out portion costs.

Freelancer (Travel)
Submits articles to travel editor for publication. Works independently. Initiates own stories and also writes specific articles or stories for publications upon request.

Freelancer (Visual Merchandising)
Initiates own designs and plans and offers services to Designers and Display Directors.

Freelance Reporter (Court Reporting)
Reporters who are in business for themselves. Develop their own contracts, follow up on recommendations of those for whom they may already have worked, and generally initiate their own assignments.

Front Desk Clerk
Responsible for direct personal contact with the guests, handling reservations, special needs, check in and check out. Familiarizes guests with a facility as well as the surrounding area. Prepares status reports on available rooms for manager. Receives guests' complaints and makes appropriate decisions about how to resolve them.

Front Desk Supervisor (Hospitality)
Directs the front desk operations in the hotel. Oversees those responsible for guests' reservations, special needs, checkin, and check-out. Reviews status reports on available rooms. Ensures that guests' complaints are handled promptly and properly.

Front Office Manager (Hospitality)
(Refer to General Index of Job Descriptions)

Garde Manger (Cold Cook)
Prepares and works with all cold meat, fish, and poultry dishes. Prepares appetizers and hors d'oeuvres such as canapes. Makes all salad dressings and mayonnaise according to recipe. Works with leftover foods to make appetizing dishes. Prepares and serves pâté maison. Makes ice and vegetable carvings.

General Accountant

Handles daily business needs, such as payroll, budgeting, accounts receivable, accounts payable, general ledger, and financial statements. Must pay close attention to all laws and regulations affecting daily business operations. They are involved in sending out all payments, royalties, dividends, rents, and other necessary expenditures.

General Manager (Food Service)

Acts as overseer to all phases of a particular group, working with the management team to plan future accounts and solve day-to-day problems.

General Manager (Hospitality)

Establishes standards for personnel administration and performance, service to patrons, room rates, advertising, publicity, credit, food selection and service, and type of patronage to be solicited. Plans dining room, bar, and banquet operations. Allocates funds, authorizes expenditures, and assists in planning budgets for departments.

Group Manager (Retail)

Supervises many departments within a retail operation.

Group Sales Manager

Concentrates on managing group sales efforts, including planning and forecasting sales and supervising sales staff. Identifies target markets and assigns specific groups to specific sales personnel. Devises and implements promotions and training programs.

Group Sales Representative (Travel)

Promotes sale of group season tickets for sports or other entertainment events. Telephones, visits, or writes to organizations, such as chambers of commerce, corporate employee recreation clubs, social clubs, and professional groups, to persuade them to purchase group tickets or season tickets to sports or other entertainment events, such as baseball, horseracing, or stage plays. Quotes group ticket rates, arranges for sale of tickets and seating for groups on specific dates, and obtains payment. May arrange for club to sponsor sports event, such as one of the races at horseracing track.

Guest Services Agent (Hospitality)

Works as a liaison between hotel guests and party providing desired services. Informs guests on services available to them in the hotel facility and assists them with making the proper connections. Concerned with any requests that guests may have and with providing answers to questions that concern guests.

Head Bartender

In charge of the entire bar. Responsible for stocking and dispensing. Responsible for hiring and firing. Must know how to mix all drinks served in the bar. Establishes drink formulas and sets up portion controls for each drink. Coordinates inventory, requisitioning, and stocking needed items, proper accounting, and receipt of proper payment for bar items.

Head Cashier (Hospitality)

Oversees the duties of the hotel's cashiers, which include receiving guests' payments when checking out of the hotel. Approves the cashing of guests' checks and the processing of certain loans. Responsible for security of the safe deposit box.

Head Waitperson

Supervises and coordinates the activities of dining room employees engaged in providing courteous and rapid service to the diners. Greets the guests and escorts them to tables. Schedules dining reservations. Arranges parties for patrons. Adjusts any complaints regarding the food or service. Hires and trains the dining room employees. Notifies the payroll department regarding work schedules and time records. May assist in preparing menus. May plan and execute the details of a banquet.

Health Club Director (Cruiselines)

Oversees uses of the health club on cruiseline. Ensures passenger understanding of use of the equipment and exercise available. Ensures safety and cleanliness of equipment. Supervises staff and approves recommended programs.

Health Technician (Electronics)

Performs the work of an electronics technician, specifically on various types of health equipment. (See *Electronics Technician*)

Hearing Reporter

Follows up and records all that is said during various types of proceedings, whether they be court trials or informal meetings. Hearings are presided over by a commissioner and there is no jury. Hearings may be conducted by various governmental agencies and departments with differing functions and responsibilities.

Home Economics Teacher
Teaches everything from balancing menus to
hygiene to food journalism.

Hostperson
Supervises and coordinates the activities of the
dining room personnel to provide fast and
courteous service to the patrons. Schedules dining
reservations and arranges parties or special
services for the diners. Greets the guests, escorts
them to tables, and provides their menus. Adjusts
complaints of the patrons.

Housekeeper
Ensures clean, orderly, attractive rooms in the
hotel or related facility. Inventories stock to ensure
adequate supplies. Issues supplies and equipment
to workers. May record data and prepare reports
concerning room occupancy, payroll expenses,
and department expenses.

Incentive Travel Specialist
Travel specialists responsible for developing
special packages for trips that have been won as a
prize or premium.

Information Broker (Word Processing)
Responsible for formulating specifications on the
basis of which information is pulled from the
database and then relayed to the client company.

Information Coordinator (Travel)
Coordinates organization and communication of
travel information as needed. Responsible for
providing accurate information to telephone
inquirers and visitors about a destination,
attraction, activity, or program. Participates in and
conducts surveys.

Information Manager
Involves specializing in database management.
Besides having a general knowledge of how organizations work and how information flows through
them, knowledge of how to set up and improve information systems is important. Knowledge of
library referencing and indexing systems is applied.
Helps a technical expert set up an electronic filing
system or corporate database. Sorts and updates
database files, advises how to design the automated
office system that would best fit with the organization's style, workflow, and procedures.

Information Packager
Edits word processing systems and their software,
applies working knowledge of word processing

and text, and finds imaginative opportunities in
which to further apply that knowledge and those
related skills.

Information Specialist (Hospitality)
Provides specific information on area attractions and
services to guests staying at the hotel. May work in
conjunction with the Concierge in providing guests
with information on restaurants, shopping areas,
museums, historical sites, theater, and local entertainment. Is well informed on the history of the area
and information available at the area's Chamber of
Commerce and Visitor and Convention Bureau.

Information Specialist (Paralegal)
Consolidates legal information after research for
easy accessibility. Lists resources for future
research by subject and sets up reference library
to maintain information in sequential order.
Advises users on how to extract the information
they need quickly and efficiently.

Informer
Person assigned by an organization as the contact
person for the press or other media for obtaining
desired information on an as-needed basis.

Inspector
Supervises cleaning staff and inspects hotel
guest rooms, corridors, and lobbies. Assigns
work to cleaning staff and trains personnel in
housekeeping duties. Posts room occupancy
records. Adjusts guests' complaints regarding
housekeeping service or equipment. Writes
requisitions for room supplies and furniture
renovation or replacements.

Instructor (Education)
Instructs students in commercial subjects (typing,
accounting, computer systems), communications
courses (reading and writing), and personality development in business schools, community colleges,
or training programs. Instructs students in subject
matter, utilizing various methods, such as lecture
and demonstration, and uses audiovisual aids and
other materials to supplement presentation.
Prepares or follows teaching outline. Administers
tests. Maintains discipline.

Insurance Agent
(See *Agent, Insurance*)

Internal Auditor
Conducts independent appraisal from within the
organization by analyzing, criticizing, and

recommending improvements to internal financial practices. Ensures the safety and profitability of investments and assets, and seeks to uncover sources of waste and inefficiency.

International Account Executive (Hospitality)
Responsible for the development of and service of international client business coming into the hotel. May also be responsible for referring clientele to international properties in other countries. May assist with providing information to client on the foreign country, its currency, passport and customs regulations, and overall familiarization with the area.

International Group Secretary
Provides secretarial support for a team headed by an account executive. Duties include transcribing letters and memos from dictaphone tapes and typing comprehensive multicountry proposals for clients; preparation of travel arrangements, and assisting with clients, brokers, and foreign visitors.

Interpreter
Translates spoken word from one language to another. Provides consecutive or simultaneous translation between languages. Usually receives briefing on subject area prior to interpreting session.

Interviewer
Interviews job applicants to select persons meeting employers' qualifications. Searches files of job orders from employers and matches applicants' qualifications with job requirements and employer specifications.

Inventory Control Manager
Ensures that all stock units are in adequate supply, both components and finished goods. Responsible for overall quality of the product. Maximizes customer service levels, inventory investment, and manufacturing efficiencies.

Inventory Coordinator
Prepares reports of inventory balance, prices, and shortages. Compiles information on receipt or disbursement of goods and computes inventory balance, price, and costs. Verifies clerical computations against physical count of stock and adjusts errors in computation or count. Investigates and reports reasons for discrepancies.

Inventory Manager
Supervises compilation of records of amount, kind, and value of merchandise, material, or stock on hand in establishment or department of establishment. Compares inventories taken by workers with office records or computer figures from sales, equipment shipping, production, purchase, or stock records to obtain current theoretical inventory. Prepares inventory reports. Makes planning decisions.

Investment Banker
Analyzes the needs of clients and makes recommendations to them on the best way to obtain the money they need. Obtains permission from each of the state governments to sell the issue in their state.

Job Analyst
Reviews all job functions within the company to continuously maintain updated details on job requirements, specific functions, and qualifications needed.

Junior Accountant
(See *Accountant*)

Junior Account Executive (Telemarketing)
(See *Account Executive—Telemarketing*)

Junior Analyst (Marketing)
(See *Market Research Analyst*)

Junior Buyer (Retail)
Performs duties of buyer trainee and also becomes involved in deciding on products for purchase and evaluating the store's needs. Learns to study the competition on a regular basis so as to evaluate and predict decisions.

Junior Consultant
(See *Consultant*)

Junior Copywriter
Studies clients from printed materials and past correspondence. May answer phone, type, file, or draft simple correspondence. May write some descriptive copy and come up with concepts for new ad campaigns. Works with the art department on presentations.

Junior Drafter
Copies plans and drawings prepared by drafters by tracing them with ink and pencil on transparent paper or cloth spread over drawings, using triangles, T-square, compass, pens, or other drafting instruments. Makes simple sketches or drawings under close supervision.

Keypunch Operator
Operates alphabetic and numeric keypunch machine, similar in operation to electric typewriter, to transcribe data from source material onto magnetic tape and to record accounting or statistical data for subsequent processing by automatic or electronic data processing equipment.

Kitchen Manager
Supervises all the production personnel in the kitchen area. Oversees the buying, storing, and preparation of all food. Takes inventory and reorders when necessary. Usually employed in operations where chefs are not employed.

Labor Relations Specialist
Responsible for being fully knowledgeable of current contracts or established policies affecting the working environment of all personnel including such areas as hiring requirements, pay policies, performance standards, leave of absence authorizations, and disciplinary procedures. When dealing with bargaining units, negotiates contracts as needed.

Law Library Manager
Manages the ordering and organizing of all materials to be housed in the law library. Responsible for keeping up-to-date on changes in the law and for obtaining new literature describing most current laws. Supervises staff. Trains staff and library users on how to use the library. Oversees telephone information service.

Law Office Administrator
Designs, develops, and plans new procedures, techniques, services, processes, and applications in the office; plans, supervises, and assists in the installation and maintenance of relatively complex office equipment; plans production, operations of service for the efficient use of manpower, materials, money, and equipment in the office.

Lawyer
Conducts civil and criminal law suits; draws up legal documents, advises clients as to legal rights, and practices other phases of the law.

Lead Agent (Travel)
A car rental agent responsible for answering customers' questions.

Lead Analyst
Assists higher level personnel in analytical studies of complex and important problems involving existing and proposed systems and their costs. Develops, examines, and implements reporting systems and procedures which provide significant contributions in terms of time saved and increased efficiency or reduced costs.

Lead Programmer
Provides specialized advice on programming languages and documentation. Maintains up-to-date knowledge of all programming language. Makes provisions for the orderly processing of changes, updatings, and modifications of programs. Coordinates all company programming efforts.

Lead Word Processing Operator
Coordinates work priorities and assigns work to word processors. May train and supervise word processors. Ensures quality of work output.

Legal Assistant
Oversees the work of other paralegals in a firm. Delegates work, handles personnel-related problems, writes appraisals of other paralegals, and supervises the hiring of paralegals when needed. Works on special projects.

Legal Secretary
Schedules appointments, court appearances; prepares documents, billing, bookkeeping, and recordkeeping. Handles subpoenas, mortgages, deeds, closings, pleadings, briefs, wills, proxies, and abstracts. May also review law journals and assist in other ways with legal research.

Legal Technician
Initiates and composes standardized legal forms routinely as needed for specific legal actions. Accepts service of legal documents, reviews for correct form and timeliness, annotates case files and status records to reflect receipt and due dates for responses. Establishes, maintains, and closes out case files or systems of legal records. Maintains tickler system, coordinates schedules with court clerks, notifies witnesses of appearances, and reminds attorneys of court appearance and deadlines for submitting various actions or documents.

Legislative Reporter
Records events, speeches, and debates that take place in the different state legislatures. Attends and reports committee meetings.

Line Cook
Responsible for any duties necessary in order to prepare and produce menu items efficiently.

Duties may include cutting and portioning, cooking, and serving items.

Litigation Paralegal
Organizes and manages documents for civil or criminal trials. Organizes and prepares pleadings, case outlines, manuals for complex litigation, discovery requests, and index documents; operates computers, and drafts pretrial and posttrial memoranda.

Loan Manager
Supervises loan personnel and approves recommendations of customer applications for lines of credit when loan officer is not able to do so. Communicates changes in policies and regulations regularly to loan personnel and customers.

Loan Officer
Interviews applicants applying for loans. Prepares loan request paper, obtains related documents from applicants. Investigates applicants' background and verifies credit and bank references. Informs applicants whether loan requests have been approved or rejected. Processes the loans.

Mail and Information Coordinator
Coordinates the information and mail services, usually at the front desk. Responsible for ensuring that outgoing and incoming mail for the facility as well as for guests is properly routed. Advises guests on most efficient procedures for receiving or sending important mail. Ensures that messages get to hotel personnel and guests on a timely and accurate basis. May also provide guests with general information about the facility and the area.

Maître d' Hôtel
In charge of the dining room in a hotel or restaurant. Supervises a team of captains, waitpersons, and junior waitpersons.

Manager (Accounting)
Organizes and directs all general accounting activities. Maintains accounting systems that ensure the proper accounting and recording of company resources; provides financial statements, analysis, and other key management reports.

Manager (Banking)
(See Bank Manager)

Manager of Programming
Trains operations staff, programmers, and systems analysts in the use of new computer equipment and software. Develops programming and systems as required, specifically in critical areas. Develops documentation standards. Anticipates and foresees future requirements for user departments.

Manager (Recreation)
Manages recreation facilities, such as tennis courts, golf courses, or arcade, and coordinates activities of workers engaged in providing services of the facility. Determines work activities necessary to operate facility, hires workers, and assigns tasks and work hours accordingly. Initiates promotion to acquaint public with activities of the facility. Maintains financial records.

Manager of Systems Analysis
Evaluates advances in computer equipment and software capabilities in light of the company's future system requirements. Coordinates the formulation of short- and long-range technical systems development plans, with special emphasis on technical feasibility. Organizes, schedules, and conducts training programs for data processing personnel and users of computer services.

Manager of Tour Operations
Supervises support functions related to the execution of a successful tour. Areas of responsibility include the bookkeeping, secretarial, telex, and computer operations areas.

Manager Trainee
Performs assigned duties, under direction of experienced personnel, to gain knowledge and experience needed for management position. Receives training and performs duties in various departments to become familiar with personnel functions and operations and management viewpoints and policies that affect each phase of the business.

Manager Trainee (Finance)
Works with financial manager while gaining an overall exposure to all aspects of the finance function of the company. Assists with budgets, purchase options, and expenses. Helps review financial reports for different product lines and assists with consolidating financial data for updated reports. May interview other department heads, customers, vendors, and other key people dealing with the finance area.

Manager Trainee (Food Service)
Assists with all functions of the area assigned. Learns the overview of the entire operation before

specializing. If in a large operation, may rotate within one area of the facility, such as the production or purchasing area, to learn all of its functions if that is the area of specialty. Usually trains by rotating among various stations in the kitchen itself and among related areas such as purchasing, the storeroom, front of the house, etc.

Manager Trainee (Retail)
Works with store manager organizing and managing the store on a daily basis. Spends time on the selling floor, learning customer service techniques and computerized systems. Assists with managing, merchandising, and analyzing stock. Directs and physically puts stock out on the floor and presents merchandise. May work with buyer learning financial planning, vendor negotiations, and branch store communications.

Manufacturing Manager
Coordinates all manufacturing operations to produce products of high quality and reliability at optimum cost and in accordance with customer shipping schedules. Participates in the preparation of the manufacturing budget. Ensures safety of employees in their exposure to varied manufacturing process hazards. Resolves various manufacturing and production problems.

Market Manager (Food Service)
Responsible for compiling information on the age, sex, and income level of restaurants' potential clientele and their dining habits and preferences. Marketing managers consider customer preferences in order to suggest appropriate sales advertising techniques. This information provides the basis for success/failure projections in certain demographic areas.

Market Research Analyst
Researches market conditions in local, regional, or national area to determine potential sales of product or service. Examines and analyzes statistical data to forecast future marketing trends. Gathers data on competitors and analyzes prices, sales, and methods of marketing and distribution. Formulates surveys, opinion polls, or questionnaires.

Market Research Director
Oversees market research for a company. Sets goals and objectives for projects. Sets timetables for completion and assigns personnel to projects. Keeps appropriate administrators informed on

findings and makes recommendations and proposes marketing strategies based on results.

Marketing Analyst (Paralegal)
Examines and analyzes statistical data to forecast future marketing trends in the paralegal field. (See **Market Research Analyst**)

Marketing Director
Directs and coordinates the development of marketing programs assigned to attain maximum penetration in the required market segments. Directs the creation, writing, and publishing of market and product plans. Explores development of product line offerings.

Marketing and Promotion Manager (Food Service)
Supervises any advertising or sales promotion for the operation. Works with food production staff to create menus and promotions with customer appeal. Often coordinates these activities with an advertising agency.

Marketing Representative (Paralegal)
Promotes and sells law-related books. Works in the marketing division of legal publishing companies.

Marketing Support Representative
Backs up the sales force by demonstrating the equipment and working with the customers after the equipment is installed; teaches the customers' word processing specialists to use the equipment and helps them find the best methods of doing the company's particular tasks.

Materials Manager
Studies receiving or shipping notices, requests for movement of raw materials and finished products, and reports of warehousing space available to develop schedules for material-handling activities. May confer with supervisors of other departments to coordinate flow of materials or products. Supervises activities of shipping and receiving personnel.

Media Director of Planning
Plans media relations in line with company goals. Reports and analyzes industry media trends. Communicates with product development to determine product market plans as they relate to media proposals and media scheduling. Oversees Media Planners.

Media Planner
Plans and administers media programs in advertising department. Confers with

representatives of advertising agencies, product managers, and corporate advertising staff to establish media goals, objectives, and strategies within corporate advertising budget. Studies demographic data and consumer profiles to identify target audiences of media advertising.

Medical Assistant
Works in hospitals or clinics cleaning and sterilizing equipment, performing various tests, and helping to maintain records.

Medical Claims Examiner
Claims examiner for the medical field. (See *Claims Examiner*)

Medical Claims Representative
Claims representative for the medical field. (See *Claims Representative*)

Medical Librarian
Records, arranges, and makes medical information available to people. Handles books, films, periodicals, documents, and other media related to the medical field.

Medical Records Administrator
Plans, develops, and administers medical record systems for hospital, clinic, health center, or similar facility to meet standards of accrediting and regulatory agencies. Assists medical staff in evaluating quality of patient care and in developing criteria and methods for such evaluation. Develops and implements policies and procedures for documentation, storing, and retrieving information and for processing medical/legal documents.

Medical Records Technician
Gathers all information on patient's condition and records it on permanent files that become the history and progress of treatment of a patient's illness or injury. Accumulates the results of a physician's examinations, information on laboratory tests, and electrocardiograms, and records these results in the records. Accuracy is particularly important because much of this information is referred to during malpractice cases, and it is also vital when processing insurance claims.

Medical Secretary
Processes many kinds of complex health insurance forms. Responsible for patient billing, records management, medical and office supply

organization, and appointments. Takes dictation and transcribes on dictaphone. Deals with medical supply vendors and pharmaceutical houses. Prepares correspondence and assists physicians with reports, speeches, articles, and conference proceedings.

Medical Technician (Electronics)
Performs the work of an electronics technician, specifically on various types of medical equipment. (See *Electronics Technician*)

Meeting Planner
Establishes objectives of the meeting, selects the site hotel and facilities, negotiates rates, sets budgets, makes air and hotel reservations, chooses speakers, plans food and beverages, arranges for all audio-visual equipment. Arranges meeting registration, exhibits, promotion and publicity scheduling, and room set-up, and arranges postmeeting evaluation. Planners are involved with negotiations that save the organization money.

Membership Coordinator
Solicits membership for club or trade association. Visits or contacts prospective members to explain benefits and costs of membership and to describe organization of club or association. May collect dues and payments for publications from members.

Membership Secretary
Compiles and maintains membership lists, records the receipt of dues and contributions, and gives out information to members of the organizations and associations. Sends out newsletters and other promotional materials on a regular basis. Answers telephone inquiries and coordinates mass mailings.

Menu Planner
Works with the Executive Chef to select all items offered on menus. Must know food service costs, preparation techniques and equipment, customer trends and preferences.

Merchandise Analyst
Evaluates available merchandise in different locations and identifies when transfers might be appropriate. Evaluates quality of merchandise from the vendors for price paid with the buyer.

Merchandise Manager
Takes charge of a group of departments, usually organized by merchandise. Coordinates and

oversees the efforts of the buyers. Develops merchandise plans, divides up the buyers' merchandise assignments, and reviews their selections. Visits the manufacturers' showrooms and travels abroad.

Merchandise Planner
Allocates merchandise from distribution point to stores as requested by buyers and merchandise managers. Ensures that merchandise is shipped properly and on a timely basis from the distribution center.

Merchandising Supervisor (Food Service)
Plans and carries out promotional programs to increase sales. Works with printers, artists, writers, and other suppliers. Must know employer's food service operations thoroughly and be able to apply market research techniques as well as budgeting and planning skills.

MIS Director
Recommends and initiates programs and/or systems which support the desired corporate profit objectives. Issues business data and management information that facilitate the businesses' planning and decision-making process at all levels. Responsible for total information service provided to user departments.

MIS Manager
Responsible for coordinating the short-term planning for MIS/EDP efforts in systems development and computer processing; for establishing guidelines for measurement of division activity to these plans; and for monitoring Division MIS/EDP performance to ensure that information is made available to all levels of management on a complete, reliable, economic, and timely basis.

MIS Specialist
Has specific knowledge of and provides service to a specialized area in the company. May concentrate on such areas as accounting, sales, production, or any other function requiring the services of the MIS department to meet its particular need.

MIS Supervisor
Ensures timely and accurate processing of incoming orders through the order preparation and data processing areas to assist in achieving a high level of customer service. Maintains external relationship with vendors of paper supplies and

forms, equipment manufacturers, equipment maintenance representatives, and leasing companies. Maintains contact with all company departments using the services of the MIS department.

National Sales Manager (Marketing)
Devises and implements sales strategies, forecasts sales, supervises in-house salespeople; establishes and attains sales goals; trains and develops sales personnel. Develops and implements marketing and advertising strategy.

Night Auditor
Brings all of the establishment's accounts up-to-date so that a day's revenue report can be made to upper management. (*In a hotel, a revenue report includes such items as a detailed account of room revenues, number of rooms occupied, average room revenue, percentage of occupancy figures, and the like.*) The night audit process is usually augmented by a computerized system. The night auditor often plays the role of the night manager.

Night Auditor (Hospitality)
(*Refer to General Index of Job Descriptions*)

Night Shift Supervisor (Word Processing)
Supervises work of word processing department during the night shift. Schedules the staff for the shift. Prioritizes work that must be completed. Responsible for maintaining the equipment and resolving routine problems that may occur in processing.

Nurse
Cares for ill, injured, convalescent, and handicapped persons in hospitals, clinics, private homes, sanitariums, and similar institutions. Observes patient and reports adverse reactions to medical personnel in charge. Administers specified medications, and notes time and amount on patient's chart. Performs routine laboratory work.

Nutritionist
Identifies the kinds and amounts of nutrients in food, translates this knowledge for schools and health care menus and restaurants and hotels; develops new foods and ingredients.

Operations Assistant (Recreation)
Responsible for assisting with overseeing the general operation of a recreational facility. Solves problems that arise concerning facilities and grounds. Contacts vendors, contractors, and

equipment repair technicians as needed. Obtains and renews necessary licenses and permits.

Office Manager
(See *Department Manager, Office*)

Operations Manager (Computer Systems)
Ensures that all jobs adhere to established conventions and may cancel any job that deviates from these conventions. Controls the processing of jobs and is responsible for obtaining the maximum utilization of the computer.

Operations Manager (Retail)
Oversees all functions of store operations, which include personnel, credit, payroll, shipping and receiving, customer service, warehousing and distribution, security, and maintenance.

Operations Research Analyst
Conducts analyses of management and operational problems and formulates mathematical or simulation models of the problem. Analyzes problems in terms of management information and conceptualizes and defines problems. Studies information and selects plan from competitive proposals that affords maximum profitability or effectiveness in relation to cost or risk.

Outside Sales Agent (Travel)
Brings new business to an agency on a referral basis.

Owner/Manager (Employment Agency)
An owner who also manages the agency. (See *Employment Agency Owner*)

Owner/Operator (Food Service)
Coordinates all employees; may be responsible for buying food and supplies; may help with menu planning; keeps the restaurant within health and sanitation guidelines; oversees payroll function. In small restaurants, may oversee marketing and promotion effort.

Owner/Operator (Travel Agency)
Delegates responsibilities to qualified managers. Encourages creative marketing and sales activities. Manages budget for the overall operation.

Packaging Specialist
Develops packaging to fit specific products for industry needs.

Page Creator (Word Processing)
Composes actual pages of catalogs relayed to home television or telephones. Involves word processing, text editing, and formatting, together with computer graphics. The system plus its computer graphics is called videotex.

Pantry Person
Draws from the storeroom all the raw materials needed to prepare all the fruit or vegetable salads, seafood cocktails, canapes, and other cold dishes. Serves these items to waiters and waitresses. May slice and portion cold meats and cheeses. Serves desserts and side dishes such as bread and butter. Makes sandwiches and prepares garnishes for other departments.

Paralegal
Assists lawyer with routine legal assignments. Maintains legal volumes to make sure they are up-to-date; assists with legal research. Helps administer estates, draft wills and trusts, complete federal and state tax returns, prepare initial and amended articles of incorporation, stock certificates, and other securities. Helps prepare court-related forms. Performs a variety of related duties upon request of the attorney.

Paralegal (Publishing House)
Assists the general counsel in the company's legal department with the areas of law that affect publishing, such as contract law and copyright law. May assist the legal publisher in planning new books about the paralegal profession or the procedures utilized by paralegals in the office.

Paralegal Instructor
Teaches paralegal students the legal procedures used by paralegals in the law office.

Paralegal Supervisor
Oversees work of paralegal responsible for researching law, investigating facts, and preparing documents to assist lawyers.

Partner (CPA Firm)
Responsible for major audit accounts. Solves complex accounting problems for clients, using standard accounting principles. Also responsible for quality of client service and volume of new business brought in to the firm. Achieves objectives through the effective management of the technicians and sales staff in the firm.

Passenger Service Agent
Provides passengers with information; assists passengers with information, assists passengers when boarding the plane.

Pastry Cook
Prepares desserts (both hot and cold), ices, and cakes for both daily use and for special occasions.

Pastry Chef
Oversees the bread and pastry needs of all kitchens and departments in a large hotel, club, or restaurant. Supervises pastry cooks and bakers. Requires ability to coordinate the activity of others. Supervises the preparation of desserts, pastries, frozen desserts, fondants, fillings, and fancy sugar decorations. Creates new recipes and produces delicate items that require mastery of fine techniques.

Peripheral Equipment Operator
Operates on-line or off-line peripheral machines, according to written or oral instructions, to transfer data from one form to another, print output, and read data into and out of digital computer. Mounts and positions materials, such as reels of magnetic tape or paper tape onto reader-sorter. Sets, guides, keys, and switches according to instructions to prepare equipment for operations. Separates and sorts printed output forms.

Personnel Assistant
Performs diversified duties in the processing and monitoring of employee benefits programs and maintenance of all employee personnel files. Sets up files on new employees. Records changes on all employee status as necessary and forwards to payroll department.

Personnel Clerk
Prepares job postings and determines eligibility to bid and successful bidder(s). Prepares monthly absenteeism reports. Prepares monthly accident reports. Assists applicants with filling out employment applications appropriately. Acts as a backup for the department secretary; performs a variety of basic personnel and clerical functions.

Personnel Director
Supervises the hiring and firing of company employees. Prepares performance reports and sets up personnel policies and regulations. In a large corporation, oversees the entire personnel function.

Personnel Manager
Responsible for developing, implementing, and coordinating policies and programs covering the following: employment, labor relations, wage and salary administration, fringe benefits administration, indoctrination and training, placement, safety, insurance, health benefits, and employee services.

Placement Director (Paralegal)
Responsible for employment orientation and job development, and may act as a liaison between the employer and the paralegal graduate seeking a position.

Plant Manager
Responsible for manufacturing of products in the required quantity and quality and for performing this function safely at a minimum cost. Recommends improvements in manufacturing methods. Sets up and approves production schedules. Regularly reviews inventories of required materials. Directs and approves all requisitions for maintenance and repair of building and equipment and for machine parts and manufacturing supplies.

Plant Safety Specialist
Coordinates safety programs. Communicates policies, programs, and regulations to appropriate personnel. Ensures compliance with governmental regulations. Enforces safety policies for chemical use, fire codes, equipment, and ventilation systems. Ensures proper guarding of machinery to avoid operator injury. Maintains records as well.

Portfolio Manager
Manages nontrust accounts, such as the pension fund of a corporation or a university endowment. Decides what stocks should be bought and sold within the portfolio.

Prep Cook
Responsible for any duties necessary in order to prepare food items for production.

President
Plans, develops, and establishes policies and objectives of the business organization in accordance with the Board of Directors and corporate charter. Plans business objectives and develops policies to coordinate functions between departments. Reviews financial statements to determine progress and status in attaining objectives. Directs and coordinates formulation of

financial programs to provide funding for new or continuing operations to maximize return on investments. May preside over board of directors. Evaluates performance of company executives.

President/Owner
Acts as president of a business and owns and operates it as well. (See *President*)

Press Coordinator
Arranges meetings and special events with the press. Contacts press either by phone or mail to detail upcoming events.

Private Secretary
As the executive's administrative partner, duties vary according to the size of the organization and the executive's responsibilities. May outline day's work for the office, schedule duties to be performed by all who work in the office; keeps everything on schedule despite interruptions. Greets callers, handles mail, keeps track of financial records, and processes data.

Product Development Technologist
Technologist working in the food service industry conducting experiments to improve flavor, texture, shelf life, or other product characteristics; develops new products or packaging materials; compares competitive products; ensures that every item meets quality standards, and interprets and solves the problems of the food service operator.

Product Manager
Oversees the research, development, and production of a particular product. Assesses need for modifications on the product based on input from market research. Estimates timely and cost-effective procedures for implementing periodic modifications. Ensures that quality of product is maintained.

Product Support Representative
(Computer Systems)
Acts as the customer's liaison with the computer manufacturer. Assists with familiarizing the customer with the computer. Acts as part trainer, part salesperson, and part adviser to the customer.

Production Coordinator
Coordinates flow of work within or between departments of manufacturer to expedite production. Reviews master production schedule and work orders, establishes priorities and availability or capability of workers, parts, or material. Confers with department supervisors to determine progress of work. Compiles reports on the progress of work.

Production Manager
Supervises and coordinates activities of those who expedite flow of materials, parts, and assemblies and processes within or between departments.

Production Manager (Food Service)
Takes leadership position in such production operation areas as engineering, scheduling, purchasing, quality control, inventory control, distribution, and human relations.

Production Planner
Ensures that inventories of stock items are maintained at reasonable levels and that orders for nonstock items are processed in a timely, effective manner. Works with plant supervisor to establish manning levels that are appropriate based on current and projected levels of activity. Requisitions all raw materials and supplies required to manufacture products.

Production Technician
Assists engineer in preparing layouts of machinery and equipment, work-flow plans, time and motion studies, and analyses of production costs to produce the most efficient use of personnel, materials, and machines.

Professional Waitperson
Serves meals to the patrons according to the established rules of etiquette. Presents a menu to the diner, suggesting dinner courses and appropriate wines, and answering questions regarding the food preparation. Writes the order on a check or memorizes it. Relays the order to the kitchen and serves the courses from the kitchen and service bars. Garnishes and decorates the dishes preparatory to serving them. Serves the patrons from a chafing dish at the table, observes the diners to fulfill any additional requests and to perceive when the meal has been completed. Totals the bill and accepts payments. May carve the meats, bone the fish and fowl, and prepare flaming dishes and desserts at the patron's table.

Program Coordinator
Oversees programs after the planning stage. Takes appropriate action to initiate planned programs, service them while in progress, and arrange for program evaluation. May assist with

recommending speakers, agendas, room setup, and promotional efforts.

Program Director
Plans and develops methods and procedures for implementing programs; directs and coordinates program activities, and exercises control over personnel according to knowledge and experience in area with which the program is concerned. Prepares program reports. Controls expenditures.

Program Director (Education)
Supervises the development of a variety of academic programs or other programs related to an educational institution. Such programs might involve parents, student organizations, industry, or other special interest groups. (See *Program Director*)

Programmer Analyst
Prepares detailed instructions for assigned programming systems or components enabling qualified personnel to proceed with implementation. Evaluates procedural and/or programming systems required to operate and support programs and systems.

Programmer Trainee
Writes the codes that make up a computer program, tests their programs, debugs them (eliminates errors), and sometimes writes the accompanying documentation that tells others why the program was written the way it was.

Project Director
Plans, directs, and coordinates activities of designated project to ensure that aims, goals, or objectives specified for project are accomplished in accordance with set priorities, timetables, and funding. Develops staffing plan and establishes work schedules for each phase of the project. Prepares project status reports for management.

Proofreader
Reads typeset (original copy) or proof of type setup to detect and mark for corrections and grammatical, typographical, or compositional errors. Reads proof against copy, marking by standardized codes errors that appear in proof. Returns marked proof for correction and later checks corrected proof against copy.

Proofreader (Paralegal)
Reviews the content of law-related manuscripts to verify facts needed in case preparation. Also can act as person who checks for improper usage or spelling or grammar errors in legal copy.

Proofreader (Word Processing)
Checks the work of the correspondence secretary and word processor for accuracy of copy.

Public Relations Specialist
Writes news releases, directs advertising campaigns, or conducts public opinion polls. Tries to create favorable attitudes about a client or its products.

Purchasing Agent
Responsible for buying the raw materials, machinery, supplies, and services necessary to run a business.

Purchasing Agent (Food Service)
Purchases foodstuffs, kitchen supplies, and equipment. Makes large contracts for several products. Purchases all supplies with the exception of capital goods such as furniture and fixed equipment.

Purchasing Assistant
(See *Purchasing Agent*)

Purchasing Manager
Responsible for the management of the procurement functions of the company. Establishes practices and procedures to be followed by buyers and other department personnel. Negotiates price and delivery. Selects vendors, assesses vendor capabilities, develops alternate sources, and evaluates vendor performance. Ensures that department records are maintained.

Purchasing Manager (Food Service)
Responsible for the actual purchase of all supplies and equipment, usually coordinated through the Executive Chef or Cook. Required to monitor and control costs and to maintain accurate inventories. Supervises purchasing agents responsible for a particular product line.

Quality Assurance Manager
Develops and maintains a system to assure that all products manufactured by the organization meet customer specifications and achieve superior quality and reliability levels. Revises and updates quality control manual. Meets with vendors, customers, and quality representatives to discuss and resolve quality problems as required.

Quality Assurance Specialist (Food Service)
Analyzes ingredients and finished products and checks standards of production, packaging, and sanitation. May be assigned to a particular type of product or food item.

Quality Control Manager (Food Service)
Travels to various units to inspect those units and make sure they adhere to company and state standards. Usually responsible for more than one operation.

Ramp Agent
Supervises baggage area to be sure baggage is sent to proper destinations.

Real Estate Manager (Food Service)
Supervises the negotiations for the acquisition and disposition of properties. Supervises staff engaged in preparing lease agreements, recording rental receipts, and performing other activities necessary to efficient management of company properties, or in performing routine research on zoning ordinances and condemnation considerations. Directs appraiser to inspect properties and land under consideration for acquisition and recommends acquisitions, lease, disposition, improvement, or other action consistent with best interests of the company. Negotiates contracts with sellers of land and renters of property.

Reception Manager
Supervises all activities of guest services, including registration of incoming guests and checkout of departing guests; provides guests with information about functions at the hotel and about the general area where the hotel is located; takes messages for guests and provides wake-up calls; handles guest relations, problems with rooms, billing, or any other routine difficulty.

Receptionist
Greets people who come into an office and directs them to the proper department. They may also do other tasks such as answering the phone and some typing. Learns the departments and key personnel in the company and what functions they perform.

Records Manager
Examines and evaluates records-management systems to develop new or improve existing methods for efficient handling, protecting, and disposing of business records and information.

Reviews records retention schedule to determine how long records should be kept.

Recreation Director (Cruiselines)
Develops safe recreation programs suitable for a cruiseline. Ensures adherence to established standards and policies. Ensures staff is properly certified for instruction when needed. Makes recommendations to activities coordinator for recreation schedules.

Regional Director
May oversee a group of regional managers. (*See* **Regional Manager**)

Regional Manager
Responsible for overseeing the activities of all operations in a particular geographical area of the country.

Regional Sales Manager
Recruits in-house personnel, recruits general agents, and assists when needed with training new sales staff with "cold calling." Holds periodic sales meetings to strengthen competitive position and explain strategies for market penetration.

Registered Representative (Account Executive or Broker)
Buys or sells securities for customers. Relays the order to members of the firm who are stationed on the exchange floors; if the security is not traded on the exchange, sells it directly in the over-the-counter market. Advises customers on the timing of the purchase or sale of securities. Counsels customers about tax shelters, mutual funds, and other investments.

Regional Vice President (Food Service)
Deals with new business development; senior management contact, both internal and external; pricing analysis; proposal development and presentation; and contract negotiations. Works with planning and achieving marketing objectives within the responsible geographic territory.

Rental Sales Representative
Negotiates car rental rates with travel agents, corporate businesses, and other commercial accounts and individual clients so as to remain competitive in the market.

Research Account Executive (Advertising)
Researches printed literature. Drafts reports from research. Gets competitive bids from suppliers.

Sits in on planning sessions. Suggests new methods of data gathering. Helps design surveys.

Research Analyst
Evaluates research findings and determines their applicability to specific projects within the company. Recommends needed research projects. Compares research findings with similar studies or surveys to determine reliability of results. Uses statistical data and measurement to examine and apply findings.

Research Analyst (Financial)
Researches and sells their research to institutional investors. Recommends portfolio managers to the stocks they believe should be bought and sold.

Research Assistant
Compiles and analyzes verbal or statistical data to prepare reports and studies for use by professional workers in a variety of areas. Searches sources, such as reference works, literature, documents, newspapers, and statistical records, to obtain data on assigned subjects. May interview individuals to obtain data or draft correspondence to answer inquiries.

Research Assistant (Paralegal)
Performs legal research by operating a computer-assisted legal research system.

Research and Development Specialist (Food Service)
Conducts research on new product lines and equipment for the food service industry. May work with food products in test kitchens or with new equipment in operating food service establishments. Reports findings to manufacturers of food products and equipment and publicizes results in trade publications to inform the industry about the possible alternatives the findings may provide for food service professionals.

Research Director
May supervise a group of research projects at a given time. (See *Project Director*)

Research Manager
(See *Project Director*)

Research Technician (Electronics)
Performs research to evaluate new methods for the electronics technician. Tests findings. May pass recommendations on to research and development. Upon request, works with other researchers and engineers to test findings.

Researcher and Evaluator (Travel)
Investigates and evaluates public relations efforts of the organization. Responsible for making recommendations on public relations programs based on goals and objectives and competition's position in the marketplace. Evaluates needs for expanding public relations efforts. Researches and recommends best strategy.

Reservationist
Sells reservations and other travel products such as tours, hotel accommodations, car rentals; operates computer reservations equipment; assists passengers in solving their travel needs.

Reservationist (Cruiselines)
Books cruises for individual clients and groups. Sells the cruise by telephone to inquirers. Explains details of the trip and accepts payment.

Reservationist (Hotel)
Responsible for confirming room reservations, either by mail or by telephone, and for writing or typing out reservation forms. Works with computer to keep guest reservations current and for billing procedures. May assist guest with other reservations for local transportation, dining, or entertainment, depending on the staff size of the hotel.

Reservations Manager
Supervises and coordinates activities of personnel engaged in taking, recording, and canceling reservations in front office of hotel. Trains front office staff. Reviews daily printouts listing guests' arrivals and individual guest folios received by room clerks. Approves correspondence going to groups and travel agents to answer special requests for rooms and rates. Evaluates computer system and manual record procedures for efficiency.

Resident Manager (Hospitality)
Administrator living on the premises to manage the day-to-day operations of the hotel or other lodging facility.

Restaurant Manager
Responsible for efficiency, quality, and courtesy in all phases of a food service operation. In large organizations, the manager may direct supervisory personnel at the next lower level. In smaller operations, they might supervise kitchen and dining room staffs directly. Knowledge of the responsibilities of all restaurant staff is essential to this position.

Revenue Officer
Investigates and collects delinquent federal taxes and secures delinquent tax returns from individuals or business firms according to prescribed laws and regulations. Recommends civil penalties when necessary. Writes reports on all actions taken.

Roasting Cook
Responsible for all meat preparation that is made to order. Also responsible for all items that are deep fried, shallow fried, sautéed, or broiled.

Robotics Technician
Performs the work of an electronics technician, specifically on various types of robotic devices. (See *Electronics Technician*)

Rooms Attendant
Coordinates service for a block of rooms in a hotel. Ensures room service operations are running smoothly. Arranges for any special requests from guests concerning accommodations. Checks the room rack and key rack frequently. Oversees the operation of switchboard and messages going to guests.

Rooms Division Supervisor
Directs all activities involved with the rooms division of the hotel. This includes staffing, housekeeping, occupancy, service, and promotion.

Rounds Cook
Replaces every member of the kitchen brigade who may be absent from each station. Must be efficient and versatile in cooking techniques.

Sales Assistant
Responsible for successful management of a selling area. Involves supervision of a selling area and customer service functions. In a large department store, may also direct inventory control and merchandise presentation and increasing the sales growth and profitability of an area.

Sales Director (Hospitality)
Responsible for research and analysis, short-term and long-range planning, determination of marketing strategies and tactics, setting of goals and objectives, budgeting, the booking of individual as well as group business, and the securing of business for the food and beverage department as well as for the rooms division.

Sales/Field Representative (Electronics)
Advises customers on installation and maintenance problems and serves as the link between the manufacturer and the customer.

Sales Manager
Coordinates sales distribution by establishing sales territories, quotas, and goals, and advises dealers and distributors concerning sales and advertising techniques. Directs staffing, training, and performance evaluations to develop and control sales programs. Prepares periodic sales reports showing sales volume and potential sales. May recommend or approve budget, expenditures, and appropriations for research and development work.

Sales Manager (Food Service)
Responsible for the development and operation of the sales department. Maintains files on past group business. Works with the social director and promotion office on contacts and may do some traveling to other areas to bring new business into the establishment. Also trains and supervises sales representatives and some account executives.

Sales Manager (Retail)
Oversees the various sales departments in wholesale and retail companies. Directs promotional sales campaigns for their merchandise or services.

Sales and Marketing Specialist (Food Service)
Plans, researches, promotes, and sells products to the food service industry.

Sales Representative
Secures orders from existing and potential customers by means of visiting the customer facility or calling by phone. Follows up on quotations submitted to customers. Submits weekly activity/call reports concerning customer quotes, orders, or problems. Provides a territory sales forecast on a monthly basis.

Sales Representative (Computer Systems)
Calls on prospective clients to explain types of services provided by establishment, such as inventory control, payroll processing, data conversion, sales analysis, and financial reporting. Analyzes data processing requirements of prospective clients and draws up prospectus of data processing plan designed specifically to serve client's needs. May also sell computers and related equipment directly.

Sales Representative (Hospitality)
Follows initial lead on a prospective client. Responsible for explaining hotel's services to government, business, and social groups to generate interest in the facility as a site for a major function. Sales representative conducts "cold calls" as well as calls to a selected prospect list. The sales representative may pass the interested client on to an account executive, who will actually set up, service, and maintain the account.

Sales Secretary
Types drafts of newsletters; keeps track of company's dealings with outside printers, suppliers, and creative people. Types, files, answers telephones, and routes mail. Takes orders, books events, or handles whatever customer request comes in for the product or service being sold.

Sales/Service Manager (Electronics)
Oversees both the sales and service efforts of a branch or many branch operations of a company. Ensures that the quality and customer service levels are maintained in the field. Receives feedback from customers through the sales and service staff. Determines what action should be taken with repeated problems.

Sales Supervisor
(See *Sales Manager*)

Sales Trainee (Hospitality)
Usually begins with front office experience to learn client relations and total product line offered by the hotel. May go on sales calls with sales representatives or assist an account executive with servicing an account.

Sales Trainee (Insurance)
Attends sales strategy sessions as an observer, or "tails" an experienced agent on calls. Assists established agents to service accounts.

Sanitation Supervisor (Food Service)
Supervises porters, dishwashers, kitchen persons, and pot washers. Ensures that dishes, cooking utensils, equipment, and floors are kept clean. Ensures that kitchen always meets health department regulations and standards.

Sauce Cook
Responsible for all preparation of sauces to be used on main items on the menu. In a middle-sized operation, the sauce cook is also the sous chef.

Schedule Planning Manager (Travel)
Approves and enforces scheduling recommendation for all air traffic coming and going into and out of the airport.

School Director
Plans, develops, and administers education programs. Confers with administrative personnel to decide scope of programs to be offered. Prepares schedules of classes and rough drafts of course content to determine number and background of instructors needed. Interviews, hires, trains, and evaluates work performance of education department staff. Assists instructors in preparation of course descriptions. Prepares budget for education programs and directs maintenance of records of expenditures, receipts, and public and school participation in programs.

School Director/Administrator
(See *School Director* and *Administrator*)

School Director (Vocational)
Directs and coordinates schools with vocational training programs. Confers with members of industrial and business community to determine manpower training needs. Reviews and interprets vocational educational codes to ensure that programs conform to policies. Prepares budgets and funding allocation for vocational programs. Reviews and approves new programs. Coordinates on-the-job training programs with employers and evaluates progress of students in conjunction with program contract goals.

School Secretary
Handles secretarial duties in elementary and secondary schools; may take care of correspondence, prepare bulletins and reports, keep track of money for school supplies and student activities, and maintain a calendar of school events.

Script Writer
Provides the creative support in a telemarketing agency. Writes all material that is to be read by the telemarketing representative.

Seafood Cook
Prepares all seafood dishes, mousses, soufflés, etc. Also prepares the fish for cold display or for hors d'oeuvres and then sends to the garde manger for final decoration.

Secretary
Performs secretarial duties for a supervisor. Takes and transcribes dictation with speed and accuracy.

Maintains correspondence and data files, arranges appointments, answers routine inquiries, and handles general office duties. Often assists in performing administrative details using initiative and judgment. Requires thorough knowledge of company policies, the organization, and how to operate in the channels of the organization. As part of the management team, must be ready to make decisions and provide relevant information to staff members on a daily basis.

Secretary (Food Service)
In large food service operations, performs a variety of administrative duties; works with customers on group business and with vendors on orders and supplies. Frees the employer to work on other areas outside the property.

Senior Accountant
(See *Accountant*)

Senior Account Executive
(See *Account Executive*)

Senior Analyst
Assists in developing the data processing procedures for solving business or mathematical problems. Assists in analyzing and evaluating proposed and existing systems.

Senior Analyst (Marketing)
(See *Market Research Analyst*)

Senior Claims Examiner
(See *Claims Examiner*)

Senior Consultant
(See *Consultant*)

Senior Copywriter
(See *Copywriter*)

Senior Drafter
Gives final approval to the plans drawn up by other drafters before presenting the plan to client. (See *Drafter*)

Senior Legal Assistant
Oversees the work of paralegals and legal assistants in the firm. (See *Paralegal* and *Legal Assistant*)

Senior Programmer
Develops flowcharts to establish logic of execution. Codes logic in programming language. Writes program language to initiate and control the program in the hardware. Reviews existing

programs and effects changes as requested. Solves production hang-ups in existing system. Writes operating instructions for computer personnel. Reviews output for the user. Supervises other programmers and gives final approval on the programs they have written. Ensures senior management receives information as requested.

Senior Systems Consultant
(See *Systems Consultant*)

Senior Underwriter
(See *Underwriter*)

Service Representative
Goes out into the field upon customer's request to service problems with purchased equipment. May diagnose the problem, correct and test the equipment to see if it is working properly. Reports problem to research and development. Tells owners and dealers about new products, service techniques, and developments in maintenance.

Service Technician (Electronics)
(See *Service Representative*)

Social Secretary
Arranges social functions, answers personal correspondence, and keeps the employer informed about all social activities.

Soup Cook
Responsible for all soups, both cold and hot, plus garnishes, stocks, etc.

Sous Chef
Principal assistant of the Chef de Cuisine. In a large operation, the sous chef will assist the Chef de Cuisine in general administrative and supervisory duties and will implement every order given. The sous chef must have the same professional background as the chef but not necessarily the same number of years of experience.

Special Events Coordinator
Performs basic function of the meeting planner and also is directly responsible for the advertising and promotion of the event, for the budget for the event, and for identifying the appropriate target market. Works with the press and media on promotion. Acts as the liaison between all participating parties.

Speaker
Person elected by an organization to present its views, policies, or decisions.

Staff Accountant

Oversees the general ledger of a firm. Reviews cost center and chart of accounts structure. Makes recommendation as to cost center/account structure which will identify the nature of expenses to their proper areas; assists in controlling annual expenditures. Reconciles daily cash flow statements and reconciles to monthly bank statements. Reconciles payroll and cash disbursement accounts. Reviews accounts payable aging and vendor statements for problems.

State Travel Director

Promotes visitor traffic within the destination, whether for pleasure, business, or convention purposes, and from within or from without the state.

Station Manager

Supervises a car rental business.

Statistical Typist

Works in all types of businesses typing statistical data from source material such as: company production and sales records, test records, time sheets, and surveys and questionnaires.

Stenographer

Takes dictation in shorthand of correspondence, reports, and other matter, and operates typewriter to transcribe dictated materials.

Stewardess (Food Service)

Supervises and coordinates activities of the pantry, storeroom, and noncooking kitchen workers, and purchases or requisitions the foodstuffs, kitchen supplies, and equipment. Inspects the kitchens and storerooms to ensure that the premises and equipment are clean and in order and that sufficient foodstuffs and supplies are on hand to ensure efficient service. Establishes controls to guard against theft and waste.

Store Manager

An executive responsible for the profitable operation of the store. Has broad merchandising responsibilities, develops staff, contributes to the store's public relations effort, and supervises the maintenance of the store. Spends significant amount of time on the selling floor and supplies other areas of management with detailed information on the operation of the store.

Storeroom Supervisor (Food Service)

Responsible for supervising, receiving, inspecting, counting, and storing of all food and other articles delivered to the storeroom. Responsible for filling out all requisitions and, under the instructions of the house auditor, for keeping a journal in ledger of all goods received and delivered. Names of purveyors, the costs and descriptions of articles, and other required information are recorded. Supervises monthly inventories with the auditor.

Superintendent of Service (Hospitality)

Responsible for overseeing all functions providing guest services in the hotel. This may include the front office and housekeeping as well as food service operations. Ensures quality service while keeping informed about any client-centered problems that may affect new or repeat business. Solves problems related to guest services.

Supervisor (Banking)

Responsible for improving the overall productivity of a department or area, motivating staff, and staying within budget. Oversees production, product development, marketing, and systems functions in the bank.

Supervisor of Data Entry Services

Directs all data input activities serving the users of centralized data input facility. Directs the development of data input procedures, performance standards, and controls. Directs the evaluation of new data entry equipment. Ensures accurate and timely completion of projects.

Supervisor of Gate Services

Observes staff to ensure that services to passengers are performed courteously and correctly. Supervises and coordinates the activities of staff engaged in admitting passengers to airplanes and assisting passengers disembarking at terminal exits of commercial flights. Reviews flight schedules, passenger manifests, and information obtained from staff to determine staffing needs. Recommends alternate procedures if needed. Evaluates performance of staff.

Supervisor (Telemarketing)

Manages groups of telemarketing communicators and is directly responsible for their performance. May also be responsible for training and scheduling of staff.

Surveyor

Interviews people and compiles statistical information. Asks questions following a specified outline on questionnaire and records answers. Reviews, classifies, and sorts questionnaires.

Compiles results in a format that is clear and concise and highlights findings relevant to the objective of the survey.

Swing Cook
(See *Rounds Cook*)

Systems Administrator (Word Processing)
Involves systems maintenance and management and systems analysis and design.

Systems Analyst
Solves the problems of adapting computer hardware and software to end-users' needs. Determines how the company can save money by adapting existing equipment. Coordinates and supervises the efforts of many computer professionals. Maintains quality control by assessing the system once it has been implemented.

Systems Consultant
Advises clients on developing, implementing, and maintaining automated programs for clients and for in-house use; on selecting hardware, writing software, and consulting with user/client when special programs must be developed.

Systems Operators Supervisor
Directs operations for optimum use of computer and peripheral equipment. Coordinates between users and other data processing functions in establishing and maintaining processing schedules. Recommends hardware changes and directs the installation of new equipment.

Systems Programmer
Prepares the computers to understand the language that the applications programmers will be using and tells the computer what peripheral equipment, such as printers and automatic teller machines, it will be controlling.

Systems Trainee (Banking)
Works in programming or part of a systems team project, refining the use of current equipment or developing systems for as yet unmet needs.

Tape Librarian
Documents and allots hardware space for all computer and peripheral equipment for schedules; produces debugging statistics and other statistical reports for the department management personnel.

Team Leader (Floor Supervisor)
Responsible for supervision of a floor in a hotel. Oversees the maintenance and upkeep, the repair and security of all rooms on an assigned floor. Supervises housekeeping staff assigned to that floor and coordinates the group to work efficiently. Submits work reports to Executive Housekeeper if requested.

Technical Secretary
Assists engineers or scientists. In addition to the usual secretarial duties, may prepare much of the correspondence, maintain the technical library, and gather and edit materials for scientific papers.

Telemarketing Center Manager
Responsible for executing the program once components have been assembled and the script written. This involves either making or receiving the calls in a way that achieves each client's objective.

Telemarketing Communicator
Delivers what everyone else sells. Coordinates or manages the allocation of the product to the proper sales and delivery channels.

Telemarketing Representative
Sells a product or "qualifies" customers for the field sales force by telephone.

Telemarketing Trainer
Instructs communicators about the product or services and how to use the scripts. Trainers also teach telemarketing efficiency, listening skills, and sales techniques.

Ticket Agent
Sells tickets to airline passengers at the airport and city ticket office; promotes and sells air travel; gives air travel and tour information; makes the flight and tour reservations; computes fares; prepares and issues tickets; routes baggage; and prepares cash reports.

Tour Director
Conducts the actual tour. Accompanies travelers as an escort throughout the trip. Solves problems and settles complaints. Has alternative plans set for the group so that tour will be successful even under adverse conditions. Coordinates the group to stay together and encourages questions about the area being visited.

Tour Escort
Assists passengers; generally assists with tours; accompanies the tour from start to finish; often

handles large sums of money; makes necessary changes in group's accommodations or itinerary as needed.

Tour Guide
Does complete narration; has specialized knowledge of a particular region or country; hired to accompany a tour only while it visits the area of special expertise.

Tour Operator
Puts together all the elements of a trip: transportation, accommodations, meals, sightseeing, and the like; negotiates rates and block space; coordinates details of the itinerary; markets the product.

Tour and Travel Account Executive
Responsible for the development and service of group tour business coming into the hotel. Brings travel and tour groups to the hotel. Consults with the tour operators and travel agents and collaborates with the hotel staff to find best strategy for servicing the group.

Tourist Information Assistant
Provides information and other services to tourists at state information centers. Greets tourists, in person or by telephone, and answers questions and gives information on resorts, historical sights, scenic areas, and other tourist attractions. Assists tourists in planning itineraries and advises them of traffic regulations. Sells hunting and fishing licenses and provides information on fishing, hunting, and camping regulations. Composes letters in response to inquiries. Maintains personnel, license-sales, and other records. Contacts motel, hotel, and resort operators by mail or telephone to obtain advertising literature.

Trader
Matches buyers and sellers of securities.

Traffic Manager
Negotiates price and service issues of all modes of transportation carrier contracts and determines the appropriate transportation mode to be utilized. Develops, maintains, and disseminates logistical data.

Trainer (Word Processing)
Trains correspondence and word processing secretaries to make fewer errors by checking their work.

Training Manager
Develops ongoing training programs for new and experienced personnel. Conducts training seminars. Writes and coordinates training manuals, working with specialists for specified details. Prepares training videotapes and/or films; maintains library of video and film training aids. Notifies employees of training sessions. Introduces topic specialists at the beginning of the program and the program agenda. Develops means of measuring the effectiveness of programs through testing.

Training Specialist
Develops and conducts training programs for specialized functions within the company upon the approval of the training manager. (See *Training Manager*)

Training Supervisor
May supervise training manager(s) as well as the entire training function for the company. Responsibilities might include overseeing training programs at various divisions and performing all budgetary responsibilities pertaining to the programs. Also may evaluate existing programs and make recommendations for modifications or new or additional programs. (See *Training Manager*)

Transportation Manager
Responsible for all aspects of transportation including inbound, between facilities, and outbound. Supervises various functions and personnel. Negotiates rates with warehouses and transportation companies. Plans, monitors, and implements the distribution department's fiscal budget. Establishes the most beneficial routing of company shipments for satisfactory customer service. Determines price levels. Plans for the department on a quarterly, yearly, and five-year basis.

Transportation Specialist
Advises industries, business firms, and individuals concerning methods of preparation of shipments, rates to be applied, and mode of transportation to be used. Consults with clients regarding packing procedures and inspects packed goods for conformance to shipping specifications to prevent damage, delay, or penalties. Files claims with insurance company for losses, damages, and overcharges of shipments.

Travel Agency Manager
Supervises the day-to-day operations of the agency. Prepares sales reports and dictates office policies. Decides on promotion and pricing of packages. Supervises, hires, and trains employees. Attends trade shows to keep informed on latest computer systems, rates, and promotions being offered by the airlines, hotels, and other related services. Initiates advertising for the agency and keeps budget.

Travel Agent
Plans itineraries and arranges accommodations and other travel services for customers of the travel agency. Plans, describes, and sells itinerary package tours. Converses with customers to determine destination, mode of transportation, travel dates, financial considerations, and accommodations required. Books customer's mode of transportation and hotel reservations. Obtains travel tickets and collects payment. May specialize in foreign or domestic service, individual or group travel, or specific geographical areas.

Travel Counselor
Advises clients on best ways to travel, destinations, costs, and safety issues. Offers advice to clients on packages available, preparation for a trip, or availability of transportation or accommodations. Researches information requested by the client.

Travel Director
Client-contact person who actually goes out with the incentive groups and on site, coordinating sightseeing trips and trouble-shooting.

Travel Editor
Buys articles submitted by freelance writers; selects unsolicited articles for publication; selects letters from readers to publish; replies to readers' letters of comment or criticism; works with layout and make-up of travel pages. May assign staff to stories almost anywhere in the world. Reviews manuscripts submitted by travel writers for content and readability. Chooses manuscripts for publication.

Travel Secretary
Coordinates all aspects of the travel function. Researches options to maintain an economical, efficient travel program. Schedules personnel for approved travel on corporate jets. Schedules personnel from approved travel authorizations on commercial flights. Makes hotel reservations. Performs clerical and secretarial duties pertaining to all travel arrangements.

Travel Specialist
Develops specialized expertise about a particular area of travel. May work for a travel agency, tour operator, publications department, or other related areas using information mastered about a specialized area of travel. May specialize in a geographic area, type of destination, or any other specific area in the travel industry.

Travel Writer
Provides practical guides, directories, and language books and brochures. Contributes feature stories to travel sections of large newspapers.

Treasurer
Directs and coordinates organization's financial programs, transactions, and security measures according to financial principles and government regulations. Evaluates operational methods and practices to determine efficiency of operations. Approves and signs documents affecting capital monetary transactions. Directs receipt, disbursement, and expenditures of money or other capital assets.

Treasurer/Controller
Has combined responsibilities of both the Treasurer and the Controller. (See *Treasurer* and See *Controller*)

Trust Officer
Manages money and securities as well as real estate and other property. Decides how assets will be managed.

Underwriter
Reviews applications, reports, and actuarial studies to determine whether a particular risk should be insured. Specializations are usually in life, property, and liability, or health insurance.

Underwriter Specialist
Specializes as an underwriter in life, property, and liability, or health insurance. (See *Underwriter*)

Underwriter Trainee
Assists the underwriter. Usually spends much time on the telephone gathering information and verifying what has been reported before the

underwriter makes final decisions.
(See *Underwriter*)

Underwriting Supervisor
Oversees the underwriting department. Ensures staff is working within appropriate guidelines and regulations when reviewing submitted materials. Evaluates performance of the staff and hires new underwriters as needed.

Unit Manager
Representative of a food service contractor who is permanently assigned to one particular client installation.

Urban Planner
Works with city or state officials to produce plans for future building and construction projects. Must be able to project an area's future population and its needs and design facilities to meet those needs.

Vegetable Cook
Prepares all garnishes such as potatoes, vegetables, egg dishes, etc.

Vending Manager
Independent businessperson who places own machines in various installations in a community or facility. Responsible for locating new machine sites, developing good public relations for the firm by handling complaints, maintaining quality control of the product and proper functioning of the machines. Handles cash funds and keeps required records.

Vice President
Plans, formulates, and recommends for approval of the President basic policies and programs which will further the objectives of the company. Executes decisions of the President and Board of Directors. Develops, in cooperation with the President and supervisors, an annual budget, and operates within the annual budget upon approval. Recommends changes in the overall organizational structure to the President. Approves public relations programs.

Vice President of Account Services
Oversees the promotion, sales, and service of a product line to a variety of customers within a defined geographical area. Develops and seeks out business of a highly complex nature and of importance to the company. Ensures efficient servicing of all accounts, once obtained. Prepares

programs for training and development of the field managers and other new and experienced personnel.

Vice President of Communications
Ensures the development and execution of advertising, public relations, public affairs, and members' relations' programs, together with effective internal and external communications to promote understanding, acceptance, and support of corporate activities and objectives by employees and the subscribing public.

Vice President of Finance
Acts under authority and responsibility delegated by corporate executive office. Conducts management studies, prepares workload and budget estimates for specified or assigned operation, analyzes operational reports, and submits activity reports. Develops and recommends plans for expansion of existing programs, operations, and financial activities.

Vice President of Human Resources
Develops Human Resources policies and programs for the entire company. The major areas covered are organizational planning, organizational development, employment, indoctrination and training, employee relations, compensation, benefits, safety and health, and employee services. Originates Human Resources practices and objectives which will provide a balanced program throughout all divisions. Coordinates implementation through Human Resources staff. Assists and advises senior management of Human Resources issues.

Vice President of Marketing (Hospitality)
In addition to overseeing the sales function, also coordinates the advertising, public relations, publicity, and community relations for the hotel. (See *Vice President of Marketing*)

Vice President of Marketing/Sales
Represents the marketing function's needs in the development of corporate policy. Formulates sales goals, marketing plans, and strategy and directs the execution of these areas for the achievement of corporate marketing objectives. Manages the sales force to achieve marketing and sales goals for assigned products.

Vice President of Merchandising
Manages several divisions of merchandise. Responsible for planning and giving buyers both

fashion and financial direction. Plans sales, inventory, and marketing by store, based on the turnover desires. Plans markups and ensures that inventory supports sales efforts.

Vice President of Operations
Directs the formulation of corporate policies, programs, and procedures as they relate to distribution, operations, research, production, engineering, and purchasing. Maximizes group and divisional short- and long-range growth and profitability.

Vice President of Production
Plans, directs, and controls production and related support functions to provide timely manufacturing and delivery of output at lowest possible costs. Manages, controls, and reviews all assigned resources: staff, technical, material, and financial. Manages budgets and expense control to ensure effective meeting of operating objectives.

Vice President of Sales
Responsible for the selling of the output of several different manufacturing facilities. Must develop effective sales policies which result in each plant's producing the optimum profit. Determines final prices and works closely with the salesstaff, the production, scheduling, and traffic staffs and research and development personnel. After the initial sale is made, the sales staff assumes continuing sales effort to such accounts.

Wage and Salary Administrator
Maintains files of updated job descriptions. Ensures that responsibilities are appropriately compensated according to established standards. Participates in and reviews local and national salary surveys to set current salary standards and pay rates for each position within the organization. Processes salary increases or other changes for personnel according to established policies.

Warehousing/Operations Manager
Determines and develops distribution strategies and practices that will support the corporate objective. Responsibilities include: identifying areas within the company that offer some opportunity for improvement; optimizing investments in all locations, in inventory, facilities, and people; and matching the corporate distribution support capabilities to the outgoing marketing, business, and operational needs. Makes use of financial and computer expertise in evaluating projects and allocation of resources.

Window Trimmer
Displays merchandise in windows or showcases of retail stores to attract attention of prospective customers. Originates display ideas or follows suggestions or schedule of manager. Arranges mannequins, furniture, merchandise, and backdrop according to prearranged or own ideas. Constructs or assembles prefabricated displays.

Wine Steward
Administers scheduling of all bar personnel, both on regular shifts and for catering work, and keeps records of their hours. Responsible for hiring, firing, and training all bar personnel, keeping customer account files, maintaining liquor and wine storage, setting standards, and ensuring that they are maintained.

Word Processing Center Manager
Responsible for word processing support given to a function or a number of departments. Trains and motivates personnel; maintains good working regulations with departments being serviced, and administers basic first-line management responsibilities. Develops new procedures, keeps records, and orders supplies.

Word Processor
Uses computers and specialized word processing equipment to enter, edit, store, and revise correspondence, statistical tables, reports, forms, and other materials. Word processing systems include keyboard, a cathode ray tube (CRT) for display, and a printer. Some equipment also has telecommunications hookups and scanners to ready manuscripts.

Chapter Sixteen

Career Resources

BOOKS

Corwen, Leonard. *Your Resume: Key to a Better Job.* 4th ed. New York: Prentice Hall, 1991.

Duncan, Melba J., with Kathleen Moloney. *How to Succeed in Business as an Executive Assistant.* New York: Macmillan Publishing Co., 1989.

duPont, M. Kay. *Business Etiquette and Professionalism.* Los Altos, CA: Crisp Publications, 1990.

Ettinger, Blanche. *Opportunities in Customer Service Careers.* Lincolnwood, IL: NTC Publishing Group, 1992.

Eyler, David R. *Job Interviews That Mean Business.* New York: Random House, 1992.

_____. *Résumés That Mean Business.* New York: Random House, 1992.

Field, Shelly. *100 Best Careers for the Year 2000.* New York: Prentice Hall, 1992.

Fruehling, Rosemary T. *Working at Human Relations.* Eden Prairie, MN: Paradigm, 1991.

Fry, Ron. *Your First Interview.* Hawthorne, NJ: The Career Press, 1991.

Girard, Joe, with Robert Casemore. *How to Sell Yourself.* New York: Warner Books, 1992.

Gordon, Barbara. *Opportunities in Commercial Art and Graphic Design Careers.* Lincolnwood, IL: NTC Publishing Group, 1992.

Hansen, Katharine. *Dynamic Cover Letters.* Berkeley, CA: Ten Speed Press, 1990.

Haynes, Marion E. *Effective Meeting Skills.* Los Altos, CA: Crisp Publications, 1990.

Irish, Richard K. *Go Hire Yourself an Employer.* 3rd ed. New York: Doubleday, 1987.

Jackson, Carole, with Kalia Lulow. *Color for Men.* New York: Ballentine Books, 1984.

Krannick, Ronald L., and Caryl Rae. *Networking Your Way to Career Success.* Manassos, VA: Import Publications, 1989.

Lauber, Daniel. *Government Job Finder.* River Forest, IL: Planning/Communications, 1992.

Lock, Robert D. *Job Search: Career Planning Guide, Book II.* 2nd ed. New York: Brooks/Cole Publishing Co., 1991.

_____. *Student Activities for Taking Charge of Your Direction and Job Search, Book III.* 2nd ed. New York: Brooks/Cole Publishing Co., 1991.

Maddux, Robert B., and Dorothy Maddux. *Ethics in Business.* Los Altos, CA: Crisp Publications, Inc., 1990.

Marano, Hara Estroff. *Style Is Not a Size.* New York: Bantam Books, 1991.

Shea, Gordon F. *Mentoring.* Los Altos, CA: Crisp Publications, 1990.

Stevens, Mark. *The Big Six.* New York: Simon & Schuster, 1991.

Zemke, Ron. *The Service Edge: 101 Companies That Profit from Customer Care.* New York: Penguin Books USA, 1989.

MAGAZINES

The Black Collegian. Black Collegiate Services, Inc., New Orleans, LA.

The Career Choices Newsletter. Career Choices Newsletter Co., Forest Hills, NY.

Career and the Disabled. Equal Opportunity Publications, Inc., New York.

EEO Bimonthly: Technical and Business Career Opportunities. CRS Recruitment Publications/CASS Communications, Inc., Northbrook, IL.

Vitality. Vitality, Inc., Dallas, TX.

Working Woman. Working Woman, Inc., New York.

REFERENCE BOOKS

CPC Annual. Bethlehem, PA: College Placement Council.

Dictionary of Occupational Titles. 4th ed. Indianapolis, IN: U.S. Department of Labor, Employment and Training Administration. The JIST Search People, JIST Works, Inc., 1991.

Encyclopedia of Careers and Vocational Guidance. 8th ed., 4 vols. Largo, FL: Careers, Inc., 1990.

Bibliography

BOOKS

Carnevale, Anthony P. *America and the New Economy*. U.S. Department of Labor Employment and Training Administration. Alexandria, VA: The American Society for Training and Development, 1991.

Carnevale, Anthony P.; Leila J. Gainer; Janice Villet; and Shari L. Holland. *Training Partnerships: Linking Employers and Providers*. U.S. Department of Labor Employment and Training Administration. Alexandria, VA: The American Society for Training and Development, 1990.

Crosby, Philip B. *Let's Talk Quality*. New York: McGraw-Hill, 1989.

Elsea, Janet, G. "The First Four Minutes." First Impression, Best Impression. New York: Simon & Schuster, 1984.

Goldenkoff, Robert, and Dana Morgan. *Federal Jobs for College Graduates*. New York: Prentice Hall General Reference, 1991.

Harkavy, Michael. *101 Careers: A Guide to the Fastest-Growing Opportunities*. New York: John Wiley & Sons, 1990.

Hirsh, Sandra, and Jean Kummerow. *Life Types*. New York: Warner Books, 1989.

Kaponya, Paul. *How to Survive Your First 90 Days at a New Company*. Hawthorne, NJ: The Career Press, 1990.

Mollay, John T. *Dress for Success*. New York: Warner Books, 1988.

Petras, Kathryn, and Ross Petras. *Jobs '92*. New York: Prentice Hall Press, 1992.

Pollan, Stephen M., and Mark Levine. *Your Recession Handbook (How to Thrive and Profit during Hard Times)*. New York: William Morrow and Company, 1991.

Scheetz, Patrick L. *Recruiting Trends 1991–92*. 21st ed. East Lansing: Michigan State University, 1991.

Strasser, Stephen, and John Sena. *From Campus to Corporation*. Hawthorne, NJ: The Career Press, 1990.

U.S. Department of Labor and Bureau of Labor Statistics. *Occupational Outlook Handbook*. 1990–91 ed., Indianapolis: 1990 JIST Works, Inc., 1990.

ARTICLES

Garber, Janet. "Workplace 1992." *Careers and the Disabled*. Greenlawn, NY: Equal Opportunity Publications, Inc., February 1992, pp. 14–17.

Gold, Carolyn. "Harness Your Stress." Company Newsletter Boston: The Sheraton Corporation, pp. 91–94.

Katz, Robert L. "Human Relations Skills Can Be Sharpened." People: Managing Your Most Important Asset. *Harvard Business Review*, 1990.

Special Edition: "Riding the Tide of Change." *The Wyatt Communicator*," Winter 1991, pp. 4–11.

Schlosberg, Jeremy. "Job Opportunity Index." *Career Futures*, Fall 1991, pp. 2–7.

U.S. Bureau of Labor Statistics. *Occupational Projections and Training Data*, pamphlet (Washington, D.C.: U.S. Government Printing Office, 1990).

Weis, William L. "No Ifs, Ands, or Butts. Why Workplace Smoking Should be Banned." *Best of Business Quarterly*, Summer 1986.

Index